ANGLO-WELSH LITERATURE
1900—1965

A Bibliography of
Anglo-Welsh Literature

1900—1965

BRYNMOR JONES, F.L.A.

Published by
The Wales and Monmouthshire Branch
of the Library Association

1970

Published with the financial support of the
WELSH ARTS COUNCIL.

Printed by
J. D. Lewis & Sons Ltd.,
Gomerian Press, Llandysul

INTRODUCTION

THIS bibliography was compiled in an attempt to delineate the school of Welsh writers of the 20th century who normally use the English language as their medium of creative expression, and are frequently described as the "Anglo-Welsh" school. The approach to the subject is enumerative, and no attempt has been made to apply literary value judgements to the authors' work. Nor is it the function of an enumerative bibliography to enter into argument as to whether the "Anglo-Welsh" school should be accepted or rejected in its entirety. Reference to Section B of this Bibliography, and particularly the general critical articles, will reveal some of the attitudes adopted by literary critics towards the Anglo-Welsh school.

The selection of authors for inclusion in a literary bibliography immediately poses certain problems. The basic principle adopted was to include writers of Welsh birth or extraction who write imaginative literature in English, locating their narratives against a Welsh background and portraying Welsh characters and idiom. A second, but I believe defensible, category comprises those novels, plays and short stories set in a Welsh locale, though their authors are not necessarily of Welsh birth. An additional lesser category consists of children's stories which display Welsh localities as a background to their narrative.

Critics have long acknowledged that many of the notable Welsh authors who have written creatively in English have been accepted into the main stream of English literature. Within the period of years covered by this Bibliography, this is particularly true of writers such as Arthur Machen, W. H. Davies, Dylan Thomas, R. S. Thomas and Vernon Watkins. The extent to which authors such as these contribute to this main stream of English letters often makes it difficult to differentiate clearly between their "Anglo-Welsh" and "English" modes of expression.

Certain works have been omitted from this compilation which, by title or implied location, are clearly not set against Welsh backgrounds. Consequently, some of the best-known titles by authors such as Richard Hughes, John Cowper Powys and Emyr Humphreys are necessarily omitted, as they are discernibly not set in Welsh localities and do not introduce Welsh themes or styles of expression. I have also excluded some works of Arthurian or of Romano-British connotation, and works relating to early periods of British history.

Because the determination of literary merit is subject to so many personal and subjective whims, it is unlikely that any two critics would agree on every decision to include or exclude entries in a bibliography devoted to an undefined "school" of authors. This makes it virtually impossible to abide consistently by a rigid line of demarcation, and I am aware of the omission of the work of authors with qualifications of birth or local association, such as Edward Thomas and Henry Treece. Differentiation on the grounds of "theme" or "locality" is doubly difficult in poetry and it would be foolish to seek to apply the yardstick of "locality qualification" to the extensive body of Anglo-Welsh verse. In assigning "localities" to prose fiction, only named or recognisable places have been noted and fictional or conjectured places are shown as such.

Historically, the most realistic factor in the development of the Anglo-Welsh school was the social and economic climate arising from the depression and industrial strife of the mid-1920's—the undeniable historical cataclysm which gave rise to the social protest of Idris Davies and Lewis Jones and other Glamorgan and Monmouthshire writers. The industrialisation and resultant social crowding of the South Wales valleys forms a recurrent and caustic theme in the literature of the Anglo-Welsh school, and contrasts sharply with the fanciful themes of some of the pre-1925 novelists who use imagined Welsh locations and improbable characters as mere background for contrived and romantic narratives.

Another prominent feature of the first quarter of the twentieth century was the literary renaissance associated with Sir John Morris-Jones, W. J. Gruffydd, T. Gwynn Jones and other writers in the Welsh language. This lively concept of a new national identity must have prompted other writers, without equal facility in Welsh, to realise the need for a channel of creative expression, parallelling the Welsh literary revival by using English as their creative medium, and introducing into that English an idiom and character portrayal both localised and recognisably Welsh. Even so, one should avoid constructing an artificial language division ; some of the leading writers of Welsh literature have also written in English, and some of the foremost Anglo-Welsh authors are fluent Welsh speakers.

The main body of this bibliography lists the work of Anglo-Welsh authors in a recurring pattern of novels, short stories, other prose, verse and drama, while Section B notes the sources of general and individual criticism. It is not claimed that the bibliography is exhaustive, as this would have necessitated consulting every literary journal published since 1900 and every daily newspaper file, many of them unindexed, over a period of 65 years. The locations noted for singly-published poems refer in the main to periodicals most easily accessible in British libraries, and are not intended as an exhaustive listing of each author's individually published poems.

I acknowledge my indebtedness to the authors of the unpublished university theses listed in Section B of the Bibliography, and to other persons prominent in Anglo-Welsh studies who read the typescript of the volume and supplied further information. I would also like to thank my professional colleagues in the National Library of Wales who frequently drew my attention to bibliographical sources, and the public librarians who readily made their bookstocks available to me. Both the Library Association and the Welsh Arts Council have given practical assistance in the publishing arrangements, but the most practical of all arrangements was undertaken by my wife, who since 1966 has twice completed the thankless task of typing the contents of this volume.

Finally the major credit for the appearance of this work must go to the Welsh Branch of the Library Association, and particularly its Bibliographies Sub-Committee. The staff of the Gomerian Press, Llandysul also deserve to be acknowledged for their courtesy and craftsmanship, and for the technical expertise which has gained for this Press a place of honour in the annual Book Design competitions of the Welsh Arts Council.

BRYNMOR JONES.

December 1969.

CONTENTS

ARRANGEMENT AND ABBREVIATIONS

1. FORM OF ENTRY

As the major part of the preparatory work for this bibliography was undertaken before the appearance of the British Text (1967) of the Anglo-American Cataloguing Rules, the form of entry adopted is mainly that of the 1908 Anglo-American Code. The type of binding has been noted and the measurements given are for the height of the book at the title-page, to the nearest half-centimetre.

Each main work, single short story or essay bears its own serial number, while an author's individual poems published in separate locations are collected at one serial number. Entries for short stories collected into an anthology are not necessarily repeated as contributions to the author's personal portion of Section A of the Bibliography. Place-names printed between inverted commas denote fictional locations for novels. The locations given are those named or readily discernible within the publication itself, and conjectured locations are shown as such. Pseudonyms are used where the author was best known by that form of name.

2. MANUSCRIPT COLLECTIONS

During the compilation of this Bibliography, the National Library of Wales received the first items of the Welsh Arts Council Manuscript Collection, by means of which the Council proposes to acquire drafts, worksheets, fair copies and correspondence of twentieth-century Anglo-Welsh writers. This material supplements other National Library manuscript collections, such as the Wil Ifan, Idris Davies, Llewelyn Wyn Griffith, Caradoc Evans and Jack Jones Collections, and a guide to this range of material is available for consultation at the Library.

NLW mss. are described systematically in the Library's published *Handlist of Manuscripts*, and typed lists are available of the Welsh Arts Council Collection. Other relevant material will be found in the scripts regularly deposited by the Welsh Region of the BBC and in the files of the *Anglo-Welsh Review*, comprising copy and correspondence, of which nos. 28-38 have been deposited to date.

3. ABBREVIATIONS

The following abbreviations are used in Section A of the text of the Bibliography :

A-W.R.	Anglo-Welsh Review
BM Cat.	The British Museum General Catalogue of Printed Books
Dock L.	Dock Leaves
LLT	Life and Letters Today
NLW	The National Library of Wales
PEN	New Poems : P.E.N. anthologies. London, 1952—
Qtly.	Quarterly
TLS	*Times Literary Supplement*
W. Mail	*Western Mail*
Wales (J.H.E.)	The magazine *Wales*, original series ; edited by J. H. Edwards.
YCP	Young Commonwealth Poets, '65, compiled by P. L. Brent ; London, Heinemann in association with Cardiff Commonwealth Arts Festival, 1965.

PROSE ANTHOLOGIES

A   1   : **FABER & FABER, LTD.**

Welsh short stories : an anthology.
London ; Faber, 1937.
491p.   18½cm.   cloth.

Contents :

Davies, Edward Tegla	The strange apeman (trans.)
Davies, Hywel	The five eggs
Davies, Rhys	Resurrection
Devereux, Blanche	The Bull Giant Head
Edwards, Dorothy	The conquered
Evans, Caradoc	The way of the earth
Evans, Margiad	Country dance
Evans, Siân	Davis
Goodwin, Geraint	Janet Ifans' donkey
Griffith, Jack	Something to be thankful for
Hughes, Richard	The stranger
Jones, Glyn	Wil Thomas
Jones, Gwyn	Shacki Thomas
Lewis, Eiluned	The poacher
Machen, Arthur	The shining pyramid
Pryce, Richard	A hewer of stone
Pughe, Ifan	The wild horses and fair maidens of Llan-gannoch
Raine, Allen	A life's chase
Richards, Frank	The black rat
Roberts, Kate	A summer day (trans.)
Thomas, Dylan	The orchards
Vaughan, H. M.	An idyll without an end
Vaughan, Hilda	A thing of nought
Williams, D. J.	A good year (trans.)
Williams, J. Ellis	Big business
Williams, R. Hughes	Siôn William (trans.)

A   2   : **EVANS, George Ewart,** *editor*

Welsh short stories.   New edition.
London ; Faber, 1959.
[vi], 7—288p.   21cm.   cloth.

Contents :

Alexander, David	Hangman's assistant
Daniel, Glyn	Death at Christmas
Davies, Rhys	The dilemma of Catherine Fuchsias
Edwards, Dorothy	The conquered
Elis, Islwyn Ffowc	The girl in the heather
Evans, Caradoc	The way of the earth
Evans, George Ewart	Introduction
Evans, George Ewart	The medal
Glynne-Jones, William	Up-ladle at three
Goodwin, Geraint	Janet Ifans' donkey
Heseltine, Nigel	Flaming tortoises
Hughes, Cledwyn	The first snow
Hughes, Richard	The stranger
Humphreys, Emyr	Mrs. Armitage
Jones, Glyn	It's not by his beak you can judge a wood-cock
Jones, Gwyn	Goronwy's house of gold
Lewis, Alun	The orange grove
Mansel, Henry	Immortality
Mathias, Roland	A night for the curing
Roberts, Kate	A summer day (trans.)
Rowe, Dilys	A view across the valley
Thomas, Dylan	The orchards
Thomas, Gwyn	Where my dark lover lies
Vaughan, Aled	The investment
Williams, D. J.	The court cupboard (trans.)
Wright, John	Gone fishing

A   3   : **JONES, Gwyn,** *editor*

Welsh short **stories.**
Harmondsworth, Middlesex ; Penguin Books, 1940.
[6],   7-169, [5]p.   18cm.   wrappers.
Contents :

Davies, E. Tegla	Samuel Jones's Harvest Thanksgiving (trans.)
Davies, Rhys	Caleb's ark
Evans, Caradoc	A mighty man in Sion
Evans, George Ewart	Let dogs delight
Evans, Siân	Davis
Goodwin, Geraint	The lost land
Gruffydd, W. J.	Dripping leaves (trans.)
Hughes, Richard	A night at a cottage
Jones, Glyn	Eben Isaac
Jones, Gwyn	Shacki Thomas
Lewis, Alun	The wanderers
Machen, Arthur	The cosy room
Richards, A. E.	Worthy is the Lamb
Roberts, Kate	Sisters (trans.)
Thomas, Dylan	A prospect of the sea
Williams, D. J.	Pwll-yr-Onnen (trans.)

A   4   : **JONES, Gwyn,** *compiler*

Welsh short stories ; selected and with an introduction by Gwyn Jones.
London ; Oxford University Press, 1956.
[4], v-xv, [1], 330p.   15cm.   cloth.
(World's Classics Series, no. 551).

Contents :

Davies, Rhys	The benefit concert
Davies, Rhys	The nature of man
Evans, Caradoc	Be this her memorial
Evans, Caradoc	A father in Sion
Evans, George Ewart	Possessions
Evans, Margiad	All through the night
Goodwin, Geraint	A sitting of eggs
Griffith, Wyn	Ifan Owen and the grey rider
Hughes, Richard	The stranger
Jones, Glyn	Price-Parry
Jones, Glyn	Wat Pantathro
Jones, Gwyn	A night at Galon-uchaf
Jones, Gwyn	Introduction
Jones, Gwyn	The brute creation
Lewis, Alun	The wanderers
Lewis, Alun	They came
Machen, Arthur	The shining pyramid
Richards, A. Edward	Worthy is the Lamb
Roberts, Kate	Old age (trans. by Wyn Griffith)
Roberts, Kate	Two storms (trans. by Dafydd Jenkins)
Thomas, Dylan	The enemies
Thomas, Dylan	A visit to Grandpa's
Thomas, Gwyn	And a spoonful of grief to taste
Thomas, Gwyn	Thy need
Vaughan, Aled	The white dove
Williams, D. J.	Pwll-yr-Onnen (trans. by Dafydd Jenkins)
Williams, Islwyn	Will Thomas's cap

A   5   : **VAUGHAN, Aled,** editor

Celtic story, Number one.
London ; Pendulum Publications, 1946.
[5], 6-167p. 18½cm. cloth.

Includes :

Davies, Howell	Baboons
Davies, Rhys	Canute
Gill, H. V.	The insufferables
Glynne-Jones, W.	"I know a bank"
Heseltine, Nigel	Homecoming
Hughes, Cledwyn	The hedgehog
Morgan, Con	Unquiet dwelling
Treece, Henry	Two at the table
Turner, M. L.	The rocking chair
Vaughan, Aled	The feud

POETRY ANTHOLOGIES

A   6   : **BELL, Sir Harold Idris and BELL, Charles Christopher,** translators

Welsh poems of the twentieth century in English verse . . . with an historical and critical essay on Welsh poetry.
Wrexham ; Hughes and Son, 1925.
x, 139p. 22½cm. cloth.

A   7   : **GRAVES, Alfred Perceval,** translator

Welsh poetry old and new in English verse.
London, New York ; Longmans, 1912.
xlii, 170p. 18½cm. cloth.
Includes translations of poems by H. Elvet Lewis : Young Wales ; The High Tide : My land ; The old melody ; My garden ; T. Gwynn Jones : To Dafydd ab Edmund : W. J. Gruffydd : The ballad of the old bachelor of Ty'n y Mynydd ; Gwerfyl Mechain.

A   8   : **GRIFFITH, Peter,** and others

Triad : thirty three poems by Peter Griffith, Meic Stephens and Harri Webb, with an introduction by Anthony Conran.
Merthyr Tydfil ; The Triskel Press, 1963.
[8], 9—58p. 20½cm. wrappers.
Wrapper illustrated with a design by Ulrich West. Limited edition of 500 copies.

A   9   : **HAWKES, Terry,** compiler

The lilting house : a selection of poems by members of the University College of South Wales and Monmouthshire, Cardiff.
London ; Fortune Press, 1955.
[8], 9—52p. 19½cm. cloth.

A   10   : **HOCKEY, Lawrence William,** compiler

Monmouthshire poetry : an anthology of poetry relating to the County or written by writers associated with Monmouthshire.
Newport, Mon. ; R. H. Johns, [1949].
[6], 7—148p. 20½cm. boards.

A   11   : **JONES, Sam,** compiler

A Bangor book of verse. Barddoniaeth Bangor.
Poems, English and Welsh, written by students of the University College of North Wales, Bangor, 1923—1924.
Bangor ; Jarvis & Foster, 1924.
xiii, [3], 84 p. 19cm. cloth.
pp. 1—38 : English poems.

A   12   : **MONMOUTHSHIRE.** County Council. Education Committee

The sweet days : (a collection of poems written by Monmouthshire school pupils).
Newport, Mon. ; Monmouthshire Education Committee, 1961.
[8], 28p. 16cm. cloth.
The collection is prefaced by Davies, W. H. "Days that have been", p. [8].

A 13 : **PLAID CYMRU** (The Welsh Nationalist Party)

Pencader poems : a collection of patriotic verse published on the day of the Rally at Pencader, September 27th, 1952.
Cardiff ; Plaid Cymru Offices, 1952.
[16]p. 18½cm. wrappers.

A 14 : **PRYS-JONES, Arthur Glyn,** *compiler*

Welsh poets : a representative English selection from contemporary writers collated by A. G. Prys-Jones.
London ; Erskine Macdonald, 1917.
[4], 5—94 [2]p. 19cm. cloth.
—Another issue. 1918.
—Another ed. 2nd ed. 1922.

A 15 : **RHYS, Keidrych,** *pseud.* (i.e. William Ronald Rees Jones), *editor*

Modern Welsh poetry.
London ; Faber, 1944.
[4], 5—146p. 19cm. cloth.

A 16 : **WILLIAMS, [David] Gwyn,** *editor*

Presenting Welsh poetry : an anthology of Welsh verse in translation and of English verse by Welsh poets.
London ; Faber, 1959.
[4], 5—128p. 19cm. cloth.
This volume comprises : (a) Welsh poems in translation and (b) English poems by Welsh authors. Ranges from the 6th to 20th centuries.

A 17 : **WILLIAMS, John Stuart** *and* **MILNER, Richard,** *editors*

Dragons and daffodils : an anthology of verse.
Llandybie, Carms. ; Christopher Davies, 1960.
[6], 7—56p. 21cm. cloth.
Wrapper bears sub-title : "Contemporary Anglo-Welsh Verse : an anthology".

Section A. II. INDIVIDUAL AUTHORS

ABSE, Dannie

Novel
A 18 : Ash on a young man's sleeve.
London ; Hutchinson, 1954.
[8], 9—200p. 18¾cm. cloth.
Location : Cardiff.
—[Excerpt from the above] : Uncle Bertie, Encounter, Vol. II, no. 4, 1954. 18—26.
—Translated version : Swedish. Stockholm, 1956.

Verse
A 19 : After every green thing.
London, New York, [etc.] ; Hutchinson, [1949].
62p. 18½cm. boards.

A 20 : Dannie Abse : [a selection of his poems].
London ; Vista Books, 1963.
[4], 5—48p. 18cm. wrappers. (Pocket Poets Series).

A 21 : Poems, Golders Green.
London, Melbourne, [etc.] ; Hutchinson, 1962.
59p. 21cm. cloth.

A 22 : Tenants of the house : poems, 1951—1956.
London, Melbourne, [etc.] ; Hutchinson, 1957.
79p. 23cm. cloth.

A 23 : Walking under water.
London, New York, [etc.] ; Hutchinson, 1952.
vii, 1, 9—47p. 23cm. cloth.

A 24 : The abandoned ; Outposts, no. 35, 1957/8, 1-4.
PEN, 1958, 13—16.
After a departure ; Dragons and daffodils : an anthology, 1960, 8—9.
The big store ; PEN 1963, 15.
Confessions, excuses and accusations ; Poetry Qtly., Vol. 10, no. 3, 1948, 167-8.
Dedicatory poem ; Stand, No. 5 [1954], 20.
Duality ; Blackburn, Thomas, *comp.*, 45—60 : an anthology of English poetry, London, 1960, 21—22.
Mavericks : an anthology. London, Editions Poetry, 1957, 32.
Kenyon Review, Vol. 17, no. 2, 1955, 255—6.
Elegy for Dylan Thomas ; Kenyon Review, Vol. 17, no. 2, 1955, 256—7.
Evens in Golders Green ; PEN 1965, 21.
Failure ; Poetry Book Magazine, Vol 6, no. 5, 1954. Special no. *Poetry from Wales*, 14.
Found ; The Poetry Review, Vol. 45, 1954, pp. 142—3.
The frontier ; Poetry (Chicago), Vol. 81, no. 4, 1953, 238—9.
The game ; Presenting Welsh Poetry, 1959, 119—20.

Ghost ; Rann, no. 14, 1951, 4.

Halls ; YCP, 178—9.

I shall accept no poet's dream : Outposts, No. 7, 1947, 11.

If the dead offend ; Poetry Quarterly, Vol. 10, no. 1, 1948, 11—3.

In Llandough Hospital ; Poetry Wales, Vol. 1, no. 2, 1965, 8—9.

Inscription on the fly-leaf of a Bible ; The Poetry Review, Vol. 46, 1955, p. 198.

Islands ; PEN 1960, 16.

The journey ; Poetry Quarterly, Vol. 9, no. 1, 1947, 72—4.

Lady in distress ; Healing of the Nations ; ed. by Vera Rich, A-W.R. Suppl., 1965, 28.

Lament of the elder ; Outposts, no. 39, 1958, 7.

Letter to Alex Comfort ; Poetry Quarterly, Vol. 11, no. 4, 1949, 211—2. Faber book of twentieth century verse ; ed. by J. Heath-Stubbs and D. Wright, 1953, 40—1.

Letter to the Times ; Partisan Review, Vol. 23, no. 1, 1956, [71—3].
Mavericks : an anthology. London, 1957, 35-6.

Looking at a map ; Mavericks : an anthology, London, 1957, 34.

Lost ; The Poetry Review. Vol. 45, 1954, p. 142.

Master ; Mavericks : an anthology. London, 1957, 31.

The meeting ; Poetry (Chicago), Vol. 81, no. 4, 1953, 239-41.

Monologue for Prince Hamlet ; Rann, No. 14, 1951, 3.

The nameless ; PEN 1963, 19.

The occupation ; Outposts, No. 21, 1952, 1—2.

On the cross we grow . . . ; Poetry Quarterly, Vol. 8, no. 4, 1946/7, 209.

On hearing the monologue of a deaf man ; Mavericks : an anthology. London, 1957, 33.

Ordinary Heaven ; Outposts, No. 15, 1949, 8—10.

Photograph and yellow tulips ; Poetry (Chicago), Vol. 81, no. 2, 1952, 105.
PEN 1953, 128.

Poem at 4 a.m. ; Outposts, No. 12, 1948, 8—9.

Postcard from Cornwall ; Encounter, Vol. III, no. 4, 1954, 67.

The race ; London Magazine, Vol. 3, no. 11, 1956, 19—20.
PEN 1957, 13—14.

The seance ; Outposts, No. 30, 1956, 5—6.

The search ; Rann, No. 14, 1951, 5.

The shunters ; Dragons and daffodils : an anthology, 1960, 7.

Song of an old man ; The Poetry Review, Vol. 45. 1954, p. 86.

Sonnet ("If you could be as of the dead . . .") : The Poetry Review, Vol. 42, no. 4, 1951, 189—90.

Suburb. Evening. Autumn ; PEN 1960, 15.

Sunday evening ; Dragons and daffodils : an anthology, 1960. 11.

Three voices : I. A Woman to a man ; II. A man to his mistress ; III. A wife to a husband; Outposts, No. 43, 1959, 1—3.

Tree ; Dragons and daffodils : an anthology, 1960, 10.

The trial ; Blackburn, Thomas, *comp.* 45—60, London, 1960, 22—5.
Kenyon Review, Vol. 18, no. 1, 1956, 68—71.
PEN 1956, 94—7.

Untitled poem. "Lady of black hair . . ." ; Poetry Quarterly, Vol. 9, no. 1, 1947, 34.

ALEXANDER, David

Stories

A 25   : Accident.
      Seven, Vol. 5, no. 1, 1944, 19—22.

A 26   : Hangman's assistant.
      Welsh Review, Vol. V, no. 1, 1946, 52—4.
      —Welsh short stories ; ed. by G. Ewart Evans, 1959, 175—9.

A 27   : So little time.
      Welsh Review, Vol. VII, no. 2, 1948, 119—21.

AMIS, Kingsley [William]

Novels

A 28   : Lucky Jim : a novel.
      London ; Gollancz, 1954.
      [6], 7—256p. 18cm. cloth.
      Location : University town (Swansea conjectured).
      Frequently reprinted (22 impressions by 1964).
      Won the Somerset Maugham Award.
      American ed. New York ; Viking Press, 1958. (Compass Books, no. 35).
      —Another ed. London ; Landsborough Publications, 1959, 222p. (Four Square Books).
      —Another ed. Penguin Books, 1961, 252 p.

      Lucky Jim ; edited and abridged by D. K. Swan. Illustrated by William Burnard.
      London ; Longmans, 1963.
      v, [1], 154p. 18½cm. wrappers. (The Bridge Series).

      Lucky Jim.
      The RussellReader ; ed. by Leonard Russell, Cassell, 1956, 377—584. (Complete version).

      [Extract from *Lucky Jim*]. *In* Chapters from the Modern Novel ; ed. by T. D. Tosswill. Bell, 1961, 17—22.

      Translated versions :
      1956 : *In* Finland, Sweden ; 1958 : Japan, Hungary, Denmark, Poland ; 1959 : Czechoslovakia ; 1960 : Argentina ; 1961 : Bulgaria, Portugal ; 1962 : Yugoslavia, Germany ; 1963 : Netherlands ; 1964 : Spain (Catalan), Israel.
      (For publication details see Annual Volumes of the UNESCO Index Translationum).

A 29   : That uncertain feeling : a novel.
London ; Gollancz, 1955.
254p. 18½cm. cloth.
Location : "Aberdarcy", Glamorgan.
—American ed. New York ; Harcourt, Brace, 1956.
—Another ed. London ; Landsborough Publications, 1960. 222p.
—Another ed. London ; New English Library, 1964. 224p. (Four Square Books).

Translated versions :
1960 : Denmark ; 1964 : Yugoslavia.

Stories
A 30   : Interesting things.
In Amis, K. My enemy's enemy. Gollancz, 1962, 151—64.
Pick of today's short stories, No. 7, 1956, 33—45.

A 31   : Moral fibre.
In Amis, K. My enemy's enemy. Gollancz, 1962, 119—48.

Other Prose
A 32   : Age-old ceremony at Mumbles ; Twentieth Century, Dec. 1956, 558.

A 33   : Mind we don't quarrel ; The Spectator, Dec. 2, 1955, 762—3.

A 34   : Where Tawe flows ; The Spectator, Aug. 13, 1954, 190—1.

Verse
A 35   : The Evans country.
London ; Fantasy Press (Oscar Mellor), 1962.
[2], 3—8, [4]p. 21½cm. wrappers.
Contents : Aberdarcy, the main square—Fforestfawr—Langwell—Pendydd—Brynbwrla, —Welch ferry, west side—To the patrons and staff of the Newton Inn, Mumbles.
All previously publ. in *The Spectator*.

A 36   : Gulls ; PEN 1956, 90.
Larger truth ; PEN 1958, 17.
Masters ; PEN 1952, 55.
Sight unseen ; PEN 1961, 15.
Wrong words ; PEN 1953, 136—7.

ANDERSON, John Redwood

Verse
A 37   : Almanac, and other poems.
London ; Macdonald, 1956.
[8], 9—127p. 21½cm. cloth.
Includes some poems of Welsh interest.

A 38   : To the Dyfrdwy, the river I love.
[London, Grasshopper Press, 1951].
[12]p. 18½cm.
A hand-printed edition of 200 copies.

ANDREW, Prudence Hastings

Novels
A 39   : The hooded falcon.
London, Melbourne [etc.] ; Hutchinson, 1960.
222p. 19½cm. cloth. (New Authors Ltd.)
Location : English—Welsh border after the Owain Glyndŵr Rebellion.

A 40   : Ordeal by silence : a story of medieval times.
London ; Hutchinson, 1961.
[6], 7—[240]p. 19½cm. cloth.
Location : Partly set in Wales : 12th century.

AREY, John Stuart

Novel
A 41   : There was no yesterday.
London ; Eyre & Spottiswoode, 1943.
[5], 6—208p. 18½cm. cloth.
Location : "Bryndyfi".

ARNOLD, A. V., *Mrs.*

Novel
A 42   : Megan of the dark isle.
London ; Alston Rivers, 1914.
[6] 319p. 19cm. cloth.
Location : Anglesey, mid-Victorian times.

ARNOLD, Arthur

Stories
A 43   : Tales from the old reading room.
Cardiff ; Western Mail, 1947.
[2], 3—238p. 16½cm. cloth.
Half-title : "Klydton Reading Room".

ASHBY, Douglas

Verse
A 44   : The harp of the hills.
Amersham, Bucks. ; Morland, 1923.
38p. 18½cm. cloth.

ASHBY, Rubie Constance

Novel
A 45   : Out went the taper.
London ; Hodder & Stoughton, 1934.
[8], 9—320p. 18½cm. cloth.
Location : Vale of "Cwm Wyddfa", nr. Llanberis, Caerns.

ASHTON, Helen

Novel
A 46   : The swan of Usk : a historical novel.
London ; Collins, 1940.
320p. 20cm. cloth.
Location : Partly in the Usk Valley and Welsh borders. Subject is the poet Henry Vaughan.

ASKEW, Alice J. de C. *and* **ASKEW, Claude Arthur Cary**

Novel
A 47 : A preacher of the Lord, by Alice & Claude
        Askew, with a coloured frontispiece by Dudley
        Tennant.
        London ; Cassell, 1913.
        viii, 311p. col. front. 19cm. cloth.
        Location : South Cardiganshire.

BADGER, Howard Charles

Verse
A 48 : Rustic rhymings.
        Kemeys, Mon. ; publ. by the author, 1957.
        32p. 23½cm. wrappers.
        Printed at the Starling Press, Risca, Mon.

BAIRACLI-LEVY, Juliette de

Novel
A 49 : The bride of Llew : a novel.
        London ; Faber, 1953.
        [6], 7—391p. 20½cm. cloth.
        Location : Links with the town of "Ferry-
        mouth", Monmouthshire.

A 50 : Look ! the wild swans. Illustrated by Olga
        Lehmann.
        Rochford, Essex, C. W. Daniel ; Manchester,
        Bairacli Books, [1947].
        [12], 13—420p. front., illus. 22½cm. wrappers.
        Location : "Rhoscomyll", Lleyn Peninsula,
        N. Wales.

BANNERMAN, Alexander

Novel
A 51 : The man with the rubber soles.
        London ; Hodder & Stoughton, [1921].
        320p. 18½cm. cloth.
        Location : Partly set in Pembrokeshire.

BARCYNSKA, Helena, *"Countess Barcynska", pseud.*

For works by the above author in the names of "Countess
Barcynska" and "Oliver Sandys", *see under*
            Evans, Marguerite Florence.

BARING, Max

Novel
A 52 : A prophet of Wales : a story.
        London ; Greening, 1905.
        viii, 9—311p. col. front. 18½cm. cloth.
        Location : A South Wales town and a North
        Wales valley.

BATEMAN, David

Verse
A 53 : Through the rainbow : a book of poems.
        Carmarthen ; Spurrell, 1933.
        [9], 10—62p. 17cm. cloth.

BAX, Clifford

Drama
A 54 : Tragic Nesta : a play in one act.
        London, New York ; French, 1934.
        [4] 5—24p. plan. 18½cm. wrappers.
        (French's Acting Edition, 172).
        Scene : Brecon Castle, c. 1120.

BEALE, Anne

Novel
A 55 : Rose Mervyn : a tale of the Rebecca Riots.
        New ed.
        London ; H. Frowde, Hodder & Stoughton,
        1916.
        viii, [2], 373, 16p. col. front. illus. 19cm.
        cloth.
        Location : Carmarthenshire ; Rebecca Riots.
        —Original edition : London, Griffith, Farran
        [1889]. (B.M. Cat.)

BEATSON, Kelland

Story
A 56 : Rachel Fairlie, B.A.
        Girls' Own Paper, April—July, 1904.
        (Background is student life at the University
        College of Wales, Aberystwyth).

BELL, David, *translator*

Verse
A 57 : Death ; translated from the Welsh "Angau"
        (Hen Benillion) ; Dock L., Vol. 2, no. 6,
        1951, 14.
        The fox ; translated from "Y Llwynog" (R.
        Williams Parry) ; Rann, No. 19 (Welsh
        number), 1953, 8.
        The owls ; translated from "Tylluanod" (R.
        Williams Parry) ; Rann, No. 19 (Welsh
        number), 1953, 19.
        The wonder of dawn ; translated from "Rhyf-
        eddodau'r Wawr" (R. Williams Parry) ;
        Welsh Review, Vol. 1, no. 3, 1939, 133.

BELL, *Sir* **Harold Idris**

Verse
A 58 : Artro revisited ; Welsh Outlook, Vol. XVIII,
        1931, 254.
        Blodeuwedd ; ibid. Vol. XI, 1924, 25.
        A Christmas Carol ; ibid. Vol. XIX, 1932, 319.
        Golden spring ; ibid. Vol. X, 1923, 26.
        "The greatest of these" : a memory of the
        War ; ibid. Vol. X, 1923, 248.
        "In our museum galleries" ; ibid. Vol. XI,
        1924, 337.
        The scientist ; ibid. Vol. XII, 1925, 145.
        A tomb-stone ; ibid. Vol. XVII, 1930, 51.

Translations

A 59 : Bones ; trans. from the Welsh "Esgyrn" (T. H. Parry-Williams) ; Welsh Review, Vol. 1, no. 3, 1939, 132.

The day after ; trans. from the Welsh of Wil Ifan ; Welsh Outlook, Vol. XVII, 1930, 212.

Eleven englynion (trans. from original Welsh stanzas) ; Welsh Review, Vol. V, no. 2, 1946, 116—9. (Previously publ. *in* Comparative Literature Studies).

The grave ; trans. from "Y Bedd" (T. Gwynn Jones) ; Welsh Outlook, Vol. I, 1914, 30.

Heaven ; trans. from the Welsh "Nefoedd" (T. H. Parry-Williams) ; Welsh Outlook, Vol. XIX, 1932, 8. Welsh Review, Vol. 1, no. 3, 1939, 133.

The Kestrel ; trans. from the Welsh "Y Cudyll Coch" (I. D. Hooson) ; Rann, no. 19 (Welsh number), 1953, 7.

Man ; trans. from the Welsh of D. Gwenallt Jones ; Dock L., Vol. 3, no. 9, 1952, 37.

Night on the sea ; from the Welsh of T. Gwynn Jones ; Welsh Poets ; [compiled by] A. G. Prys-Jones, 1917, 14.

Ode to Autumn (W. J. Gruffydd) ; The Land of My Fathers, London, 1915, 73.

Revenant ; trans. from the Welsh of Alafon ; Welsh Outlook, Vol. I, 1914, 312.

Rhydcymerau ; trans. from the Welsh of D. Gwenallt Jones ; Poetry Book Magazine, Vol. 6, no. 5, Fall 1954, 11.

Sonnet written in time of war ; from the Welsh of R. Williams Parry ; Welsh Poets [compiled by] A. G. Prys-Jones, 1917, 13.

Tempora mutantur ; trans. from the Welsh of W. J. Gruffydd ; Welsh Poets [compiled by] A. G. Prys-Jones, 1917, 15.

Welsh harp stanzas : translations of Welsh "Hen benillion" ; Dock L., Vol. 2, no. 6, 1951, 9—13.

BELLYS, Gwilym, *pseud.* [i.e. *William Davies*]

Novel

A 60 : Howell Gwynedd : a tale of the time of Owen Glyndwr.
Denbigh ; Gee & Son, *printers*, 1914.
175p. 17½cm. limp cloth.
Appendices.
Location : Country around Flint.
[Note : T.p. notes three other titles by this author : Huwcyn y Mynydd : The stranger : Uchmor Llwyd. Copies not traced. No copies shown in British Museum or N.L.W.].

BERRIDGE, Elizabeth

Novel

A 61 : Upon several occasions.
London, Melbourne [etc.] ; Heinemann, 1953.
251p. 18cm. cloth.
Location : "Bryntanat", a Welsh border village.

BERRY, Ron

Novels

A 62 : Hunters and hunted.
London, Melbourne [etc.] ; Hutchinson, 1960.
[12], 13—208p. 19½cm. cloth. (New Authors Limited).
Location : "Blaenddu" in a South Wales Valley.

A 63 : Travelling loaded.
London ; W. H. Allen, 1963.
[4], 5—224p. 19½cm. cloth.
Location : "Cadwallader County" and "Abbey Town".

BETHELL, Llewelyn Slingsby

Verse

A 64 : The Red Dragon.
Oxford ; Blackwell, 1920.
[6], 7—56p. front. 19½cm. wrappers.
(Adventurers All Series, no. XXVIII).
Title-page decorated with raised engraving.

BIELSKI, Alison J.

Verse

A 65 : Twentieth century flood, and other poems.
Dulwich, London ; Outposts Publications, 1964.
[4], 5—28p. 20½cm. wrappers.

A 66 : Apocalypse ; The Poetry Review, Vol. 52, no. 3, 1961, 187.

Family history ; YCP, 179—80.

A game of chess ; Dock L., Vol. 7, no. 20, 1956, 35.

Nocturne ; Poetry Wales, I, 1965, 3.

Sea ; A.-W.R., Vol. 13, no. 31, undated, 26—7.

Stranger in Wales ; Poetry Wales, Vol. 1, no. 2, 1965, 10—11.

Token ; A.-W.R., Vol. 14, no. 33, 1964, 7—8.

Twentieth-century flood ; ibid. 6—7.

Voyage ; ibid. Vol. 12, no. 30, undated, 54.

BINGHAM, Leslie J.

Verse
A 67 : The survivors : [a poem].
London ; Outposts Publications, 1964.
[2], 3—32p. 20½cm. wrappers.
(Author has Swansea connections).

BONIFACE, Eleanor

Stories
A 68 : S'Nellie's Welsh fairy tales.   Illustrated by
Wynona Garfitt.
Newtown ; Welsh Outlook Press, 1929.
[12], 108p. illus. 21½cm. cloth.
—Excerpts from the above tales published in
The Welsh Outlook, Vols. XIV and XV, 1927
and 1928.

A 69 : The dancing stones ; Welsh Outlook, Vol. XX,
1933, 253—4.

A 70 : The grove of Heaven ; ibid. [55]—6.

A 71 : The king of the cats ; ibid. Vol. XIX, 1932,
107—8.

A 72 : "Owain by the grace of God . . ." ; ibid. 309.

A 73 : The Rose of Mona ; ibid.   Vol. XX, 1933,
[128]—9.

A 74 : Saint Beuno and the bird ; ibid. [20].

Verse
A 75 : Old holy things of Wales.
Newtown ; Welsh Outlook Press, [1937].
28p. 19cm. boards.

A 76 : Welsh ways and days.
Ditchling ; Pepler & Sewell, 1935.
10p. illus. 19cm. wrappers.

A 77 : Chapel ; Welsh Outlook, Vol. XX, 1933, 268.
Church ; ibid. 304.
Gossip ; ibid. 309.
Hiraeth ; ibid. 241.

BOORE, Walter Hugh

Novel
A 78 : The valley and the shadow.
London, Melbourne [etc.] ; Heinemann, 1963.
[4], 5—190p. 19½cm. cloth.
Location : Village of "Bryncoed".

Story
A 79 : The finger.
A-W.R., Vol. 11, no. 28, undated, 37—41.

Verse
A 80 : Eternity is swift.   Foreword by Henry Treece.
London, Mitre Press, 1959.
61p. 19cm. cloth.
—Title poem "Eternity is swift" *in* The Poetry
Review, Vol. 47, 1956, 141.

A 81 : Winter seas.
London ; Fortune Press, 1953.
[6], 7—39p. 20cm. cloth.
Includes poems of Welsh interest.

A 82 : The anniversary ; English, Vol. 9, no. 50, 1952,
112.

The blackbird ; The Poetry Review, Vol. 52,
no. 3, 1961, 146.

Heritage ; ibid. Vol. 43, no. 4, 1952, 205.

I am remote from self ; Poetry Quarterly,
Vol. 12, no. 4, 1950/51, 202.

Late evening ; English, Vol. 11, no. 66, 1957,
243.

Meeting place ; Outposts, No. 33, 1957, 8.

She lay in death ; English, Vol. 10, no. 60,
1955, 240.

Thoughts before sleep ; The Poetry Review,
Vol. 47, 1956, 33.

Winter ; English, Vol. 12, 1959, [230].

BOWEN-ROWLANDS, Lilian

Novel
A 83 : The piteousness of passing things.
London ; New Century Press, 1900.
vii, 138p. 18½cm. cloth.
Location : Pembrokeshire.

BOYLE, Brian Leworthy

Verse
A 84 : A moment out of time : poems.
Southend-on-Sea ; Citizen Publishing Co.,
[1963], 11p. wrappers.

BROMLEY, Elizabeth

Verse
A 85 : All the year round in North Wales, and other
poems.
Shrewsbury ; Wilding and Son, 1921.
[4], 5—42p. 18½cm. wrappers.
British Museum Catalogue : Colwyn Bay, 1921.
31p. [1st ed.]
2nd ed. NLW copy.

BROOKES, Ewart

Novel
A 86 : Ride the wild wind.
London, Melbourne [etc.] ; Jarrolds, 1958.
[4], 5—256p. 19½cm. cloth.
Location : Partly in a Welsh seaport.

BROOKS, Jeremy

Novels
A 87 : Henry's war.
London ; Macmillan, 1962.
[6], 186p. 20cm. cloth.
Location : Partly set in North Wales.

A 88 : Jampot Smith.
London, Melbourne [etc.] ; Hutchinson, 1960.
256p. 18½cm. cloth.
Location : Llandudno, Caerns.

BROSTER, Dorothy Kathleen

Novel
A 89 : Ships in the bay !
London, Heinemann, 1931.
436, [1]p. 18cm. cloth.
Location : St. David's, and Pembrokeshire.

BROWNE, Edith Ophelia

Novel
A 90 : Thus Merlin said.
London ; Hutchinson, [1934].
[8]—9—286, [1], 56p. 18½cm. cloth.
Llewelyn ap Gruffydd and 13th century Wales.

BRYNLEY, David

Novel
A 91 : Seth : a novel.
London ; Chatto & Windus, 1955.
[6], 7—317p. 19½cm. cloth.
Location : "Lyden", a fishing village and "Cwmglen", a mining town.

BURNETT, Yelva

Novel
A 92 : A Welsh wooing.
London ; Newnes, [1920].
96p. 15½cm. wrappers. (Friendship Library, no. 67).

BURTON, P[hilip] H.

Drama
A 93 : Granton Street : a play in three acts.
[Port Talbot, Glam. ; F. S. Powell], 1934.
[4], 91p. 18½cm. wrappers.
Scene : "Abernansant", a Glamorgan mining town.

A 94 : White collar : a play in three acts.
[Port Talbot, Glam. ; F. S. Powell], 1938.
[4], 114p. 18cm. wrappers.
Scene : "Abernansant", a Glamorgan mining town.

BURTON, Richard

Story
A 95 : A Christmas story.
London, Melbourne [etc.] ; Heinemann, 1965.
28, [2]p. front. illus. cloth. 21½cm.

BUTLER, Suzanne

Novel
A 96 : Vale of tyranny.
London ; Hodder & Stoughton, 1954.
[4], 5—252p. 19cm. cloth.
Location : Partly set in "Vale End", Monmouthshire, 19th century.

BYRNE-THOMAS, Lilian

Verse
A 97 : Smoke : a collection of poems [with] illustrations by C. Ford-Dunn.
Newport, Mon. ; R. H. Johns, 1945.
[6], 7—56p. front. illus. 18½cm. wrappers.

CADWALADR, Dilys

Stories
A 98 : The divorce.
Welsh Outlook. Vol. XV, 1928, 128—9.

A 99 : The murder.
Welsh Outlook. Vol. XVI, 1929, 23.

Other Prose
A 100 : The high places ; Welsh Outlook. Vol. XV, 1928, 276—7.

A 101 : The pagan ; ibid. Vol. XVI, 1929, 278—80.

A 102 : Sidelights on eternity ; ibid. 83—4.

Verse
A 103 : The veil ; translated from the Welsh "Y Llen" by R. C. Ruck.
Dock L., Vol. 4, no. 12, 1953, 8—16.
[Original Welsh version was the Crown Poem of the 1953 National Eisteddfod at Rhyl].

A 104 : A British spy, on the eve of his execution, to his brother ; Welsh Outlook, Vol. XV, 1928, 339.

CADWALADR, J.J.

Verse
A 105 : Songs for music, and other verses.
London ; Drane, [1914].
[5], 6—66p. 15½cm. cloth.

CANAWAY, William Hamilton

Novels
A 106 : My feet upon a rock.
London, Melbourne [etc.] ; Hutchinson, 1963.
[6], 7—224p. 19½cm. cloth.
Location : Mountain of "Moel Eifion" and
village of "Nant-y-Bont", Snowdonia.

A 107 : The seal.
London ; M. Joseph, 1959.
[6], 7—174p. 19½cm. cloth.
Location : Welsh coastal area.

Verse
A 108 : The sewin ; PEN 1955, 60.

CARR, Glyn, *pseud.* [*i.e. Frank Showell Styles*]

Novels
A 109 : Death of a weirdy.
London ; Bles, 1965.
[8], 9—223p. map. 18cm. cloth.
Location : "Cwm Conan" valley and village.

A 110 : Death on Milestone Buttress.
London ; Bles, 1951.
285p. 18½cm. cloth.
Location : Snowdonia.

A 111 : Death under Snowdon.
London ; Bles, 1954.
[6], 7—239p. 18½cm. cloth.
Location : Snowdonia.
Cardiff Public Libraries' copy autographed by
"Glyn Carr", [i.e. F. Showell Styles].

A 112 : Murder of an Owl.
London ; Bles, 1956.
[8], 9—287p. map. 18½cm. cloth.
Location : Snowdonia.

CARTER, Barbara Barclay

Prose
A 113 : Old Nurse, by Barbara Barclay Carter, with an
introduction by Viola Meynell.
London ; Cape, 1936.
[8], 9—287p. 20cm. cloth.
Location : Breconshire.

CASTLE, Agnes *and* CASTLE, Egerton

Novel
A 114 : The hope of the house.
London, New York [etc.] ; Cassell, 1915.
viii, [2], 3—339p. 19cm. cloth.
Location : House of "Treowen", nr. Pen-y-fal
Mountain, Mon.

CHAMBERLAIN, Brenda

Prose
A 115 : Mountains of rock.
Welsh Review, Vol. IV, no. 3, 1945, 190—7.

A 116 : Silkie and tide race.
Welsh Review, Vol. VII, no. 3, 1948, 176—83.

A 117 : Ynys Enlli.
Welsh Review, Vol. VI, no. 2, 1947, 82—95.

Verse
A 118 : The green heart : poems.
London ; Oxford U.P., 1958.
viii, 76p. 18cm. cloth.
The ms. in unpublished form won the Arts
Council (Welsh Committee) Poetry Award
for 1956.

A 119 : Blodeuwedd ; Wales, Vol. VI, no. 24, 1946,
19—21.
Christmas Eve by the Baltics ; Poetry in
Wartime ; ed. by M. J. Tambimuttu,
1942, 28—9.
Dead climber ; ibid. 29—31.
Dead ponies ; ibid. 27.
Elegy ; Poetry Qtly., Vol. 4, no. 4, 1942, 130.
"Even as an alder . . ." (From *The Green
Heart*) ; Poetry Qtly., Vol. 7, no. 1, 1945.
[Excerpt from] *The Green Heart* "O Great Bear
in the sky . . . trapped by the circumstance
of time" ; ibid. Vol. 11, no. 3, 1949, 147.

Fisherman husband ; Presenting Welsh Poetry,
1959, 114.

For Alun ; Wales, New Series, 4, Summer
1944, 7.

From Blodeuwedd ; Poetry London X ; ed.
by Tambimuttu, 1944, 33—4.

Island fisherman ; Botteghe Oscure, IV, 367.

I think of you in a time of storm ; Life and
Letters, Vol. 65, June 1950, 191—2.

Poem for five airmen burnt to death inside
their aeroplane in Cwm Pen Llafar and for
the mothers who mourn them ; Welsh
Review, Vol. III, no. 1, 1944, 18—20.

Poems ; Botteghe Oscure, V, 293—303 :
Contains : Women foregathered on the
strand—Lovesong—Song of a woman from
the western island—Shrove Tuesday—
The green heart, I—V.

Reproof from Schlotheim (*From* The Green
Heart) ; Poetry Qtly., Vol. 7, no. 4, 1945,
129.

Seal cave ; ibid. Vol. 13, no. 3, 1951, 112—3.

Shapely mountains well named ; ibid. Vol. 12,
no. 2, 1950, 81.

Song ; Welsh Review, Vol. III, no. 1, 1944, 17.

Song—Talysarn ; Modern Welsh Poetry ; ed. by K. Rhys, 1944, 18.

To Dafydd Coed mourning his mountain-broken dog ; ibid, 19.

Voices speak from the Crevasse ; Poetry Qtly., Vol. 5, no. 4, 1943, 134.

You who in April laughed ; Poetry Qtly., Vol. 5, no. 2, 1943, 48. Modern Welsh Poetry ; ed. by K. Rhys, 1944, 18.

CHAPIN, Harold

Drama
A 120   : Elaine : comedy in three acts.
         In The comedies of Harold Chapin.
         London, Chatto & Windus, 1921, 117—77.
         Scene : "Llangwilloc", N. Wales.

A 121   : The threshold : a play in one act.
         London, New York ; French, 1921.
         [4], 5—15 [1]p. 18½cm. wrappers.
         Scene : Miner's house, Rhondda Valley.
         —American ed. 1921.

CHARLES, Thomas Owen

Novel
A 122   : Dear old Wales : a patriotic love story.
         Pittsburgh, U.S.A. ; American Printing Co., 1912.
         [12], 13—189 [2]p. illus. 19½cm. wrappers.
         Location : "Llangwenllian" at foot of Nant-y-Garth Pass, Denbs.

CHRISTIE, Kate

Novel
A 123   : Morgan.
         London ; Collins, 1957.
         [8], 9—254p. 19cm. cloth.
         Location : Seaside town of "Llandafy".

CLARK, Gwyn

Drama
A 124   : Going out is it ? a play in one act.
         London ; Samuel French, 1961.
         [4], 23, [2] p. plan. 18½cm. wrappers.
         (French's Acting Edition).

A 125   : Job's comforter : a comedy in one act.
         London ; Samuel French, 1961.
         [4], 18, [2]p. plan. 18½cm. wrappers.
         (French's Acting Edition).

CLARKE, Isabel Constance

Novel
A 126   : Children of the shadow.
         London ; Hutchinson, [1924].
         [8], 9—352, 48p. 19cm. cloth.
         Location : Partly at the house of "Pendre", N. Wales.

CLEWES, Howard

Novel
A 127   : Sailor comes home.
         London, New York [etc.] ; Longmans, Green, 1938.
         [6], 274p. 18½cm. cloth.
         Location : South Wales dockland areas.

COLLINS, William John Townsend

Stories
A 128   : The romance of the echoing wood . . . with introduction by Arthur Machen and epilogue by William Henry Davies. Decorations by E. F. Powell.
         Newport, Mon. ; R. H. Johns, 1937.
         [8], 43p. 25cm. illus. boards.
         Limited ed. of 220 copies : NLW has signed copy no. 141.—Variant binding. Copy no. 32 of limited ed. in NLW, cloth binding has autographs of W. J. T. Collins, A. Machen, W. H. Davies, E. F. Powell and R. H. Johns.

A 129   : Tales from the new Mabinogion . . . arranged and decorated by Fred Richards.
         London ; publ. privately at the Baynard Press, 1923.
         82p. illus. 20cm. Vellum.
         Limited ed. of 150 copies. NLW has copy no. 52.
         —Another ed. London ; Black, 1923.
         80p. 20cm. cloth.

Verse
A 130   : "Autumn sunshine".
         Newport, Mon. ; R. H. Johns, 1934.
         [4] 5—62 [1]p. 18½cm. cloth.
         100 copies printed in Garamond type, on English unbleached hand-made paper, and signed by the author. (NLW copy unsigned).

A 131   : "In gold and purple" : verses new and old including "More West Ward Rhymes".
         Newport, Mon. ; R. H. Johns, 1931.
         133, [2]p. 18½cm. cloth.
         Three hundred and twenty-five numbered copies printed in Garamond type on English unbleached hand-made paper, and signed by the author.

A 132 : Pembrokeshire poems.
Newport, Mon. ; R. H. Johns, 1931.
[2], 3—24p. 18cm. wrappers.
NLW copy has "author's note" : "All the
verses in this booklet, with the exception of
"Grey Days and Gold", were included in a
volume published earlier in 1931, "In Gold
and Purple"."

A 133 : "Pilgrimage", and other poems.
Newport, Mon. ; R. H. Johns, 1944.
[8], 69, [1]p. 18½cm. cloth.

CONRAN, Anthony [Edward Marcell]

Verse
A 134 : Collected poems, Volume 1 : early poems,
1951—58.
Oxford ; Clive Allison, 1965.
iv, 56p. 21½cm. cloth.

A 135 : Collected poems, Volume Two : Mythological
poems, 1959—61.
Denbigh ; Gee & Son, 1965.
iv, [2], 59—120p. 21½cm. cloth.

A 136 : Asymptotes (opus 7).
[Bangor ; publ. by the author], 1963.
28p. 21½cm. wrappers.

A 137 : Formal poems.
Llandybie (Carms.) ; Christopher Davies,
1960.
[4], 5—51p. 22½cm. cloth.
Awarded the 1958 £100 prize by the Welsh
Committee of the Arts Council of Great
Britain.

A 138 : Guernica.
[Denbigh ; Gee & Son, n.d.]
[8]p. 21½cm. wrappers.

A 139 : Icons (opus 6).
Bangor ; [publ. by the author], 1963.
12p. 21cm. wrappers.

A 140 : Metamorphoses.
[Pembroke Dock] ; Dock Leaves Press, 1961.
[6], 7—27p. 18½cm. cloth.

A 141 : The mountain (opus 2). *Revised ed.*
[Denbigh ; Gee & Son, *printers*], 1963.
16p. 21½cm. wrappers.
Originally published March, 1960, in *New
Echoes*, University College of North Wales
Arts Festival Supplement.

A 142 : Sequence of the blue flower.
[Oxford ; Clive Allison, 19— ?]
(Copy not seen).

A 143 : Stelae, and other poems.
[Oxford ; Clive Allison, 19—?]
(Copy not seen).

A 144 : Affair of birds ; YCP, p. 180.
A crown for Anna Daniel ; A-W.R., Vol. 11,
no. 28, undated, 18—9.
Consists of : The Well—The Swing-gate—
The Fledgling.

The dead ; trans. from the Welsh of D.
Gwenallt Jones ; Poetry Wales, Vol. 1,
no. 2, 1965, 12.

For Dylan Thomas, on hearing he was dead ;
Poetry Book Magazine, Vol. 6, no. 5, 1954.
Special no. *Poetry From Wales*, 25.
Dock L., Vol. 5, no. 13, 1954, 6—7.
The winning poem in a competition for the
Dylan Thomas Award, adjudicated by
Louis MacNeice.

From Llangollen ; A-W.R., Vol. 11, no. 271,
undated, 14.

Instead of a gift ; Critical Qtly., Vol. 5, no. 3,
1963, 250.

Lament for W. J. Gruffydd ; Dock L., Vol. 5,
no. 15, 1954, 45.

Poems ; Critical Qtly., Vol. 2, no. 4, 1960,
352—4. *Contents :* Zion—The blade—In
this weekday country—Open Sesame.

Rhydcymerau ; trans. from the Welsh of
D. Gwenallt Jones ; Poetry Wales, Vol. 1,
no. 2, 1965, 13.

Success ; Critical Qtly., Vol. 5, no. 3, 1963,
250.

Swallow ; ibid. Vol. 3, no. 4, 1961, 335.

To George, an old tortoise ; ibid. Vol. 1,
no. 4, 1959, 317.

A winter's tale ; ibid. Vol. 5, no. 3, 1963, 249.

CONROY, Ellen

Drama
A 145 : Evan Evans : a drama of Welsh life in three
acts.
Wales (J.H.E.), Vol. 3, 1913, February, 70-6 ;
March, 150—4 ; April, 212—6.

COOMBES, Bert Lewis

Stories
A 146 : The flame.
New Writing ; ed. by J. Lehmann, No. 3,
Spring, 1937, 131—4.
Penguin New Writing, No. 4, 62—66.

A 147 : Machine man.
New Writing ; ed. by J. Lehmann. No. 5, Spring 1938, 193—5.

A 148 : A miner's record—I.
New Writing and Daylight ; ed. by J. Lehmann, 1942, 46—62.

A 149 : Thick candles.
Penguin New Writing ; No. 21, 45—8.

A 150 : Twenty tons of coal.
New Writing, New Series, III, Christmas 1939, 159—174.
Penguin New Writing, No. 9, 35—59.

Prose
A 151 : Miners day. Illustrations by Isobel Alexander.
Harmondsworth, Middlesex ; Penguin Books, 1945.
[4], 5—128p. illus., port. 17½cm. wrappers.

A 152 : These poor hands : the autobiography of a miner working in South Wales.
London ; Gollancz, 1939.
286p. 19½cm. cloth.

Essays
A 153 : The Vale of Neath.
Wales, Vol. VII, no. 25, 1947, 216—221.

A 154 : Valley of Wales.
Anvil : life and the arts ; ed. by Jack Lindsay.
London, Meridian Books, 1947, 22—28.

A 155 : The way we live now.
Penguin New Writing ; No. 2, 9—15.

CORDELL, Alexander, *pseud.* [i. e. *George Alexander Graber*]

Novels
A 156 : The Hosts of Rebecca.
London ; Gollancz, 1960.
[8], 9—240p. 19½cm. cloth.
Location : Carmarthenshire, 1838—9.

A 157 : Rape of the fair country : a novel.
London ; Gollancz, 1959.
[8], 9—302p. 18½cm. cloth.
—New York ; Doubleday, 1959.
335p. boards.
Location : Monmouthshire [Garndyrus].

COURAGE, John, *pseud.* [i.e. *Richard Goyne*]

Novel
A 158 : Death of a village.
London, Melbourne [etc.] ; Stanley Paul, 1954.
[6], 7—192p. 18½cm. cloth.
Location : The village of "Llanader", N. Wales.

COURT, Lily

Verse
A 159 : Lyrics of leisure.
Penmaenmawr ; Venture Press, 1946.
[7], 8—42p. illus. 19cm. cloth.

COVE, Ernest George

Drama
A 160 : Those who wait : a play in one act.
Cardiff ; Educational Publishing Co. [1920].
[8], 9—35p. 15½cm. wrappers. (E.P.C. Welsh Drama Series, no. 18).
Scene : "Cwmyllwyd", S. Wales.

COXHEAD, Elizabeth

Novel
A 161 : One green bottle.
London ; Faber, 1951.
[6], 7—281p. 18⅙cm. cloth.
Location : North Wales : "Cae Capel" : rock-climbing areas.

CRAWSHAY-WILLIAMS, Eliot

Novels
A 162 : Rough passage : a novel.
London, New York ; John Long, [1950].
[4], 5—240p. 18½cm. cloth.
Partly located in Wales.

A 163 : Speckled virtue.
London ; John Long, [1940].
303p. 18½cm. cloth.
Location : A Welsh country house, "Brynglas".

A 164 : The Wolf from the west, tracing the glorious tragedy of Glyndŵr.
London, New York [etc.] ; John Long, [1947].
224p. 18½cm. cloth.
Reconstructs the life and times of Owain Glyndŵr.

Verse
A 165 : Barrage : a collection of poems.
London, New York ; John Long, [1944].
[9], 10—55p. 18½cm. wrappers.
Some poems of Welsh interest.

A 166 : Flak : a collection of poems. Wood engravings by Sibyl C. Williams.
London, New York [etc.] ; John Long, n.d.
56p. 18½cm. wrappers.
Includes poems of Welsh interest.

A 167 : The gutter and the stars.
London ; Erskine Macdonald, 1918.
[6], 7—86p. 18cm. boards.
Some poems on Welsh themes.

A 168   : No one wants poetry. Wood engravings by
Myfanwy Haycock.
Newtown ; Welsh Outlook Press, [1938].
[4], 5—66p. illus. 21½cm. boards.
Includes poems of Welsh interest.

A 169   : Songs on service.
Oxford ; B. H. Blackwell, 1917.
xi, 104, [4]p. 18cm. cloth.

A 170   : Our coast ; Welsh Outlook, Vol. XVII, 1930,
143.

Where now is sanctuary ? ; This and That,
London, 1947, 22.

Story
A 171   : God on the war ; Welsh Review, Vol. II,
no. 2, 1939, 66—76.

CRONIN, Archibald Joseph
Novel
A 172   : The Citadel.
London ; Gollancz, 1937.
[7], 8—446p.
Location : Partly in the Welsh mining town
of "Blaenelly".
Frequently reprinted.
—Another ed. London ; The New English
Library, 1965.
352p. 18cm. wrappers.
(Four Square Books Series).

Translated versions :
France : Le citadelle. 1949. 2 versions.
Spain : La ciudadela. 1949.
Holland : De citadel. 1948.
Greece : To Kastro. 1949.
Poland : Cytadela. 1948.
Finland : Sisarengas. 1948.

CROSLAND, Thomas William Hodgson
Prose
A 173   : Taffy was a Welshman.
London ; Ewart, Seymour & Co., 1912.
[9], 10—179p. 19cm. cloth.
Note : Includes a preface in which the author
denies that he was "Draig Glas" (q.v.).

CUDBIRD, G. M.
Verse
A 174   : Sonnet and song.
Cardiff ; Priory Press, 1946.
60p. 20cm. wrappers.

CUTTING, Vivien
Verse
A 175   : Tree of knowledge.
Newtown ; Montgomeryshire Printing Co.,
1952.
[8], 36p. 21½cm. wrappers.

A 176   : Above Gwynllyn, Rhayader ; Welsh Review,
Vol. IV, no. 1, 1945, 23.
Bombed sites ; ibid. 22.

Jephthah's daughter ; ibid. Vol. VII, no. 3,
1948, 198.

DANIEL, Glyn Edmund
Novel
A 177   : Welcome death.
London ; Gollancz, 1954.
[4], 5—231p. 18cm. cloth.
Location : "South Glamorgan village of
Llanddewi". (Text).
Reprinted : Harmondsworth, Penguin Books,
1962.
[6], 7—253p. 18cm. wrappers.
(Penguin Books, 1743).

Story
A 178   : Death at Christmas.
Welsh short stories ; ed. by G. Ewart Evans,
2nd ed. 1959, 71—82.

DAVID, Tudor
Stories
A 179   : The inhabitant ; Dock L., Vol. 8, no. 22,
[1958], 28—33.

A 180   : The interview ; ibid. Vol. 5, no. 14, 1954,
24—8.

A 181   : The treasure of the golden hair ; Y Ddinas,
Vol. 12, no. 9, 1958, 23.

DAVIES, Beryl M.
Verse
A 182   : Earth song.
[Brecon ; "Brecon & Radnor Express"], 1946.
[3], 4—33p. 18cm. cloth.

A 183   : Two things, and other poems.
[Brecon ; "Brecon & Radnor Express", 1944].
[3], 4—31[1]p. 18½cm. cloth.

DAVIES, Betty Eynon
Drama
A 184   : The four-leaved clover : a play in one act.
Cardiff ; Educational Publishing Co., 1920.
[4], 5—31p. 15½cm. wrappers.
(E.P.C. Welsh Drama Series, no. 39).
Scene : Farmhouse, S. Wales.

A 185   : Home : a play in one act.
Newtown ; Welsh Outlook Press, [1925].
[5], 6—28p. 18½cm. wrappers.
Scene : Kitchen in a small inn.

A 186 : The matchmaker : a play in one act.
Newtown ; Welsh Outlook Press, [1922].
[5], 6—39p. 15cm. wrappers.
Scene : A South Wales village.

DAVIES, Charles

Novel
A 187 : Welshman's way.
London ; (L. & V. Woolf at the) Hogarth
Press, 1927.
[4], 5—127p. 16½cm. wrappers. (Hogarth
Stories, 2).

Stories
A 188 : Cockadoodleoo.
Welsh Review, Vol. V, no. 3, 1946, 201—7.

A 189 : Count your blessings.
Writing Today, 2 ; ed. by D. Val Baker.
Staples P., 1945, 76—88.

A 190 : Pikelets and a penny.
Welsh Review, Vol. II, no. 3, 1939, 159—64.

Verse
A 191 : Anglesey ; Wales, Vol. V, no. 7, 1945, 64.

The eagle ; A Book of Aberystwyth Verse ;
ed. by C. Davies and E. K. Prosser, [1926],
10.

A feather in my cap ; ibid. 11.

"I was a stranger . . ." ; Welsh Outlook,
Vol. XII, 1925, 136.

Miss Saranna ; A Book of Aberystwyth Verse ;
ed. by C. Davies and E. K. Prosser, [1926],
12—3.

Noon ; ibid. 14.

Old Uncle Ned ; Welsh Outlook, Vol. XVIII,
1931, 24—5.

A portrait ; Welsh Outlook, Vol. XII, 1924,
333.

Portrait ; Wales, Vol. IV, no. 6, 1944/5, 13—4.

Portrait of several selves (for B.J.M.) ; Modern
Welsh Poetry ; ed. by K. Rhys, 1944, 20—2.

Roads ; Welsh Outlook, Vol. XI, 1924, 109.

There is a poem everywhere ; Modern Welsh
Poetry ; ed. by K. Rhys, 1944, 22.

Trearddur Bay ; Wales, Vol. VII, no. 26,
1947, 287.

DAVIES, Constance

Verse
A 192 : The French polisher : W. B. in memoriam ;
Modern Welsh Poetry ; ed. by K. Rhys,
1944, 23—6.

Mother ; Wales, Vol. V, no. 8/9, 1945, 20.

New triads ; Modern Welsh Poetry ; ed. by
K. Rhys, 1944, 26—7.

Night driving ; Wales, Vol. V, no. 8/9, 1945,
60.

A Picture ; ibid. Vol. V, no. 7, 1945, 74.

Rhaiadr ; Modern Welsh Poetry ; ed. by K.
Rhys, 1944, 27—8.

Snowdon ; Battlefield ; Wales, New Series, 2,
1943, 70.

DAVIES, D. (of Molleston)

Story
A 193 : Pembrokeshire stories, by D. Davies (of
Molleston).
London ; Stockwell, n.d.
[4]. 5—93p. 18½cm. limp boards.

DAVIES, David Thomas

Stories
A 194 : Billy Hopkins : [a study in boy-nature].
The Dragon, May 1904, 222—8.

A 195 : A bit of life : [a short story].
The Dragon, Dec. 1903, 71—4.

A 196 : Old Peg.
The Welsh Outlook, Vol. II, 1915, 22—24.

Drama
A 197 : The barber and the cow.
Oxford ; Blackwell, 1926.
[8], 108p. 18½cm. boards. (British Drama
League Library of Modern British Drama,
No. 15).
Scene : "Llanybryn", a village in Wales.

A 198 : Pancakes : a play in one act ; translated from
the Welsh by the author.
London ; J. G. Miller, 1960.
[3], 4—16p. 18½cm. wrappers.
Scene : Kitchen of a miner's home.
Welsh version entitled "Ffrois".

A 199 : Where is he ? a one-act play.
Stratford-upon-Avon ; Shakespeare Head
Press, 1917.
[7], 8—28p. 19cm. wrappers.
Scene : Glamorgan : miner's home.
Welsh version entitled : Ble Ma' Fe ?

DAVIES, Dudley Garnet

Verse
A 200 : Poems.
Calcutta and Simla; Thacker, Spink, 1921.
[6], 49p. 19cm. cloth.

A 201 : Carmarthenshire ; They Look at Wales : an anthology of prose and verse, 1941, 16—7.

The caverned harp ; Welsh Outlook, Vol. XI, 1924, 53.

The cliffs of Aberystwyth ; Wales (J.H.E.), Vol. 6, Aug. 1914, 297.

The cradle of the dawn ; ibid. May 1914, 156.

Home thoughts from England ; Welsh Outlook, Vol. XVIII, 1931, 300.

A little Welsh maid ; Wales (J.H.E.), Vol. 6, July 1914, 273.

Moon ; The Poetry Review, Vol. 45, 1954, 88.

Mycenean tombs ; ibid. Vol. 46, 1955, 201.

Nature's little optimist ; Wales (J.H.E.), Vol. 6, March 1914, 11.

Sonnet to Homer ; ibid. June 1914, 193.

To a mound on Garn-goch, Llangadock ; ibid. Vol. 5, Nov. 1913, 47.

DAVIES, Evan   *"Dyfrig"*

Verse
A 202 : 1914—1918.
London ; Stockwell, [1936].
[2], 78p. front. (port.) 18cm. cloth.

DAVIES, Gloria Evans

Verse
A 203 : Words for Blodwen.
London ; Chatto & Windus ; Hogarth Press, 1962.
(Phoenix Living Poets Series).
40p. 22½cm. cloth.

A 204 : Cat ; PEN 1957, 37.
Celebration ; PEN 1965, 58.

DAVIES, Glyn Dŵr

Stories
A 205 : Shop closed, and other stories.
Ilfracombe ; Stockwell, 1953.
[2], 3—44p. 18½cm. wrappers.

DAVIES, Gwyn

Novels
A 206 : Ann's vocation.
Glasgow ; Pickering & Inglis, *printers*, [1947].
16p. 22cm. (The Lily Library, no. 227).
Location : Llandore and "Gower Island".

A 207 : Davy, the Welsh boy.
London ; Pickering & Inglis, 1947.
[10], 11—160p. col. front., illus. 18cm. cloth.
Location : Breconshire, early 19th century.

A 208 : Hugh the blacksmith.
London ; Kingsgate Press, 1946.
[4], 5—96p. col. front. 18cm. cloth.
Location : Black Mountains and Welsh Border areas.

A 209 : When spring returns.
London ; Victory Press, 1947.
[4], 5—223p. col. front., 18½cm. cloth.

DAVIES, Helen G.

Novels
A 210 : Mingled wine.
London ; J. Long, 1926.
318p. 18½cm. cloth.
Location : North Wales.

A 211 : Peter Curtis and his.
London ; J. Long, 1926.
318p. 18½cm. cloth.
Location : Partly located in a South Wales mining area.

DAVIES, Howell

Stories
A 212 : Baboons.
Celtic Story, Number One ; ed. by Aled Vaughan, 1946, 116—22.

A 213 : This is what happened.
Welsh Outlook, Vol. X, January 1923, 9—11.

A 214 : Tomos-the-little-man.
Welsh Review, Vol. IV, no. 4, 1945, 247—50.

Verse
A 215 : Alchemy ; A Book of Aberystwyth Verse ; ed. by Charles Davies and E. K. Prosser. [1926], 15.

Dead man's joy ; ibid. 18.

Folly ; ibid. 17.

The kiss of death ; Welsh Outlook, Vol. V, 1918, 76.

My captain ; ibid. 75.

Our dead ; The Dragon, April 1919, 69.

Sounds of summer ; Poetry Qtly., Vol. 3, no. 2, 1941, 43.

Swallow wings ; A Book of Aberystwyth Verse ; ed. by Charles Davies and E. K. Prosser, [1926], 16.

A tavern song ; Welsh Outlook, Vol. XII, 1925, 51.

DAVIES, Idris

Prose

A 216 : Land of my mothers ; Wales, no. 4, March 1938, 141—4.

A 217 : Shadows and cakes ; ibid. no. 3, 1937, 115-6.

Verse

A 218 : The angry summer : a poem of 1926. London ; Faber, 1943. [4], 5—56p. 21½cm. cloth.

A 219 : Gwalia deserta. London ; Dent, 1938. [6], 26p. 18½cm. cloth.

A 220 : Selected poems of Idris Davies. London ; Faber, 1953. [4], 5—68p. 21cm. cloth.

A 221 : Tonypandy, and other poems. London ; Faber, 1945. [4], 5—70p. 21½cm. cloth.

A 222 : The black tips of Rhondda ; Bristol Writers and Artists Association. Bristol Packet [No. 2], [1945], 24. Little Reviews Anthology, 1946, 154.

Capel Hebron ; A Book of Wales ; ed. by D. M. & E. M. Lloyd, 1953, 261.

Childhood ; Writing Today, 3, Staples P., 1946, 38.

The coast of Kerry ; Wales, New Series, 3, January 1944, 7—8.

The county of Monmouth ; Praise of Wales ; comp. by Maxwell Fraser, 1950, 53.

Dai's Empire ; Wales, No. 4, March 1938, 153.

Deacon at Bethany ; Wales, New Series, 3, January 1944, 9.

Derby Day, 1946 ; Wales, Vol. VI, no. 24, 1946, 17.

Early morning ; Rhyme and reason ; ed. by David Martin. Fore Publications, 1944, 7.

Excerpt from "Gwalia Deserta", Stanza XV ; Modern Welsh Poetry ; ed. by K. Rhys, Faber, 1944, 29—30.

Excerpt from "Gwalia Deserta" : "O what can you give me ? . . . Sing the silver bells of Wye !" ; *In* The colour of saying : an anthology of verse spoken by Dylan Thomas; ed. by R. N. Maud and A. T. Davies, 1963, 49—50.

From Ammanford to Fleur-de-Lys ; Modern Welsh Poetry ; ed. by K. Rhys, 1944, 31—2.

Hywel and Blodwen ; Modern Welsh Poetry ; ed. by K. Rhys, 1944, 28—9. Poetry Book Magazine, Vol. 6, no. 5, Fall, 1954, 10.

In Cheltenham ; Bristol Packet, Bristol ; Bristol Writers' Association [1944], 34.

In gardens in the Rhondda ; A Book of Wales ; ed. by D. M. and E. M. Lloyd, 1953, 48—9.

In Glasnevin Cemetery ; Dock L., Vol. 3, no. 8, 1952, 28.

In Memoriam ; PEN 1952, 101.

Interlude ; Wales, No. 1, 1937, 17. Modern Welsh Poetry, 1944, 31.

Irish railway station ; Wales, No. 4, March 1938, 152. The First 'Comment' Treasury, 1937, 35.

The lay preacher ponders ; The Faber book of twentieth-century verse ; ed. by J. H. Stubbs and D. Wright, 1953, 122—3.

The leopard ; Modern reading, 14 ; ed. by R. Moore, 1947, 103.

London Welsh ; Wales, New Series, 3, January 1944, 7. Little Reviews Anthology, 1945, 176—7.

Mining valley ; Welsh Review, Vol. II, no. 3, 1939, 140.

Mists upon the sea ; Dock L., Vol. 2, no. 6, 1951, 36.

Monmouthshire, Wales ; Pencader Poems, 1952, [14].

Morning comes again ; Wales, No. 20, 1939, 271.

Mrs. Evans Fach ; A Book of Wales ; ed. by D. M. and E. M. Lloyd, 1953, 182.

Near Rhymney ; Wales, No. 4, March 1938, 152—3.

One February evening ; LLT, Vol. 22, no. 25, [1939], 408—9.

Out of Gwalia ; Rhyme and reason ; ed. by David Martin, Fore Publications, 1944.

Pembroke coast ; Modern reading, 14 ; ed. by R. Moore, 1947, 104.

The places of my boyhood ; A Book of Wales ; ed. by D. M. and E. M. Lloyd, 1953, 46.

The poet ; Welsh Review, Vol. II, no. 3, 1939, 140.

Renaissance ; Modern Welsh Poetry, 1944, 33. Wales, No. 1, 1937, 18.

Respice finem ; Welsh Outlook, Vol. XIX, 1932, 36.

Re-union ; ibid.   98.

Rhymney ; A Book of Wales ; ed. by D. M. and E. M. Lloyd, 1953, 46—7.

The sacrifice ; LLT., Vol. 20, no. 17, 1939, 50.

The seeker ; Wales, Vol. V, no. 7, 1945, 68.

Snowflake ; Welsh Review, Vol. III, no. 4, 1944, 249.

Sonnet ; Modern Welsh Poetry, 1944, 32. Wales, No. 1, 1937, 17.

Tiger Bay ; Wales, New Series, 3, January 1944, 8.

Two framed pictures ; LLT., Vol. 21, no. 19, 1939, 49.

William Morris ; Wales, No. 3, Autumn 1937, 83.
Modern Welsh Poetry ; ed. by K. Rhys, 1944, 30.

DAVIES, Idris Garmon

Verse
A   223   : Jewels and dust [by ' Garmon '].
Abertridwr (Glam.), Cymric Federation Press, 1947.
[3], 4—48p. illus. port. 22cm. wrappers.
Includes some poems on Welsh themes.

DAVIES, Jonathan

Verse
A   224   : Burdens in bloom : poems of nature and devotion.
Newtown ; Montgomeryshire Printing Co. [1937].
48p.   18cm.   wrappers.

DAVIES, Naunton Wingfield   *"Naunton Covertside"*

Novels
A   225   : The King's guide : a romance.
London ; Drane, n.d. [Preface 1901].
viii, 352 [4]p. 18cm. cloth.
—Another edition.   London ; Simpkin Marshall, 1901.

A   226   : The Reverend Jack.
London ; Drane, n.d.
[6] + [7], 8—455p. 19cm. cloth.
Location : "Llanybont", rural area.

A   227   : The secret of a hollow tree : a novel.
London ; Drane n.d.
vii, [1], 317p. 18cm. cloth.
Location : Llantrisant, Glam.

Drama
A   228   : The arrogance of power : a drama of 1925.
Cardiff ; Educational Publishing Co., 1920.
[4], 5—128p. 15½cm. wrappers. (E.P.C. Welsh Drama Series, no. 35).
Scene : Manor Glyn, Glamorgan.
—[*Also* : Act V. A rewritten version. Published separately].

A   229   : The conversion : a comedy in one act.
Cardiff ; Educational Publishing Co., 1920.
[8], 9—32p. 15½cm. wrappers. (E.P.C. Welsh Drama Series, no. 33).
Scene : A house in Glamorganshire.

A   230   : The epidemic : a sketch.
Cardiff ; Educational Publishing Co., 1920.
[4], 5—24p. 15½cm. wrappers. (E.P.C. Welsh Drama Series, no. 31).
Scene : A Glamorgan farm.

A   231   : The great experiment : a play in four acts, by Naunton Davies and Stanley Drewitt.
Cardiff ; Educational Publishing Co., n.d.
[6], 7—143p. 15cm. wrappers. (E.P.C. Plays, no. 17).
Scene : "Wenallt Castle".

A   232   : The human factor : a play in four acts.
Cardiff ; Educational Publishing Co., 1920.
[6], 7—143p. 15½cm. wrappers. (E.P.C. Welsh Drama Series, no. 36).
Scene : Glamorgan, 1910.

A   233   : The schemer : a play in three acts and three scenes.
Cardiff ; Educational Publishing Co., 1920.
[8], 9—128p. 15½cm. wrappers. (E.P.C. Welsh Drama Series, no. 34).
Scene : Partly in Glamorgan, 1913.

A   234   : The second son : a play in three acts.
Cardiff ; Educational Publishing Co., 1920.
[6], 7—160p. 15½cm. wrappers. (E.P.C. Welsh Drama Series, no. 30).
Scene : Cardiganshire.

A 235   : The village wizard : a comedy in one act.
Cardiff ; Educational Publishing Co., 1913.
[3], 4—24p. 18cm. wrappers.
Scene : Tailor's work-room.
Welsh version by J. Ifano Jones, entitled
Dewin y Pentref.

DAVIES, Noëlle

Verse
A 236   : Middle country.
Newtown, Mont. ; Welsh Outlook Press, 1936.
[4], 5—48p. 24cm. wrappers.

A 237   : A ballad of the last battle (*c.* 1409) ; Pencader
Poems, 1952, 8—11.
Moonrise in the hills ; The Jongleur, Autumn
1931, no. 18 [unpaged].
The Old Man of Pencader ; Pencader Poems,
1952, [1].
September gold ; The Jongleur, Spring 1932,
no. 20 [unpaged].

DAVIES, Nora E.

Verse
A 238   : After seeing Epstein's Lazarus ; Dock L.,
Vol. I, no. 2, 1950, 30—1.

Cardigan Bay ; ibid. Vol. I, no. 1, 1949, 21.

Christmas Eve ; ibid. 22.

Creative art ; ibid. Vol. 3, no. 7, 1952, 6.

The dance of Spring ; ibid. Vol. I, no. 2.
1950, 31—2.

I shall have died ; ibid. Vol. I, no. 1, 1949,
21.

The music room ; ibid. Vol. 2, no. 4, 1951,
41.

On first seeing a coloured women (sic) in a
London church ; ibid. Vol. I, no. 1,
1949, 20—1.

DAVIES, Oliver

Verse
A 239   : Between-time poems.
London, New York ; John Lane, 1909.
vii, [5], 106 + [14]p. 18½cm. cloth.

A 240   : Plain song.
London ; Staples Press, 1949.
[4], 5—70p. 22cm. cloth.

A 241   : Songs and signs.
Oxford ; Blackwell, 1920.
viii, 62p. 19½cm. wrappers.

A 242   : Songs at random.
London ; Dent, 1912.
63p. 19cm. cloth.

A 243   : Ar hyd y nos ; Dock L., Vol. 3, no. 8, 1952, 13.

Caress the world ; A-W.R., Vol. 9, no. 23
[undated], 41.

The day before ; Welsh Poets ; comp. by A. G.
Prys-Jones, 1917, 28—9.

Y Ddraig Goch ; Welsh Outlook, Vol. V,
1918, 151.

Elms ; Exiles ; Welsh Review, Vol. 1, no. 5,
1939, 248—9.

Happy-go-lucky ; Welsh Poets ; comp. by
A. G. Prys-Jones, 1917, 26.

Home-sickness ; ibid. 27—8.

Our allies ; A-W.R., Vol. 9, no. 23 [undated],
42.

Stranelake ; Welsh Poets ; comp. by A. G.
Prys-Jones, 1917, 25—6.

Themes ; A-W.R., Vol. 9, no. 23 [undated],
42.

Token-time ; ibid. 41.

To one who detracted ; Welsh Outlook, Vol.
XII, 1925, 51.

Up to you ; The Poetry Review, Vol. 41
no. 2, 1950, 66.

DAVIES, Rhys

Novels
A 244   : Arfon.
London ; Foyle [1931].
[4], 68p. 21½cm. cloth.
Limited ed. of 400 copies, numbered 1 to 400
and twelve copies lettered A to L. NLW has
signed copy no. 3.

A 245   : A bed of feathers.
London ; The Mandrake Press, [1929].
[4], 5—93p. front. 15cm. cloth.
Location : A mining valley.

A 246   : The black Venus.
London, Toronto ; Heinemann, 1944.
[4], 200p. 18½cm. cloth.
—Another ed. London ; Pan Books, 1949.
254p.
Location : Welsh rural area.

Translated version :
Swedish. Den svarta Venus.
Stockholm, Fritzes Bökforlog, 1948.
—Helsingfors, Söderstrom, 1948.

A 247   : Count your blessings.
London, New York ; Putnam, 1932.
[6], 7—319p. 18½cm. cloth.
Location : "Craig Ddu".

A 248   : The dark daughters.
London, Toronto ; Heinemann, 1947.
[4], 298p. 18½cm. cloth.

A 249   : Girl waiting in the shade.
London, Melbourne [etc.] ; Heinemann, 1960.
[4], 207p. 18½cm. cloth.
Location : Partly in Wales.

A 250   : Honey and bread.
London ; Putnam, 1935.
[6], 7—365p. 18½cm. cloth.
Location : Glamorgan, early 19th century.

A 251   : Jubilee blues.
London, Toronto ; Heinemann, 1938.
[4], 315p. 19cm. cloth.
Location : Glamorgan mining valley.

A 252   : Marianne.
London, Melbourne ; Heinemann, 1951.
[4], 301p. 18cm. cloth.
Location : "Mainly South Wales coast"
(Wrapper).

A 253   : The perishable quality : a novel.
London, Melbourne [etc.] ; Heinemann, 1957.
[4], 238p. 19½cm. cloth.
Location : South Wales town of "Bylau", and
London.

A 254   : The red hills.
London, New York ; Putnam, 1932.
[9], 10—250p. 18½cm. cloth.
Location : A Welsh mining village.
—Another ed. New York ; Covici, Friede,
1933.

A 255   : Rings on her fingers.
London ; Shaylor, 1930.
[8], 9—256p. 18½cm. cloth.
—Another ed. Collector's ed. Shaylor, 1930.
—American ed. New York ; Harcourt,
Brace, [1930].

A 256   : The stars, the world and the women . . . with
a foreword by Liam O'Flaherty and an
illustration by Frank C. Pape.
London ; William Jackson (Books), 1930.
[6], 7—53p. front. 25cm. cloth. (Furnival
Books, no. 4).
550 copies signed by the author, 500 only
being for sale.
NLW has signed copy no. 28.

A 257   : A time to laugh.
London, Toronto ; Heinemann, 1937.
[6], 432p. 19½cm. cloth.

A 258   : Tomorrow to fresh woods.
London, Toronto ; Heinemann, 1941.
[6], 315p. 18½cm. cloth.
Location : Mining valley town of "Wern".

A 259   : Under the rose.
London, Toronto ; Heinemann, 1940.
[6], 333p. 19cm. cloth.
Location : Morlais House, the village of
"Sarn".

A 260   : The withered root.
London ; R. Holden, 1927.
[8], 280p. 18½cm. cloth.
Location : S. Wales mining valley.
—Another ed. New York ; H. Holt, 1928.

Short story volumes
A 261   : Aaron.
London ; Archer, 1927.
[2], 3—11p. 25¾cm. wrappers.
One hundred copies printed. NLW has
signed copy no. 80.
Location : A Welsh valley.

A 262   : Boy with a trumpet.
London, Melbourne ; Heinemann, 1949.
[6], 265p. 18½cm. cloth.
Contents : The dilemma of Catherine Fuchsias
—Boy with a trumpet—Canute—A Human
condition—Fear—The fashion plate—The
foolish one—The beard—Wigs, costumes,
masks.

A 263   : The collected stories of Rhys Davies.
London, Melbourne ; Heinemann, 1955.
viii, 416p. 19½cm. cloth.

A 264   : Daisy Matthews and three other tales by
Rhys Davies, with wood engravings by
Agnes Miller Parker.
Waltham St. Lawrence ; The Golden Cockerel
Press, 1932.
[4], 64p. illus. 24cm. cloth.
Limited ed. of 325 copies. NLW has signed
copy no. 22.
Contents : Daisy Matthews—The wanderer—
The sleeping beauty—Lovers.

A 265   : The darling of her heart, and other stories.
London, Melbourne [etc.] ; Heinemann, 1958.
[6], 233p. 19½cm. cloth.
Contents : All through the night—A spot of
bother—Afternoon of a faun—The darling
of her heart—Man up a tree—A visit to
Eggeswick Castle—The wedding at The
Lion—Period piece—Tears, idle tears.
(Two of these stories have non-Welsh
locations).

A 266   : A finger in every pie.
London ; Heinemann, 1942.
[6], 177p. 18½cm. cloth.
Contents : The wages of love—Abraham's
glory—Charity—Mourning for Ianto—The

nature of man—A pearl of great price—
Nightgown—Alice's pins—The dark world
—Ancient courtship—Over at rainbow
bottom—The pits are on the top—Weep not,
my wanton—The zinnias—Pleasures of the
table—Tomos and the harp—The parrot—
Queen of the Côte d'azur.

A 267 : Love provoked.
London, New York ; Putnam, 1933.
[6], 7—301p. 18½cm. cloth.
Contents : Daisy Matthews—The romantic
policewoman—Lovers—Doris in Gomorrah
—The journey—The wanderer—The bard
—The sleeping beauty—A bed of feathers—
Faggots—Arfon.

A 268 : A pig in a poke : stories.
London : Joiner & Steele, 1931.
280p. 18½cm. cloth.
Contents : Death in the family—A pig in a
poke—The new garment—Conflict in Morfa
—The song of songs—The stars, the world
and the women—The lily—Mrs. Evans
number six—The sisters—A gift of death—
Evelyn and Ivor—The doctor's wife—
Blodwen—Hunger.

A 269 : Selected stories.
London, Dublin ; Maurice Fridberg, 1945.
[4], 5—127p. 18cm. wrappers. (Hour-
Glass Library Series, ed. by Reginald
Moore).
Contents : Resurrection—The contraption—
Revelation—Death in the family—Conflict
in Morfa—Wrath—Arfon—The Bard—
The Journey—Cherry-blossom on the Rhine.

A 270 : The song of songs, and other stories.
London ; Archer, [1927].
53p. front. (port.) 21cm. wrappers.
Limited ed. of 100 copies privately printed.
NLW has signed copy no. 14.
Contents : A gift of death—The sisters—Mrs.
Evans Number Six—History—The lily—
The song of songs.

A 271 : The things men do : short stories.
London ; Heinemann, 1936.
266p. 19cm. cloth.
Contents : The two friends—The contraption—
Wrath—Cherry-blossom on the Rhine—The
friendly creature—Glimpses of the moon—
The funeral—Caleb's ark—Resurrection—
Half holiday—The farm—On the tip.

A 272 : The trip to London : stories.
London, Toronto [etc.] ; Heinemann, 1946.
[4], 128p. 18½cm. cloth.
Contents : The benefit concert—A dangerous
remedy—The last struggle—Price of a
wedding ring—The trip to London—
Gents only—The public-house—River, flow
gently—Spectre de la rose—Death of a
canary—Orestes.

A 273 : A woman.
London ; Capell, at the Bronze Snail P., 1931.
[8], 9—39p. 23cm. cloth.
165 copies printed for sale. 17 presentation
copies printed and lettered A—L. (NLW
has presentation copy I). Text, with some
variation, is partly the text of Chap. I of
Count Your Blessings.

Single Stories
A 274 : The benefit concert.
Best World Short Stories, 1947 ; ed. by J.
Cournos and S. Norton, 23—32.
Welsh short stories ; ed. by Gwyn Jones, 1956,
9—21.

A 275 : Canute.
Celtic Story, Number One ; edited by Aled
Vaughan, 1946, 10—9.
Little Reviews Anthology, 1947—48, 8—17.
Welsh Review, Vol. V, no. 2, 1946, 85—93.

A 276 : The dark world.
The Toc H gift book ; edited by Hilda Hughes.
2nd ed. [London ; Muller, 1945].

A 277 : Deplorable story.
Wales, No. 3, Autumn 1937, 90—8.

A 278 : The dilemma of Catherine Fuchsias.
Welsh short stories ; ed. by G. Ewart Evans,
1959, 17—35.

A 279 : Fear.
Pick of today's short stories, No. 2, 1950, 71—6.

A 280 : Harvest moon.
Little Reviews Anthology, 1946, 18—26.
Modern international short stories ; ed. by D.
Val Baker [1946], 14—22.

A 281 : The last struggle.
English story. Fifth series ; ed. by Woodrow
Wyatt, 1944, 107—18.

A 282 : The nature of man.
Stories of the Forties. Vol. 1 : ed. by R.
Moore and W. Wyatt, Nicholson & Watson,
1945, 92—7.
Welsh short stories ; ed. by Gwyn Jones, 1956,
1—8.

A 283 : On the tip.
Voyage ; ed. by D. Val Baker. Sylvan Press,
1945, 13—20.

A 284 : Petticoat House [excerpt from a work in
progress] ; Modern Reading, no. 15 ; ed.
by R. Moore, 1947, 89—105.

A 285 : Spectre de la rose.
English story. Sixth series ; ed. by Woodrow
Wyatt, 1945, 81—92.

A 286 : The stars, the world and the women.
Modern Reading, no. 6. London, [1943],
52—73.

A 287 : The wedding at the Lion.
Wales, September 1958, 51—62.

Other Prose
A 288 : From a notebook ; Wales, Vol. IV, no. 5,
1944, 64—70.

A 289 : From my notebook. [No. II] ; Wales, New
Series, 2, October 1943, 10—2.

A 290 : From my notebook (III) ; Wales. Vol. VI,
no. 2, 1946, 13—8.

A 291 : Time and the Welsh mountains ; Countryside
character ; comp. by Richard Harman.
London ; Blandford Press, 1946, 209—19.

Drama
A 292 : [The maid of Cefn Ydfa : a play].
No published version traced. Welsh version
"Y Ferch o Gefn Ydfa" ; trans. by T. J.
Williams-Hughes.
Liverpool, Brython Press, 1938.

A 293 : No escape : a play in three acts from his novel
"Under the Rose", by Rhys Davies in
collaboration with Archibald Batty.
London ; Evans, 1955.
[9], 10—72p. front. plan. 21½cm. wrappers.
Scene : Morlais, a Welsh farmhouse.
—*Also in :* Ring up the curtain. Heinemann,
1955, 101—94.

DAVIES, Thomas Edmund Coedfryn

Verse
A 294 : Passion flowers.
Carmarthen ; Spurrell, [1928].
[9], 10—71p. front. (port.) plate. 18cm.
wrappers.

A 295 : Woodland breezes : a collection of miscellaneous poems, by T. Edmund Davies (ab
Coedfryn).
Carmarthen ; Spurrell, [1925].
[5], 6—68p. front. (port.) plates. 18½cm.
wrappers.
—Another ed. 2nd ed. [Sub-title : Short
poems].
Carmarthen, Spurrell, [1926].
[7], 8—70 [2]p. front. (port.) plates.
18½cm. wrappers.

A 296 : Field-fever ; Welsh Outlook, Vol. XIII, 1926,
328.

Gwalia ; ibid. 328.

Magdalene ; ibid. 188.

O why these tears ! ; ibid. 121.

An Oriental passing ; ibid. 121.

Sailor love ; ibid. 162.

DAVIES, William Henry (1871—1940)

Note : The publication history of the works of W. H.
Davies would properly constitute a personal
bibliography in its own right. A complete
chronology of his published volumes will be
found in Stonesifer, Richard J., *W. H.
Davies : a critical biography.* See Section B :
97.
As the majority of his published poems are
on general themes, and cannot discernibly
be proved to be written against a specifically
Welsh locale or on a Welsh theme, a selection
only of the works of W. H. Davies is appended
below. Entries A 297—325 comprise volumes
of the complete and collected poems, prose
works relevant to his personal history and a
selection of W. H. Davies' many contributions
to anthologies and periodical publications.

Prose
A 297 : The adventures of Johnny Walker, tramp.
London ; Cape, 1926.
[4], 5—256p. 18½cm. cloth.
—Another ed. London ; Brown, Watson,
1963.
[6], 7—238p. 18cm. wrappers. (Digit
Books).

A 298 : The autobiography of a super-tramp . . . with
a preface by Bernard Shaw.
London ; Fifield, 1908.
xiv, 295p.

Reprinted : 1908, 1911.
—Another ed. 4th ed. Fifield, 1917.
—Another ed. 5th ed. Fifield, 1920.
—American ed. New York ; Knopf, 1917.
—Another ed. London ; Cape, 1926.
(Travellers' Library Series).
—Another ed. Cape, 1930. (Life & Letters
Series).
—Another ed. London ; Allen & Unwin,
1951. (Windsor Selections Series).
—Another ed. London ; Brown, Watson, 1960.

A 299 : Later days.
London ; Cape, 1925.
[6], 7—223p. 19cm. cloth.

A 300 : A poet's pilgrimage.
London ; Melrose, 1918.
[8], 9—378p. 18½cm. cloth.
Includes Welsh locations.

A 301 : The true traveller.
London ; Duckworth, 1912.
viii, 292 [4], 20p. 18½cm. cloth.

Verse

A 302 : The complete poems of W. H. Davies, with
an introduction by Osbert Sitwell and a
foreword by Daniel George.
London ; Cape, 1963.
xxxiv, 616p. 19½cm. cloth.
Wrapper : . . . "contains, it is believed, all the
poems written and published by W. H.
Davies. It supersedes *Collected Poems* which
appeared first in 1942 . . ." [Total of 749
poems].

A 303 : Collected poems.
London ; Fifield, 1916.
vii, [1], 9—160p. front. (port.) facsim.
18½cm. cloth.
Includes facsimile of the poet's script.
—Another impression. Cape, 1923. 4th imp.
1925. 5th imp.

A 304 : Collected poems : second series.   With a
portrait by Augustus John.
London ; Cape, 1923.
157p. port. cloth.
—2nd impression. Cape, 1923.

A 305 : Collected poems of W. H. Davies.
London ; Cape, 1928.
xx, 399p. 19cm. cloth.
—2nd impression. Cape, 1929.

A 306 : The poems of W. H. Davies.
London ; Cape, 1934.
[4], 5—475p. 19cm. cloth.

A 307 : The poems of W. H. Davies, 1940.
London ; Cape, 1940.
525p. front. (port.) 19½cm. cloth.

A 308 : Collected poems.
[London ; Cape, 1942]. Copy not traced.
(Noted in *Complete Poems*, 1963).
—Another impression. With introduction by
Osbert Sitwell. Cape, 1943.
Further impressions : 1945, 1947, 1948, 1951,
1955.

Verse   *Collected in anthologies* (by date of publication).
Locations of more than one poem in the same
anthology :

A 309 : The child and the mariner ; Georgian Poetry,
1911-12 ; ed. by E. H. Marsh. London,
Poetry Bookshop, 1912—13, 55—9.
Days too short ; ibid. 60.
In May ; ibid. 61.
The heap of rags ; ibid. 62.
The kingfisher ; ibid. 63.

A 310 : Thunderstorms ; Georgian Poetry, 1913—
1915 ; ed. by E. H. Marsh, 1915, 65.
The mind's liberty ; ibid. 66.
The moon ; ibid. 67.
When on a summer's morn ; ibid. 68.
A great time ; ibid. 69.

The hawk ; ibid. 70.
Sweet stay-at-home ; ibid. 71.
A fleeting passion ; ibid. 72.
The bird of paradise ; ibid. 73.

A 311 : Brothers ; *In* An Annual of new poetry.
London, Constable, 1917, 19.
The bell ; ibid. 20.
In England ; ibid. 21.
Jove warns us ; ibid. 22.
Angel and mystery ; ibid. 23.

A 312 : The white cascade ; Georgian Poetry, 1916—
1917 ; ed. by E. H. Marsh. London, 1918
(i.e. Nov. 1917), 159.
Easter ; ibid. 160.
Raptures ; ibid. 161.
Cowslips and larks ; ibid. 162.

A 313 : Lovely dames ; Georgian Poetry, 1918-19 ; ed.
by E. H. Marsh. London, 1919, 29.
When yon full moon ; ibid. 30.
On hearing Mrs. Woodhouse play the
harpsichord ; 31.
Birds ; ibid. 32.
Oh, sweet content ! ibid. 33.
A child's pet ; ibid. 34.
England ; ibid. 35.
The bell ; ibid. 36.

A 314 : The captive lion ; Georgian Poetry, 1920—22 ;
ed. by E. H. Marsh. London, 1922, 37.
A bird's anger ; ibid. 38.
The villain ; ibid. 39.
Love's caution ; ibid. 40.
Wasted hours ; ibid. 41.
The truth ; ibid. 42.

A 315 : Thunderstorms ; *In* The Golden Treasury of
Modern Lyrics ; arr. by Laurence Binyon.
London, Macmillan, 1924, 200.
The example ; ibid. 214—5.
The hawk ; ibid. 311—2.
A thought ; ibid. 314—5.

A 316 : Logic ; *In* Then and Now. London, Cape,
1935, 26.
The woods and the banks ; ibid. 58.
Lemorna Cove ; ibid. 111.
Charity ; ibid. 126.
Hunting joy ; ibid. 140.
Wild oats ; ibid. 209.

A 317 : Joy and pleasure ; *In* The Oxford book of
modern verse, 1892—1935 ; [comp.] by
W. B. Yeats. Oxford U.P., 1947, 128—9.
Truly great ; ibid. 129—30.
Leisure ; ibid. 131.
The sluggard ; ibid. 132.
The best friend ; ibid. 132-3.
School's out ; ibid. 133.

A 318 : Songs of joy ; *In* The Oxford book of Victorian
verse ; [comp.] by Arthur Quiller-Couch.
1948, 970.

Truly great ; ibid. 971.
Money ; ibid. 972.
In May ; ibid. 972—3.
Leisure ; ibid. 973—4.
The elements ; ibid. 974.

A 319 : One poet visits another ; *In* The Faber book
of twentieth-century verse ; ed. by J.
Heath-Stubbs and D. Wright, 1953, 124.
The truth ; ibid. 124—5.
A lovely woman ; ibid. 125—6.

A 320 : Joy and pleasure ; *In* Modern Verse, 1900—
1950. (Comp. by Phyllis M. Jones). 2nd
ed. enl. 1955. Oxford U.P., 1955, 63—4.
Leisure ; ibid. 64—5.
School's out ; ibid. 65.
Days that have been ; ibid. 65—6.

A 321 : The moon ; *In* Modern verse in English ; ed.
by David Cecil and Allen Tate. London,
Eyre & Spottiswoode, 1958, 155.
A great time ; ibid. 155.
The bird of Paradise ; ibid. 155—6.
The kingfisher ; ibid. 156—7.

A 322 : Days too short ; *In* Poems of Our Time,
1900—1960. Dent, 1959, 46.
School's out ; ibid. 68.
In the snow ; ibid. 79.
A great time ; ibid. 86.
A thought ; ibid. 119.

A 323 : The happy child ; *In* Poems of Our Time,
1900—1962. Dent, 1959, 34.
Sweet stay-at-home ; ibid. 53.
The example ; ibid. 63.
Thunderstorms ; ibid. 65.
The kingfisher ; ibid. 66.
The rain ; ibid. 66.
The moon ; ibid. 86.
The villain ; ibid. 125.
The beautiful ; ibid. 137.
The mourner ; ibid. 250.

A 324 : The inquest ; *In* The colour of saying : an
anthology of verse spoken by Dylan
Thomas ; ed. by R. N. Maud and A. T.
Davies, 1963, 50—1.
One poet visits another ; ibid. 51.
The poet ; ibid. 52.

Verse   *Single locations*
A 325 : At night ; The Spectator, Feb. 10, 1923, 241.

Common joys ; The British Annual of Literature, 1938, Vol. I, 25.

Days that have been ; Presenting Welsh
Poetry, 1959, 105.
A Book of Wales ; ed. by D. M. & E. M. Lloyd,
1953, 341.

Dogs ; *In* Manning-Sanders, Ruth, *comp.*
Birds, beasts and fishes. Oxford U.P. 1962,
23.

Dreams of the sea ; *In* Hope, Ronald, The
Harrap book of sea verse, 1960, 49.

Eldorado's gold ; English Review, Aug. 1912,
1—2.

The example ; *In* A tale that is told ; comp. by
Arthur B. Allen, 1960, 159.

First joys, *from* "Infancy" ; Love for life ;
ed. by John Hadfield, 1961, 29.

The hospital waiting-room ; *In* Reeves,
James, *comp.* The Cassell book of English
poetry, 1965, 959.

I am the poet Davies, William ; ibid. 960.

The inquest ; ibid. 961.

The inquest ; *In* Palgrave, F. T. *ed.* The
Golden Treasury. 5th ed. (with a new
Fifth Book ed. by John Press), Oxford U.P.,
1964, 435—6.

Joy supreme ; English Review, Jan. 1912, 204.

The kingfisher ; *In* The Oxford book of English
verse, 1250—1918 ; [comp.] by Sir Arthur
Quiller-Couch, 1948, 1100.

The last years ; Welsh Review, Vol. 1, no. 1,
1939, 16.

Leaves ; The Spectator, Sept. 8, 1923, 319.

Leisure ; The Oxford book of English verse,
1250—1918 ; [comp.] by Sir Arthur Quiller-
Couch. New ed. repr. 1948, 1101—2.
In Other men's flowers ; [comp.] by A. P.
Wavell. London, Cape. New ed., 1958,
68—9.

Money ; The Oxford book of English verse,
1250—1918 ; [comp.] by Sir Arthur
Quiller-Couch. New ed. repr. 1948, 1101.

Nature's friend ; A tale that is told ; [comp.]
by Arthur B. Allen, 1960, 159—60.

Old or young ? ; The Dragon, Lent Term
1927, 19. [Signed by the author].

On a cold day ; *In* Manning-Sanders, Ruth,
comp. Birds, beasts and fishes. Oxford U.P.,
1962, 112.

One token ; The Spectator, Sept. 8, 1923, 319.

The sea ; *In* Hope, Ronald, The Harrap book
of sea verse, 1960, 192—3.

See where young love ; The Spectator, June 2, 1923, 925.

Sheep ; Presenting Welsh Poetry, 1959, 104.

The truth ; *In* Ball, W. J. *and* Thornley, G. C. The golden road to English literature, Book 1. London, Longmans, 1960, 56—7.

Violet and oak ; The Spectator, Feb. 10, 1923, 241.

The Welshman's heaven ; Wales (J.H.E.), Vol. 6, March 1914, 39. [Repr. from *The New Statesman*].

When yon full moon ; Welsh Poets : comp. by A. G. Prys Jones, 1917, 30.

A woman's charms ; English Review, Jan. 1912, 205.

Worms ; Welsh Review, Vol. 1, no. 1, 1939, 16.

DAVIES, William Thomas Pennar [*i.e. "Davies Aberpennar"*].

Prose
A 326   : Imaginary conversation : I. Keidrych Rhys and Dafydd ap Gwilym. Wales, Vol. VII, no. 29, 1948, 523—31. (Broadcast by the B.B.C., Nov. 19, 1947).

Verse
A 327   : Admonition to the four elements ; Dock L., Vol. 5, no. 15, 1954, 46—7.

Beware, wass ; Modern Welsh Poetry ; ed. by K. Rhys, 1944, 17.

Confessio amantis ; Poetry Book Magazine, Vol. 6, no. 5, Fall 1954, 22.

For Gwenhwyfar and Blodeuwedd ; Modern Welsh Poetry ; ed. by K. Rhys, 1944, 17.

Poem for D. Robert Griffiths ; ibid.   15—6.

Poem for Gwyn and Kathe ; ibid.   14.

Poem for Keith Scott ; ibid.   17—8.

Poem for M.A.J.D. ; ibid.   13.

Tudur Aled ; ibid.   13.

DAVIS, Alastair

Verse
A 328   : Ballad of the beauty of Wales. London ; [publ. by the author], 1933. 10p.   18cm.   wrappers.

A 329   : The birth of youth, and other poems. London ; Spottiswoode, Ballantyne, 1931. [10], 56, [2]p.   20cm.   cloth. Limited ed. of 225 copies.

A 330   : The hills of dream ; and other poems. London ; Spottiswoode, Ballantyne, 1930. [10], 65, [4]p.   18½cm.   cloth.

A 331   : A song of spring, and other poems. Oxford ; Blackwell, 1936. xii, 51p.   19cm.   cloth.

A 332   : Carleon-on-Usk (sic) ; Welsh Outlook, Vol. XVIII, 1931, 72. Owain Glyndŵr ; Pencader Poems, 1952, [p. 11].

DEVEREUX, Blanche

Novel
A 333   : Star of Mercia : historical tales of Wales and the Marches . . . with an introduction by Ernest Rhys. London ; Cape, 1922. [4], 5—160p.   18½cm.   cloth.

DORLING, Henry Taprell,   *"Taffrail"*

Novel
A 334   : Mystery at Milford Haven. London ; Hodder & Stoughton, 1936. [v], [1], 7—320p.   19cm.   cloth. Map on endpaper.

DOWDING, Walter

Story
A 335   : Gwri, the star and the Gorsedd. Welsh Review.   Vol. II, no. 1, 1939, 6—11.

Verse
A 336   : Celtic Renaissance ; Pencader Poems, 1952 [p. 15].

The cloud ; Poetry Qtly., Vol. 2, no. 3, 1940, 74.

"Crabbed age and youth" ; Wales.   New Series, I.   July 1943, 72.

I'r hen iaith a'i chaneuon ; Modern Welsh Poetry ; ed. by K. Rhys, 1944, 34.   Also in A Book of Wales ; ed. by D. M. & E. M. Lloyd, 1953, 269.

[*Extract from*] I'r hen iaith a'i chaneuon ; Praise of Wales ; comp. by Maxwell Fraser, 1950, 34.

Poems of Brynmawr.
I : The poet's dream ; Welsh Outlook, Vol. XVIII, 1931, 8.
II : Spring in Brynmawr ; ibid. 39.
III : Brynmawr in Autumn ; ibid. 80—1.
IV : Snowdrops ; ibid. 120.

Wales—a mourning ; Modern Welsh Poetry ; ed. by K. Rhys, 1944, 34—5.

"DRAIG GLAS", *pseud.* [i.e. *Arthur Tyssilio Johnson*]

Prose
A 337   : Madge Carrington and her Welsh neighbours.
London ; Stanley Paul, [1911].
[6], 7—301, [3]p. 19cm. cloth.
Subsidiary pp. of advertisements.

A 338   : The perfidious Welshman.
London ; Stanley Paul, 1910.
[4], 5—157, [2]32p. 19cm. cloth.
Subsidiary pp. of advertisements.

A 339   : The Welshman's reputation : a reply to a recent satire on the Welsh, entitled "The Perfidious Welshman", by "An Englishman".
London ; Stanley Paul, 1911.
160p. 19½cm.
—Another ed. Cheaper ed.
London ; S. Paul, 1914.
158p. 19½cm.

DYER, John

Prose
A 340   : The ragged mountain. Illustrated by Josef Herman.
London ; Chatto & Windus, 1965.
[8], 215p. illus. 19½cm. cloth.
Location : A Rhondda Valley mining village.

EATON, Henry W.

Novel
A 341   : An errant esquire : a romance of the conquest of Wales.
New York ; printed for private circulation, 1901.
x, 342p. 19½cm. cloth.
One hundred copies printed : NLW has copy no. 34.

EDE, J. P.

Verse
A 342   : Llandudno lays.
Ilfracombe ; Stockwell, [1942].
[4], 5—24p. 18cm. wrappers.

EDELMAN, Maurice

Novel
A 343   : Who goes home ?
London ; Wingate, 1952.
[7], 8—255p. 18cm. cloth.
Location : Partly set in the Welsh parliamentary constituency of "Cwmbrau".

EDWARDS, Dorothy

Novel
A 344   : Winter sonata.
London ; Wishart, 1928.
[8], 254, [3]p. 18½cm. cloth.
Story
A 345   : Rhapsody.
London ; Wishart, 1927.
—Another issue. 1932.
[8], 234p. 18½cm. cloth.
Extract from the above : The Conquered.
Welsh short stories ; ed. by G. Ewart Evans.
2nd ed., 1959, 219—31.

EDWARDS, *Sir* Francis, *translator*

Verse
A 346   : Translations from the Welsh.
Privately printed at the Chiswick Press, 1913.
xii, 159p. 17cm. cloth.
For private circulation.
Includes translations of some 20th century poets, e.g. Elfed, Wil Ifan and Sir John Morris-Jones.

EDWARDS, John

Drama
A 347   : The call of the sea.
Newtown, Mont.; Welsh Outlook Press, [1925].
18p. 13½cm. wrappers.
Scene : Cottage on the Welsh coast.
Welsh version entitled "Galw'r Môr", 1924.

EDWARDS, Oliver

Verse
A 348   : Allensbank ; Welsh Review, Vol. III, no. 1, 1944, 41.

Apology to my friends for not having answered their letters ; Rann, no. 15, 1952, 4—5.

Appeasement ; Welsh Review, Vol. III, no. 1, 1944, 40—1.

The cat and the man ; ibid. no. 4, 1944, 250—1.

The search ; Rann : an Ulster quarterly of poetry, no. 9, 1950, 7.

The two ; ibid. no. 2, 1948, 9.

View ; ibid. no. 13 [October 1951], 3.

ELIAS, Frank

Novel

A 349 : Beach mystery.
London ; Lutterworth Press, [1946].
[6], 7—192p. 18½cm. cloth.
Location : "Moelvre Bay" (Anglesey). 1860—
1870.

ELLIS, Joseph E. *"Brynford"*

Novel

A 350 : "The White vest".
Abergele ; J. H. Williams, *printer*, 1940.
[4], 5—142p. port. 18cm. wrappers.
Serialised in the "Abergele Visitor", 1931.
Location : The Vale of Clwyd.

ELLIS, Thomas Evelyn [*afterwards Thomas Evelyn Scott-Ellis, 8th Baron Howard de Walden*]

Drama

A 351 : The cauldron of Annwn.
London ; *printed by* T. Werner Laurie, 1922.
xix, [1], 327p. 22½cm. Vellum.
Edges uncut. Private edition for subscribers
only.
Contents : Three verse-plays : Children of
Don—Dylan—Bronwen.

A 352 : Children of Don.
London ; Edward Arnold, 1912.
[6], 7—95p. 18½cm. wrappers.
Scene : A cavern.
[Libretto of a music-drama in three acts and
a prologue. Music by Josef Holbrooke.
London, Novello, 1912].
—Another ed. E. Arnold, 1912.
[6], 7—95p. front. 19cm. cloth.

A 353 : Dylan, son of the wave.
London ; Simpkin, Marshall, Hamilton,
Kent & Co., 1918.
[8], 9—73p. front. 19cm. cloth.
[Based on legend of Gwyddno, King of
Ceredigion and Seithenyn, Keeper of the
Dykes].

A 354 : Pont Orewyn : drama.
Cardiff ; Educational Publishing Company,
1914.
[4], 5—18p. 15cm. wrappers.
Scene : A packbridge.

Verse

A 355 : The song of Gwyn ap Nudd.
Cardiff ; Western Mail, *printers*, [1913].
[4]p. wrappers.
An inset in the programme of a concert at
Cardiff, Nov. 20, 1913.

ETHERIDGE, Ken

Verse

A 356 : Poems of a decade.
Hull ; Guild Press, 1958.
[2], 3—16p. 22cm. wrappers. (Guild Poets
Series).

A 357 : Songs for courage.
Llandyssul ; J. D. Lewis & Sons, *printers*, 1940.
[8], 9—74p. 21½cm. cloth.

A 358 : Abstract ; Wales, No. 2, Summer 1937, 14.

Acrimony in autumn ; Dock L., Vol. 2, no. 6,
1951, 24.

Airmen drinking ; Wales, New Series, 4, 1944,
51.

Annunciation ; Wales, No. 4, March 1938,
138—9.
Modern Welsh Poetry, ed. by Keidrych
Rhys, Faber, 1944, 39—40.
The First Comment Treasury, London,
1937, 39.

Blades in the slag ; Life & Letters Today,
Vol. 16, no. 8, 1937, 56.

Carnations ; Modern Welsh Poetry, 1944, 40.
Welsh Review, Vol. II, no. 3, 1939, 142.

Corpus delicti ; Wales, January 1959, 46.

Country walk ; Wales, No. 2, August 1937, 65.

Credo ; Outposts, No. 4, 1945, unnumbered.
Wales, No. 2, August 1937, 65.

Early snow ; Modern Welsh Poetry, 1944, 41.

Epitaph ; Wales, No. 2, August 1937, 68.

Flowering Cosmos ; ibid. 67—8.

Harvest ; ibid. 68.

The house in the woods ; Prospect, no. 7/8,
Winter 1946—7, 35.

Male nude ; Wales, Dec. 1958, 30.

Mask ; Modern Welsh Poetry, 1944, 42.
Wales, No. 1, Summer 1937, 15.

The new Hellas ; More Poems from the
Forces ; ed. by K. Rhys, 1943, 76—7.

An old collier ; Modern Welsh Poetry, 1944,
43.

Old woman warming her hands ; Welsh
Review, Vol. V, no. 2, 1946, 98—9.

Prince of Wales ; Wales, Dec. 1958, 29.

Shadows ; ibid. 28.

Sleeping Men ; Wales, New Series, 3, 1944, 73.

Snow ; ibid. 72.

Song for courage ; Wales, New Series, I, 1943, 25.
More Poems from the Forces, 1943, 75.

Spring fragment ; Modern Welsh Poetry, 1944, 40—41.
Wales, No. 1, Summer 1937, 16.

To a young sailor ; More Poems from the Forces, 1943, 77.

Winter streams ; Dock L., Vol. 2, no. 4, 1951, 18.

Young Starlings ; Wales, No. 2, August 1937, 66.

Drama
A 359   : The folly of Seithenyn.
Best one-act plays of 1944—45 ; ed. by J. W. Marriott.
Harrap, 1946, 119—143.

A 360   : The lamp ; a play in one act.
London ; H. F. W. Deane, 1937.
[5], 6—21p. wrappers.
Award-winning play in 1937 British Drama League Festival.
Scene : A colliery (underground).

A 361   : Prospect of Amanw : a verse play in one act.
Ammanford ; [publ. by the author], 1956.
20 leaves. 26cm. Typescript.

A 362   : Underground.
London ; J. B. Pinker, [1936].
[6], 23p. Typescript. Wrappers.
Scene : A road in colliery workings.
Award-winning play in 1936 British Drama League Festivals.

Story
A 363   : The brook.
Welsh Review, Vol. 1, no. 6, 1939, 306—12.

EUSTACE, Alice

Novel
A 364   : The make-believe lover.
London ; John Long, 1924.
[6], 7—318, [1]p. 18½cm. cloth.
Location : Partly located in the Rhondda mining valley of "Pendyrys".

EVANS, David
Verse
A 365   : Above Brynamman ; Wales, no. 6/7, 1939, 204.

From my swivel rock ; ibid. 204—5.

(From R.B.'s album) ; Wales, New Series, I, 1943, 24.

Poem I ; Wales, no. 5, Summer 1938, 178.
Modern Welsh Poetry ; ed. by K. Rhys, 1944, 43—4.
Poem II ; Wales, no. 5, Summer 1938, 178—9.
Modern Welsh Poetry ; ed. by K. Rhys, 1944, 43—44.
Sona dialect ; Wales, no. 8/9, 1939, 240.
Modern Welsh Poetry, 1944, 44—5.
Synthesis ; Wales, no. 6/7, 1939, 204.
Modern Welsh Poetry ; ed. by K. Rhys, 1944, 45.
This political time-plotted day ; Wales, New Series, I, 1943, 23.
Modern Welsh Poetry, 1944, 45—6.

EVANS, [David] Caradoc   (1883—1945)
Novels
A 366   : Morgan Bible.
London ; Andrew Dakers, 1943.
[4], 5—111p. 18cm. cloth.
Location : A village inland from "Aberbedw-on-the-Sea".

A 367   : Mother's marvel.
London ; Andrew Dakers, [1949].
[4], 204p. 18cm. cloth.
—Another ed. 1951 (Paperback).

A 368   : Nothing to pay : a novel.
London ; Faber, 1930.
310p. 18cm. cloth.
Autobiographical : draper's trade. Based on personal experience in Cardiff.

A 369   : This way to heaven.
London ; Rich & Cowan, 1934.
[6], 7—335p. 18cm. cloth.
No apparent Welsh location.

A 370   : Wasps : a novel.
London ; Rich & Cowan, 1933.
[8], 9—288p. 18½cm. cloth.
Location : "Red Ford" in a West Wales valley.

Stories
A 371   : Capel Sion.
London ; A. Melrose, [1916].
vii [1], 225, [6]p. 18½cm. cloth.
—2nd edition. 1917.
Contents : Redemption—The word—The tree of knowledge—Three men from Horeb—The pillars of Sion—The widow's mite—Calvary—Sons of their father—A mighty man in Sion—A sacrifice unto Sion—The deliverer—Judges—A keeper of the doors—The acts of Dan—The comforter.

A 372 : The earth gives all and takes all.
London ; Andrew Dakers, 1946.
xxxv, [1], 65p. front. (port.) 18cm. cloth.
Publ. posthumously.
Contents :
pp. v—vi : Without bitterness : introduction
by Marguerite Caradoc Evans.
pp. vii—xxxiv : Caradoc, by Professor George
H. Green.
Stories : The earth gives all and takes all—To
keep a rainbow white—Oldest brother—
Big Servant—A Jew names Joshua . . .
[Title supplied]—Pen Clock . . . wanted a
mint [Title supplied]—Clogs for love.

A 373 : My neighbours.
London ; A. Melrose, 1919.
[i—vi], vii, [1], 242p. 18cm. cloth.
—Another ed. New York ; Harcourt, Brace
& Hare, 1920.
Contents : The two apostles—According to the
pattern—Earthbred—For better—Love and
hate—Treasure and trouble—Saint David
and the prophets—Joseph's house—Like
brothers—A widow woman—Unanswered
prayers—Lost treasure—Profit and glory.

A 374 : My people : stories of the peasantry of West
Wales.
London ; Melrose, 1915.
v, 275p. 18½cm. cloth.
—Reprinted, 1915.
3rd ed. 1916.
—Reprinted 1916, 1917.
—6th ed. 1919 (with frontispiece portrait).
—Another ed. London, Dobson, 1953.
155p. 18cm. cloth. (Twentieth Century
Classics Series).
Contents : A father in Sion—A heifer without
blemish—The way of the earth—The
talent Thou gavest—The glory that was
Sion's—The devil in Eden—The woman
who sowed iniquity—A just man in Sodom
—Be this her memorial—The Redeemer—
As it is written—A bundle of life—Greater
than love—Lamentations—The blast of God.

Also in NLW : Collection of newspaper
cuttings relating to the controversy provoked by "Two Welsh Studies" of Caradoc
Evans and their subsequent publication in
"My People" above.

A 375 : Pilgrims in a foreign land.
London ; Andrew Dakers, 1942.
[4], 155p. 18½cm. cloth.
Wrapper : Sub-title : "Tales of the Welsh".
Contents : Your sin will find you out—Bliss
is in the mist—Do not borrow your brother's
head—Robbers do not look for treasure in
coffins—A wife from off is well off—One
repentant sinner is worth two pews in
Heaven—The hangman's rope is made of
words—Do not praise your marriage day
in the morning—Where faith is blind, God

is bright—The capel always wins—Twins
with one head, trouble ; twins with two,
peace—Changeable as a woman with
child—Cobbler, stick to your bench—A
widow with a full purse needs no husband—
Pews for saints and fire for sinners, but no
nest for the soul-less—Who loses his money
loses his brains—Bellyful of religion, bellyful
of madness.

A 376 : Be this her memorial.
In Smith, A. J. *and* Mason, W. H., *editors.*
Short story study. London, E. Arnold,
1961, 62—71. (incl. biographical notes
on Caradoc Evans).
Welsh short stories ; ed. by Gwyn Jones, 1956,
22—7.

A 377 : The coffin.
Full Score ; ed. by Fytton Armstrong.
London ; Rich & Cowan, [1933].
Best short stories of 1942, No. 1, English,
105—10.

A 378 : A father in Sion.
Welsh short stories ; ed. by Gwyn Jones, 1956,
28—37.

A 379 : Horse Hysbys and Oldest Brother.
Welsh Review, Vol. IV, no. 2, 1945, 100—3.

A 380 : Joseph's House.
Welsh Review, Vol. IV, no. 1, 1945, 29—33.

A 381 : The milky way.
English story. 6th series ; ed. by Woodrow
Wyatt, 1945, 51—60.

A 382 : Two Welsh studies.
The English Review, April 1915, 25—36.
Comprises two stories : The man who walked
with God—Be this her memorial.

A 383 : The way of the earth.
Welsh short stories ; ed. by G. Ewart Evans.
2nd ed. 1959, 96—105.

A 384 : Who steals an egg will steal all.
New voices : Atlantic anthology ; ed. by
Nicholas Moore and Douglas Newton, 1945,
136—9.

A 385 : Your sin will find you out.
Wales, No. 8/9, 1939, 214—9.

Other Prose

A 386 : Caradoc Evans' Journal, 1939—44. [A frag-
mentary journal of the war period ; edited
by Marguerite Caradoc Evans].
Welsh Review, Vol. IV, no. 2, 1945, 104—11.
Vol. IV, no. 3, 1945, 201—8.

Drama
A 387 : Taffy : a play of Welsh village life in three acts.
London, New York ; Melrose, [1924].
[4], 5—86 [2]p. 18½cm. cloth.
Scene : A Cardiganshire village.
NLW has album of Press cuttings and reviews relating to the London theatre performance of this play.

EVANS, E[van] Eynon

Prose
A 388 : On driving a bus.
Welsh Review, Vol. III, no. 4, 1944, 295—300.

Drama
A 389 : According to the doctor : a comedy in three acts.
London ; Samuel French, 1960.
[4], 76p. plan. 21½cm. wrappers.

A 390 : Affairs of Bryngolau : a comedy of Welsh life.
London ; Samuel French, 1936.
[5], 6—100p. 15½cm. wrappers. (Welsh Drama Series, no. 121).
Scene : Mining town of "Tremynydd", S. Wales.

A 391 : All through the night : a comedy in three acts.
London, New York ; Samuel French, 1947.
[9], 10—96p. plan. 18½cm. wrappers.
Scene : Mining village of "Tre-nant".

A 392 : Bachelor brothers.
London ; Samuel French, 1953.
[4], 83p. plan. 18½cm. wrappers.
Scene : Tŷ Graig, a Welsh farm house.

A 393 : Bless this house : a comedy in three acts.
London ; Samuel French, 1954.
[4], 76p. 21½cm. wrappers. (French's Acting Edition, no. 226). Scene changes from the Midlands to "Penrytown", Wales and to Herefordshire.

A 394 : Cobbler's wax : a comedy of Welsh life.
Aberdare, Glam. ; Stephens and George, *printers*, 1937.
[5], 6—84p. plan. 18½cm. wrappers.
Welsh version entitled "Cŵyr Crydd", by J. Ellis Williams.

A 395 : Cold coal : a drama of Welsh life.
London ; Samuel French, 1939.
[6], 7—88p. 18½cm. wrappers.

A 396 : Half a loaf : a comedy in three acts.
London ; Samuel French, 1950.
[7], 8—112p. plan. 18½cm. wrappers. (French's Acting Edition, no. 1997).
Scene : "Cwmglas", Welsh industrial town.

A 397 : Jailbird Johnnie : a play in one act for women.
London ; Samuel French, 1960.
[6], 23, [2]p. plan. 18½cm. wrappers. (French's Acting Edition).

A 398 : Kith and kin : a comedy-drama in three acts.
Aberdare, Glam. ; Stephens & George, [1946].
[7], 8—92p. plan. 18cm. wrappers.

A 399 : Maria : a comedy in four acts.
Aberdare, Glam ; Stephens & George, 1942.
[5], 6—83p. plan. 18½cm. wrappers.
Scene : "Pencarth", a Welsh farmhouse.

A 400 : Wishing well : a comedy.
London ; Samuel French, 1946.
104p. plan. 18½cm. wrappers. (French's Acting Edition, no. 142).
—Welsh version : *Dwy frân ddu*, trans. by J. Ellis Williams.

Story
A 401 : Prize onions, and other stories.
Llandebie, Carms. ; Christopher Davies, 1951.
[5], 6—66p. 18½cm. wrappers.
Wrapper : "Silurian Books".
Contents : The organ blower—Prize onions—The rivals of Rhydfach—Plain cooking—The new allotments.

EVANS, Evan R.

Novel
A 402 : The Lord of Corsygedol : a tale of Welsh life in the sixteenth century.
London ; Griffon Press, 1902.
viii, [1], 10—204p. 19cm. cloth.
Location : Commote of Mawddwy and the Mawddach Estuary.

EVANS, George Ewart

Stories
A 403 : Ben Knowledge.
Wales. Vol. IX, no. 31, 1949, 4—10.

A 404 : Beyond the trees.
Wales. New Series, I, July 1943, 53—9.
Little Reviews Anthology, 1945, 66—70.

A 405 : The destination.
Bugle Blast. 2nd Series, 1944, 104—10.

A 406 : Feet and the man.
Pick of today's short stories, no. 3, 1952, 56—62.

A 407 : Folk tale.
Welsh Review. Vol. 1, no. 4, 1939, 196—8.

A 408 : Gold key.
English story. First series ; ed. by Woodrow and Susan Wyatt, 1941, 187—91.

A 409 : He saith among the trumpets, Ha, Ha.
Wales. No. 5, 1938, 167—70.

A 410 : The journey.
Wales. Dec. 1958, 8—15.

A 411 : Let dogs delight.
Life and Letters Today, Vol. 24, no. 31, 1940, 310—8.

A 412 : The medal.
Welsh short stories ; ed. by G. Ewart Evans. 2nd ed., 1959, 167—74.

A 413 : Pause for conversation.
Wales. No. 2, Aug. 1937, 46—52.

A 414 : Possessions.
Welsh short stories ; ed. by Gwyn Jones, 1956, 37—50.

A 415 : The powder monkey.
Wales. Vol. VII, no. 28, Feb.—March, 1948, 432—41.

A 416 : The singer.
Wales. Vol. IV, no. 6, Winter 1945, 73—7.

A 417 : Theirs is the kingdom.
Life and Letters Today, Vol. 21, no. 22 [1939], 68—73.

Other Prose
A 418 : The voice of the children.
Cardiff ; Penmark Press, 1947.
182p. 18½cm. cloth.
Autobiography of a South Wales childhood.
Also in : Welsh Review, Part I : Vol. IV, no. 3, 1945, 184—90. Part II : Welsh Review, Vol. IV, no. 4, 1945, 238—44.

Verse
A 419 : Ailsa Craig ; Wales, Vol. V, no. 7, 1945, 33.

Airman at a railway terminus ; ibid. 59—60.

At the seaside ; Wales. No. 6/7, 1939, 203—4.
Modern Welsh Poetry, ed. by K. Rhys, 1944, 46—7.

The clerk ; More Poems from the Forces ; ed. by K. Rhys, 1943, 82. Wales. New Series, I, 1943, 25.

The dead pheasant ; Wales. No. 40, 1959, 19.

The Golden Bird : (a radio poem for five voices) ; Dock. L., Vol. 8, no. 22, [1958], 13—27. Running-title notes author as "George Ewart Thomas".

North from the Prescelly Mountains ; Dock L., Vol. 6, no. 16, 1955, 27—8.

Poem ["Forty years in the world's turning"] ; Dock L., Vol. 2, no. 4, 1951, 12.

Poem ["Progress in the peaceable blue of a sky in summer . . ."]. Wales. No. 10, 1939 276.

Modern Welsh Poetry ; ed. by K. Rhys, 1944, 47.

Poem ["To a flat sky . . ."] ; Wales. New Series, 3, 1944, 73.

The recruit ; More Poems from the Forces ; ed. by K. Rhys, 1943, 81.
Wales. New Series, I, 1943, 26.

Seeing is not seeing ; A-W.R., Vol. 11, no. 28, undated, 55.

The statue ; Dock L., Vol. 4, no. 11, 1953, 45.

The two birch trees ; ibid. Vol. 2, no. 5, 1951, 35.

Winter 1939 ; Modern Welsh Poetry ; ed. by K. Rhys, 1944, 48.

EVANS, Howel
Novel
A 420 : A Little Welsh girl.
London, New York ; Hodder & Stoughton, 1919.
[10], 11—315p. 18½cm. cloth.
Location : "Llanhwyll", Welsh mountain area.

EVANS, Hugh John
Verse
A 421 : Llangollen poems.
Llangollen ; Hugh Jones, 1920.
[4], 44p. 16cm. wrappers.

EVANS, Kilsby D[avies]
Prose
A 422 : Bevin Boy—pre-war.
Welsh Review, Vol. III, no. 4, 1944, 217—219.

Drama
A 423 : The lost daffodil, and six other plays.
Cardiff ; Educational Publishing Company, 1950.
[4], 5—71p. 18cm. wrappers.
Contents : Arthur's Cave—Dewi and Boia—First Prince of Wales—Harry Morgan's way—The lost daffodil—The triumph of Ifor Bach.
Note : Total of six plays only (cf. title).

A 424 : Outwitted, and two other plays.
Cardiff ; Educational Publishing Company, 1950.
[4], 5—64p. 18cm. wrappers.
Contents : Bill Jones' jewel—Outwitted—The biter bit.

A 425 : Royalist Gold, and three other plays.
Cardiff ; Educational Publishing Co., 1950.
[4], 5—64p. 18½cm. wrappers.
Contents : Royalist gold—The mysterious King
Gado—The story of Gwenllian—The wiles
of Abermarlais.

EVANS, Lilly Margaret

Verse
A 426 : Windows.
Llandysul ; J. D. Lewis & Sons, 1934.
[6], 7—27p. 21½cm. wrappers.

EVANS, Margiad

Novels
A 427 : Country dance. Illustrated by Peggy Whistler.
London ; A. Barker, 1932.
xii, 96p. col. front. col. illus. 22½cm. cloth.
Location : Welsh border, rural areas in the
1850's.

A 428 : The wooden doctor.
Oxford ; Basil Blackwell, 1933.
xviii, 220p. 18½cm. cloth.
Location : Partly set in "Abercarrog", in
Welsh hills.

Stories
A 429 : All through the night.
Welsh Review, Vol. III, no. 3, 1944, 159—67.
Welsh short stories ; ed. by Gwyn Jones, 1956,
51—64.

A 430 : The black house.
Welsh Review, Vol. I, no. 5, 1939, 242—6.

A 431 : The lost fisherman.
Welsh Review, Vol. V, no. 1, 1946, 9—28.

A 432 : A party for the nightingale.
Welsh Review, Vol. VII, no. 4. 1948, 285—93.
Pick of Today's short stories, no. 2, 1950,
86—98.

A 433 : Solomon.
Life and Letters, Vol. 48, no. 103, 1946,
171—81.

A 434 : Thomas Griffiths and Parson Cope.
Penguin Parade, no. 11 ; ed. by D. Kilham
Roberts, 1945, 73—85.

A 435 : The wicked woman.
Life and Letters, Vol. 9, 1933—4, 468—73.

Other Prose
A 436 : Autobiography.
Oxford ; Basil Blackwell, 1943.
v, [1], 158p. front. 19½cm. cloth.
2nd edition. London ; A. Barker, 1952.
v, 192p. 19cm. cloth.

A 437 : A little journal of being alone.
Life and Letters Today, Vol. 24, no. 31, 1940,
255—68.

A 438 : A ray of darkness.
London ; A. Barker, 1952.
[8], 9—191p. 18½cm. cloth.

Verse
A 439 : Poems for obscurity.
London ; Andrew Dakers, 1947.
[4], 5—48p. 18½cm. cloth.

A 440 : Christmases ; Cornhill Magazine, Vol. 170,
1018, 1958/59, 270.

Cure ; PEN 1957, 44—5.

The forest ; London Magazine, Vol. 1, no. 8,
1954, 11.

Lullaby for me ; Orion : a miscellany. London,
Nicholson & Watson, 1945, 76.

Lying on a hillside, after a storm ; Welsh
Review, Vol. VI, no. 1947, 96.

The passionate refusal ; ibid. Vol. IV, no. 1,
1945, 20—1.

Poem ("I must be dead . . .") ; PEN 1957, 45.

Poem ("Lift with reproaches . . .") ; Life and
Letters, Vol. 65, June 1950, 216.

Resurrection ; Welsh Review, Vol. IV, no. 1,
1945, 21.

Sonnet ("Not in disgrace . . ."), Cornhill
Magazine, Vol. 167, no. 1001, 1954, 453.

A sparrow singing ; Welsh Review, Vol. IV,
no. 4, 1945, 246.

The summer wind ; London Magazine,
Vol. 4, no. 5, 1957, 63.

There is a castle ; Welsh Review, Vol. VI,
no. 2, 1947, 96.

To my daughter ; PEN 1958, 36.

To my sister Siân ; Cornhill Magazine,
Vol. 168, no. 1006, 1955/56, 332—3.

Travellers' joy ; Life and Letters, Vol. 65,
April 1950, 48.

The will ; ibid. 49—50.

EVANS, Marguerite Florence "Countess Barcynska" "Oliver Sandys"

Of the numerous works written under the names of "Countess Barcynska" and "Oliver Sandys", the titles noted below are those which are discernibly written against a Welsh background and in which some Welsh characters appear.

Novels

A 441 : Black harvest.
London, Melbourne [etc.] ; Hurst & Blackett, 1960.
191p. 18cm. cloth.
Location : Part of the story set in Welsh areas.

A 442 : Butterflies in the rain.
London ; Hurst & Blackett, 1958.
[4], 5—192p. 18cm. cloth.
Location : "Dovesea", on the Welsh coast.

A 443 : Conjuror.
London, New York [etc.] ; Rich & Cowan, [1950].
236p. 18½cm. cloth.
Location : Mid-Wales (?) : some Welsh characters.

A 444 : The constant rabbit.
London, New York [etc.] ; Hurst & Blackett, [1949].
224p. 18½cm. cloth.
Location : Partly in a Welsh country mansion.

A 445 : Dot on the spot.
London, New York [etc.] ; Hurst & Blackett, [1949].
224p. 18½cm. cloth.
Location : Partly in a Mid-Wales village.

A 446 : Gorgeous brute.
London, New York [etc.] ; Rich & Cowan, [1949].
224p. 18½cm. cloth.
Location : Partly Tresaith, Cards.

A 447 : Learn to laugh again.
London, New York [etc.] ; Hurst & Blackett, n.d.
[6], 7—190p. 18½cm. cloth.
Location : Welsh seaside town.

A 448 : Luck is a lady.
London, New York [etc.] ; Rich & Cowan, [1945].
190p. 18½cm. cloth.
Location : Partly set in village of "Badarn" near "Fairbay" (Cardiganshire).

A 449 : Miss Paraffin.
London, New York [etc.] ; Hurst & Blackett, [1944].
180p. 18cm. cloth.
Location : Partly at "Devil's Pocket", Cards.

A 450 : Miss Venus of Aberdovey.
London, Melbourne [etc.] ; Rich & Cowan, 1956.
191p. 18½cm. cloth.
Location : Pennal, Mont. and Aberdovey.

A 451 : A new day.
London ; Hurst & Blackett, 1957.
[6], 7—192p. 18½cm. cloth.
Location : Partly in Wales.

A 452 : No faint heart.
London ; Hurst & Blackett, [1943].
176p. 18½cm. cloth.
Location : Welsh setting.

A 453 : Poppet and Co.
London, New York [etc.] ; Hurst & Blackett, [1944].
Location : Partly at "Reba", Cardiganshire.

A 454 : Publicity Baby.
London ; Hurst & Blackett, [1935].
288 [32]p. 18½cm. cloth.
Location : Part of the story set in Mid-Wales.

A 455 : Singing uphill.
London ; Hurst & Blackett, 1940.
[2], 222p. 18½cm. cloth.
Location : Welsh setting.

A 456 : Sunset is dawn.
London, New York [etc.] ; Rich & Cowan, 1953.
200p. 18½cm. cloth.
Location : Aberystwyth, Cards.

A 457 : The tears of peace.
London, New York [etc.] ; Rich & Cowan, [1944].
206p. 18cm. cloth.
Location : Coastal village of "Morfa".

A 458 : Those dominant hills.
London, New York [etc.] ; Rich & Cowan, 1951.
260p. 18cm. cloth.
Location : Partly Cardiganshire.

A 459 : Tiptoes.
London ; Hurst & Blackett, [1935].
288p. 18½cm. cloth.
Location : University town of "Redwood" (Aberystwyth ?).

A 460 : The wise and the steadfast.
London, Melbourne [etc.] ; Hurst & Blackett, 1961.
184p. 18cm. cloth.
Location : Partly set in "Porthsea", Wales.

A 461 : The wood is my pulpit.
London ; Rich and Cowan, [1943].
192p. 18½cm. cloth.
Location : Welsh setting.

A 462   : Yesterday is tomorrow.
London, New York [etc.] ; Rich & Cowan,
1950.
240p. 18cm. cloth.

Other Prose
A 463   : Full and frank : the private life of a woman
novelist.
London ; Hurst & Blackett, 1941.
208p. front. (port.), ports. 21¼cm. cloth.
—Reprinted, 1947. 184p.

A 464   : Unbroken thread : an intimate journal of the
daily life in the Welsh countryside of
England's best-loved novelist.
London, New York [etc.] ; Rider [1948].
[6], 7—184p. front. (port.), plates. 21cm.
cloth.

EVANS, William   *"Wil Ifan"*

Prose
A 465   : Here and there.
Cardiff ; Western Mail and Echo, 1953.
[4], 5—100p. 21½cm. wrappers.
Essays reprinted from the "Western Mail".

Verse
A 466   : Further poems.
Cardiff ; Western Mail & Echo, 1955.
[6], 7—52p. 21½cm. wrappers.
Illustrated wrapper.

A 467   : A quire of rhymes.
Cardiff ; Educational Publishing Co. [1918].
48p. 15½cm. wrappers.

A 468   : Short poems.
Cardiff ; Western Mail & Echo, 1943.
[6], 7—40p. 21cm. cloth.

A 469   : Songs of the heather heights.
London ; Hodder & Stoughton, [1921].
viii, 79p. 14cm. wrappers.

A 470   : Where I belong, with the voices of river, wood
and counterpane.
Cardiff ; Western Mail & Echo, 1946.
[2], 3—24p. illus. 18½cm. wrappers.
Based on the author's Welsh poem "Bro Fy
Mebyd".

A 471   : Some Welsh poets translated, I : Welsh
Outlook, Vol. XIX, 1932, 118—9.
    1. Ifan the Pedlar : from the Welsh of Waldo
Williams.
    2. Embarking and 3. The Wood Pigeon,
from the Welsh of R. Williams Parry.

A 472   : Some Welsh poets translated, II : ibid.
149—51. 1. April ; 2. October ; 3. The
Stars ; 4. The Hedgerows of May ; 5. Had'st
Thou but Love ; 6. The Gipsy, from the
Welsh of Eifion Wyn.

A 473   : Some Welsh poets translated, III : ibid.
188—9. Includes translations of some of
the poems of W. Crwys Williams.

A 474   : Some Welsh poets translated, IV : ibid. 202—3.
Includes translations of some of the work of
Islwyn.

A 475   : Some Welsh poets translated, V : ibid. 244—5.
Includes translations of Mafonwy, Moelwyn
and James Evans.

A 476   : Some Welsh poets translated, VI : ibid. 268—9.
Includes translations of Gardde, W. J.
Gruffydd and T. H. Parry-Williams.

A 477   : The dove of God ; Welsh Outlook, Vol. I,
1914, 315.

[English poems included in] Darnau adrodd
1932.
The cripple child at the Sunday School treat,
50—1.
Pine logs, 49. Porthcawl, 54.
The wind of the West, 51.

The eyes of Norah Kilsant ; Welsh Outlook,
Vol. XVII, 1930, 321.

In the hedge ; ibid. 234.

In memoriam : R.M.L., the translator ; ibid.
Vol. V, 1918, 318.

Mist ; ibid. Vol. II, 1915, 64.

On seeing a fallen tree trunk rotting in the
soil ; ibid. Vol. XVI, 1929, 158.

Over eighty ; ibid. 378.

Poplars ; ibid. Vol. II, 1915, 472.

Rhiannon (M. K.) ; ibid. Vol. XIX, 1932, 62.

The tell-tale stain ; ibid. Vol. XVIII, 1931,
105.

Two wrecks (The Titanic & The Lusitania) ;
ibid. Vol. II, 1915, 238.

Vanished dreams ; translated by ' Mariduni-
ensis ' from the Welsh "Nos y Cyngherdd".
The Dragon, Nov. 1915, 22.

Other Prose
A 478   : The Militia Razor.
Welsh Outlook, Vol. X, May 1923, 135—6.

A 479   : Trees.
Welsh Outlook, Vol. XVII, 1930, 14—5.

EVERETT-GREEN, Evelyn

Novels
A 480   : The Lord of Dynevor : a tale of the time of
            Edward the First.
            London, Edinburgh ; Nelson, [1905].
            —Another ed. [1920].
            [9], 260, [6]p. col. front., col. plates, 18½cm.
            cloth.
            BM Cat. : Originally published 1892 [1891].

A 481   : Cambria's chieftain.
            London, Edinburgh [etc.] ; Nelson [1903].
            xii, 13—384p. 18½cm. cloth.
            Location : Sycharth and Glyndyfrdwy.

FARDO, George

Verse
A 482   : Poetical and humorous works of G. Fardo,
            relating to Powysland and North and South
            Wales.
            Bath ; Wilkinson Bros., *printers*, 1903.
            [2], 3—300p. 19cm. cloth.
            NLW has variant binding of this ed., incl. a
            frontispiece portrait of the author.

FELIX-JONES, Ivor

Novel
A 483   : The walking voice.
            London ; Duckworth, 1927.
            [6], 7—216p. 19cm. cloth.
            Location : Fishing village of "Aber-Abel".

FERRIS, Paul

Novel
A 484   : Then we fall.
            London, Melbourne [etc.] ; Hutchinson, 1960.
            [6], 7—200p. 19½cm. cloth.
            Location : "Narberth", a Welsh seaport.

Story
A 485   : The boat.
            Dock L., Vol. 2, no. 6, 1951, 20—2.

FINNEMORE, John

Novels
A 486   : The custom of the country : an idyll of the
            Welsh mountains.
            London ; Lawrence and Bullen, 1898.
            [6], 246p. 19cm. cloth.
            Location : "Trefaen" in the area of "Mynydd
            Bach" (Cardigan Bay).

A 487   : The Red Men of the Dusk : a romance . . .
            with eight illustrations by Lawson Wood.
            London ; C. A. Pearson, 1899.
            [5], 6—328p. front. plates. 19½cm. cloth.

Location : In the Welsh hills, and border
counties.
Reprinted. A. & C. Black, 1911, 1918.
—Another edition. A. & C. Black, 1926.
[7], 8—328p. col. front. 18½cm. cloth.

FINNEMORE, John *and* **FINNEMORE, Emily
Pearson**

Novel
A 488   : From a Welsh hillside.
            London ; A. & C. Black, 1923.
            v, 229, [3]p. 18cm. cloth.

FIRBANK, Thomas

Novel
A 489   : Bride to the mountain : a romance.
            London ; Harrap, 1940.
            [4], 5—256p. map. 18½cm. cloth.
            Location : "Marchllyn" Valley, North Caerns.

FISHER, Alan Magness

Novel
A 490   : Accommodation found.
            Newport, Mon. ; R. H. Johns, 1952.
            [4], 5—180p. 18cm. cloth.
            Location : Partly in Newport, Mon.

FLETCHER, Harry Lutf Verne

Novels
A 491   : The devil has the best tunes.
            London ; Macdonald, 1947.
            [4], 5—253p. 18½cm. cloth.
            Location : Radnorshire : Rebecca Riots.

A 492   : Forest Inn.
            London ; Macdonald, 1946.
            vii, 8—222p. 18cm. cloth.
            Location : Radnorshire.

A 493   : High pastures.
            London ; Macdonald, 1957.
            [4], 5—192p. 18½cm. cloth.
            Location : Radnorshire.

A 494   : The rising sun.
            London ; Macdonald, 1951.
            [4], 5—240p. 18½cm. cloth.
            Location : Welsh border country.

A 495   : The storm.
            London ; Macdonald, 1954.
            [6], 7—221p. 18½cm. cloth.
            Location : "Newpool" and "Llanithon" :
            (Radnorshire ?).

A 496   : The whip and the tongue.
            London ; Macdonald, 1949.
            [6], 7—224p. 18½cm. cloth.
            Location : Welsh border country.

A 497 : The woman's house.
London ; Macdonald, [1947].
[4], 5—188p. 18½cm. cloth.
Location : Welsh hill country.

Stories
A 498 : That reminds me.
Writers' Parade : short stories, No. 1.
London. Kangaroo Books, undated, 6—7.

A 499 : The voice of the bird.
English. Vol. 3, no. 18, 1941, 252—5.

FLETCHER, John Kyrle

Novel
A 500 : My Lord Worcester : the story of the fall of
Raglan and Chepstow. Newport, Mon. ;
A. W. Dawson, 1901.
[9], 10—171p. 18cm. cloth.
Another ed.—2nd ed. Newport, Mon. ;
Williams Press, Ltd., 1925.
[5], 6—141p. 20cm. boards.

FLETCHER, Joseph Smith

Novel
A 501 : The pigeon's cave : a story of Great Orme's
Head in 1806.
London ; S. W. Partridge, 1904.
165, [3], 32p. illus. 18½cm. cloth.
—Another impression, 1913 ; 1933.
Location : Llandudno, Caerns.

FORD, Donald [Frank William]

Novels
A 502 : The following seasons : a novel.
London ; Bodley Head, 1959.
[8], 9—287p. 18½cm. cloth.
Location : A Welsh valley : farming com-
munity.

A 503 : There is still a river.
London ; Constable, 1954.
[6], 7—334p. 18½cm. cloth.
Location : The Welsh valley of "Sarn".

A 504 : Wise men make answer.
London ; Constable, 1955.
[6], 7—285 [1]p. 18cm. cloth.
Location : The Welsh valley of "Sarn".

Story
A 505 : The green door.
Penguin New Writing, no. 39 ; ed. by John
Lehmann, 39—47.

FOX, Charles Arundel Overbury

Verse
A 506 : A New Zealander's treasury of verse.
Bishopston, Swansea ; publ. by the author,
1953.
127p. 23cm. cloth.
Includes poems on Swansea and Gower.
Swansea Central Public Library has no. 188
of an edition of 200 copies.

FOXALL, Raymond

Novel
A 507 : Song for a prince : the story of Llywelyn the
Great.
London ; Hale, 1959.
[9], 10—192p. 19cm. cloth.

FRANCIS, John Oswald

Prose
A 508 : The legend of the Welsh, and other papers.
London, Cardiff ; Educational Publishing Co.
[10], 11—120p. 18¾cm. wrappers.
Includes essays of literary interest.

A 509 : Antipholus of Tanybwlch ; The Dragon,
Dec. 1909, 57—60.

A 510 : Betsi : a Welsh idyll ; Wales (J.H.E.), Vol. 3,
Feb. 1913, 85—7.

A 511 : The conflict of youth and ego : an extract
from the play Change ; They Look at
Wales : an anthology of prose and verse,
1941, 29—31.

A 512 : In fulfilment of a promise ; The Dragon,
April 1921, 154—6.

A 513 : Said the slave of the lamp ; The Dragon,
Feb. 1906, 113—4.

A 514 : Two sides of the border. From "The Legend
of the Welsh" ; They Look at Wales, 1941,
32—5.

Drama
A 515 : The bakehouse : a gossip's comedy (in one act).
Cardiff ; Educational Publishing Co., 1920.
[4], 5—39p. 15½cm. wrappers. (E.P.C.
Welsh Drama Series, no. 12).
Scene : "Aberpandy", S. Wales.

A 516 : The beaten track : a Welsh play in four acts.
London, New York ; Samuel French, 1927.
[10], 11—110, [2]p. 15½cm. wrappers.
(Welsh Drama Series, no. 81).
Welsh version entitled "Ffordd yr Holl
Ddaear" by Magdalen Morgan.

A 517 : Birds of a feather : a Welsh wayside comedy in
one act.
Newtown ; Welsh Outlook Press, [1927].
[6], 7—28p. 21½cm. wrappers.

Welsh version entitled "Adar o'r Unlliw".
—3rd edition. Cardiff ; William Lewis Ltd.,
[1946]. 32p. 15cm. wrappers.
—4th edition. London, New York ; Samuel
French, [1951].
Also in : Short modern plays ; sel. by G. Boas.
London ; Macmillan, 1935, 117—41.

One-act plays of today. 5th series,
ed. by J. W. Marriott. Harrap, 1931,
29—52.

A 518 : Change : a Glamorgan play in four acts.
Aberystwyth ; Gwasg y Ddraig Goch (W.
Jones), 1913.
viii, 134p. wrappers. (Welsh Plays Series,
no. 2).
Scene : Cottage on the Twmp, "Aberpandy".
—Another ed. New York, Doubleday, Page,
1914.
—Another ed. Cardiff ; Educational Publish-
ing Co., 1920. vi, 122p. 15½cm. wrappers.
(E.P.C. Welsh Drama Series, no. 13).
Change was awarded the Lord Howard de
Walden Prize, 1912. Welsh version by
Magdalen Morgan entitled "Deufor Gyf-
arfod".

A 519 : Cross currents : a play of Welsh politics in
three acts.
Cardiff ; Educational Publishing Co., [1923].
[4], 5—100p. 15½cm. wrappers. (E.P.C.
Welsh Drama Series, no. 59).
Scene : Farm near Dinas, North Wales.
Welsh version by R. Silyn Roberts entitled
"Gwyntoedd Croesion". (E.P.C. Welsh
Drama Series, no. 62).

A 520 : The crowning of peace : a short pageant of
the peace of nations . . . with a translation
into Welsh by T. Gwynn Jones.
Cardiff ; Welsh Council of the League of
Nations Union, 1921.
[2], 3—40p. 15cm. wrappers.
Originally published (English version only) :
London, League of Nations Union, 1919.
—Another ed. Cardiff, Educational Publ. Co.,
1922.
[8], 9—55p. 15½cm. wrappers.
(E.P.C. Welsh Drama Series, no. 54).

A 521 : The dark little people : a comedy of the Welsh
tribes, in three acts.
Cardiff ; Educational Publishing Co., [1922].
[6], 7—94, [2]p. 15½cm. wrappers. (E.P.C.
Welsh Drama Series, no. 56).
Scene : Farm above village of "Pontewyn".
Welsh version by John Hughes entitled
"Y Bobl Fach Ddu".

A 522 : His shining majesty : a one act comedy.
Cardiff ; William Lewis, n.d.
[4], 5—26, [2]p. 15cm. wrappers.
Scene : "Riverside Patch", common land in
rural Wales.

A 523 : Howell of Gwent : a romantic drama in three
acts.
London, New York ; Samuel French, 1934.
[8], 9—98, [4]p. 15½cm. wrappers. (Welsh
Drama Series, no. 113).

A 524 : Hunting the hare : a one act comedy.
Liverpool ; Hugh Evans, n.d.
34 leaves. Typescript. 16½cm. wrappers.
—Another ed. Cardiff, William Lewis, n.d.
[4], 5—27, [1]p. 15½cm. wrappers.

A 525 : John Jones : an episode in the history of Welsh
letters.
Newtown ; Welsh Outlook Press, [1927].
[6], 7—28, [1]p. 21½cm. wrappers.
Scene : "Careg Goch Castle".
Welsh version by Magdalen Morgan.

A 526 : King of the river : a one-act comedy.
Cardiff ; William Lewis, [1943].
[4], 5—30p. 15cm. wrappers.

A 527 : Little village : a Welsh farce in three acts.
London ; New York ; Samuel French, [1930].
[4], 5—138p. 15cm. wrappers. (Welsh
Drama Series, no. 97).
Scene : "Little Village", part of "Portifor",
on Welsh coast.

A 528 : The perfect husband : a Welsh farce in one
act.
Newtown ; Welsh Outlook Press, [1927].
[6], 7—23p. 21½cm. wrappers.
Scene : Village of "Pontewyn".

A 529 : The poacher : a comedy in one act.
Cardiff ; Educational Publishing Co., [1914].
44p. wrappers. (E.P.C. Welsh Drama Series,
no. 10). Frequently reprinted.
Welsh version by Mary Hughes entitled
"Y Potsier".

The poacher : a comedy in one act.
In One-act plays of today. 4th series, ed. by
J. W. Marriott. Harrap, 1928, 233—57.

A 530 : The Sewing Guild : a woman's comedy in one
act.
Cardiff ; William Lewis, n.d.
[4], 5—30, [1]p. 15cm. wrappers.
Scene : "Aberton", a market town.

A 531 : Tares in the wheat : a country comedy in three
acts.
Cardiff ; William Lewis, n.d.
[6], 7—94p. 15cm. wrappers.
Scene : "Trefelyn", a rural village.
(NLW copy has ms. note : "Rewritten and
title altered to "The Sheep and the Goats").

A 532 : Torches on the river : a one act comedy.
Liverpool : Hugh Evans, n.d.
36 leaves. Typescript. 16½cm. wrappers.

FRANCIS, M. E. *pseud.* [*i.e. Mary Blundell*]

Novels
A   533   : The runaway.
           London ; Hutchinson, [1923].
           [4], 5—288, 40p. 18½cm. cloth.
           Location : North Wales.

A   534   : Young Dave's wife : a novel.
           London ; Hutchinson, [1925].
           [8], 9—284, 48p. 19cm. cloth.
           Location : North Wales farming communities.

GALLICHAN, Walter M.   *"Geoffrey Mortimer"*

Novel
A   535   : The conflict of Owen Prydderch.
           Edinburgh ; Morton ; London ; Simpkin,
           Marshall, 1905.
           [4], 300, [15]p. 18½cm. cloth.
           Location : Village of "Llanfair", Berwyn
           Mountains area.

GALLIE, Menna

Novels
A   536   : Man's desiring.
           London ; Gollancz, 1960.
           [4], 5—192p. 19½cm. cloth.
           Location : Crynant, S. Wales and the Mid-
           lands.

A   537   : The small mine.
           London ; Gollancz, 1962.
           [5], 6—191p. 19½cm. cloth.
           Location : "Cilhendre", near Swansea, Glam.

A   538   : Strike for a kingdom.
           London ; Gollancz, 1959.
           [4], 5—200p. 18½cm. cloth.
           Location : "Cilhendre", Tawe Valley.

GARLICK, Raymond

Stories
A   539   : Angharad and the Sphinx.
           Dock L., Vol. 1, no. 2, 1950, 33—7.

A   540   : The golden mountain.
           Dock L., Vol. 1, no. 1, 1949, 27—30.

Other Prose
A   541   : The words in my life : passages from an
           autobiography.
           A-W.R., Vol. 13, no. 31, undated, 15—19.

Verse
A   542   : Blaenau observed : a broadcast poem.
           Pembroke Dock, Pemb. ; Dock Leaves Press,
           1957.
           [6], 7—18p. 20½cm. wrappers.

A   543   : Landscape and figures : selected poems,
           1949—63.
           London ; The Merrythought Press, 1964.
           [10], 11—44p. 21½cm. wrappers.
           This edition limited to 150 signed copies
           printed on Antique Wove paper, plus 10
           signed copies printed on Antique Laid paper
           and specially bound in hard cases. NLW
           has signed copy no. 66 of the former.

A   544   : Poems from Pembrokeshire.
           [Pembroke ; Dock Leaves Press, 1954].
           Pamphlet. 20½cm.
           (Dock Leaves Pamphlets, no. 2).

A   545   : Poems from the mountain-house.
           London ; Fortune Press, [1950].
           [4], 5—32p. 18½cm. boards.

A   546   : Requiem for a poet.
           Pembroke Dock ; Dock Leaves Press, 1954.
           Pamphlet. 21½cm.
           (Dock Leaves Pamphlets, no. 1).
           Commissioned by the B.B.C. and broadcast
           in the series "Radio Odes".

A   547   : The Welsh-speaking sea.
           Pembroke Dock ; Dock Leaves Press, 1954.
           [10], 11—46p. 18cm. cloth.

A   548   : Aros a myned ; trans. from the Welsh "Aros a
           Mynd" of Ceiriog. Based on an original
           translation by Elin Garlick.
           Dock L., Vol. 1, no. 1, 1949, 27.

           Baling out ; Healing of the Nations ; ed. by
           Vera Rich. A-W.R. Supplement, 1965, 6.

           Ballet ; English, Vol. 7, no. 41, 1949, 225.

           David Dominic Davies ; A-W.R., Vol. 10,
           no. 26, 1960, 60—1.

           Doves ; ibid. Vol. 15, no. 35, 1965, 51.

           Eclogue ; English, Vol. 8, no. 43, 1950, 30.

           Education ; Dock L., Vol. 3, no. 7, 1952, 19.

           The elate island (for the Prior and Monks of
           Caldey) ; Rann, No. 19 (Welsh number),
           1953, 13.

           Feeding the fish ; A-W.R., Vol. 12, no. 30,
           undated, 41—2.

           For a young poet ; English, Vol. 10, no. 59,
           1955, 187.

           Home thoughts from abroad ; A-W.R.,
           Vol. 12, no. 30, undated, 40.

           Lady Llanfair ; Wales, no. 41, 1959, 35.

Letter to London ; Dock L., Vol. 4, no. 10, 1953, 29.

Mair y Mynyddoedd [Mary of the Mountains] ; Dock L., Vol. 3, no. 8, 1952, 33.

Mushrooms ; Dock L., Vol. 2, no. 4, 1951, 42.

Note on the Iliad ; A-W.R., Vol. 12, no. 29, undated, 10—1.

Old masters ; PEN 1958, 40.

Opera ; Dock L., Vol. 1, no. 1, 1949, 26.

Orchestra ; ibid. 25—6.

Orison ; ibid. 26—7.

Peacocks ; A-W.R., Vol. 15, no. 35, 1965, 51.

Poem from Manorbier : PEN 1954, 102.

Poem from the mountain-house ; Prospect, Vol. 2, no. 11, 1949, 11.

Pryddest ; The City ; Y Ddinas, Vol. 9, no. 9, 1955, 14.

Seven on a theme ; Wales, Nov 1958, 26—9.

Stanzas from Esztergom ; Dock L., Vol. 1, no. 2, 1950, 54—5.

Still life ; A-W.R., Vol. 15, no. 35, 1965, 51-2.

Theory of images ; ibid. Vol. 12, no. 30, undated, 41.

Vowels ; ibid. Vol. 13, no. 31, undated, 20.

Walking in the forest ; ibid. Vol. 12, no. 30, undated, 40—1.

GEORGE, Arthur   (of Penrieth, Pembs.)

Verse
A 549 : Alun, and other poems.
Carmarthen ; Spurrell, [1913].
[5], 6—102, [1]p.   front. (port.)   18½cm.
wrappers.

GIBBON, Muriel Morgan

Novel
A 550 : Jan : a novel.
London ; Hutchinson, [1921].
[9], 10—288p.   18½cm.   cloth.
Location : "Brynavon".

GILBERTSON, Belfrage

Verse
A 551 : Poems of Merioneth.

London ; Stockwell, [1930].
[3], 4—16p.   18cm.   boards.

GILL, Hugh Valentine

Stories
A 552 : The black four-master, and other stories.
Llandybie ; Christopher Davies, 1955.
[7], 8—154p.   18½cm.   cloth.
Contents : The upside down world—The cave of the thief—The traitor—The cider-making—Hills in the sky—The insufferables—The black four-master—Miracle at Eithinog—Killer — Vixen — Castaway — Noson Lawen—The power of bees—Solomon's head—Grand partnership—Adventurers.

A 553 : The insufferables.
Celtic Story, No. 1 ; edited by Aled Vaughan, 1946, 20—5.

A 554 : The upside down world.
Welsh Review, Vol. VI, no. 4, 1947, 285—9.

GLYN, Megan, *pseud.* [*i.e. Margaret G. Parry*]

Novels
A 555 : Arian : a novel in two parts.   Part one : Poverty Hall.   Part two : The three lovers.
Amlwch Port, Anglesey ; Megan Glyn Publishers, [1950].
[6], 7—214p.   18½cm.   cloth.

A 556 : Hovering chariot.
London ; The Delyn Press, [1951].
[4], 5—192p.   18½cm.   cloth.
Location : Village of ' Cregingwag '.

A 557 : Simon Peter : a novel of Welsh life—1870 to September 1939.
[No publisher's imprint].
Liverpool ; Daily Post Printers, [1947]. Wrapper and spine give "Mercury Press".
[5], 6—163p.   18cm.   cloth.
Location : Village of "Eilfaen".

A 558 : Simon Peter : a novel of Welsh life—1870 to September 1939.
Braille version. Vols. 1 to 3 in Braille type.
London ; National Institute for the Blind, [1950].
4to.   3 vols.   cloth.

GLYNNE-JONES, William

Novels
A 559 : The childhood land.
London ; Batsford, 1960.
[6], 7—157p.   20cm.   cloth.
"Working-class children in a small Welsh industrial town in the 1910's." (British National Bibliography).
Location : "Abermor", Carms. [Llanelly].

A 560 : Farewell innocence.
London ; Werner Laurie, 1950.
[6], 7—286p. 18½cm. cloth.
Location : Steel foundry : Llanelly, Carms.

A 561 : Ride the white stallion.
London ; Werner Laurie, 1950.
[4], 5—231p. 18½cm. cloth.
Location : "Abermor" [Llanelly], Carms.

Stories
A 562 : He who had eaten of the eagle : short stories.
Glasgow ; W. Maclellan, 1948.
[4], 5—161p. 18½cm. cloth.
Contents : Prologue—Spell—Steel foundry—
The mills are starting Monday—Man,
woman and child—Saved—A visit to Dai's
—"Night out"—Resurrection of Reuben
Cardigan—Dafydd and the elders—Resist-
ing arrest—Ianto, Betty Jane and the
insurance man—Turkey for five—The
bride—Dead men could tell tales—Old
Weary—He who had eaten of the eagle—
Speed—Pagan love song—The merry love
to dance—The last day.

A 563 : The champion ; Dock L., Vol. 1, no. 3, 1950,
10—7.

A 564 : Cinder gatherers ; Seven, Vol. 5, no. 4 [1945],
47—54.

A 565 : "Come into the parlour, Daniel" ; Pick of
today's short stories, No. 3, 1952, 77—85.

A 566 : Dead men could tell tales ; Seven, Vol. 5,
no. 3 [1945], 15—6.

A 567 : God's honour ; Adam International Review,
No. 234, 1953, 26—8.

A 568 : "I know a bank" ; Celtic Story, Number One ;
edited by Aled Vaughan, 1946, 46—60.

A 569 : Moving pictures ; New short stories, 1945—6 ;
ed. by J. Singer. Glasgow, Maclellan, [1946],
165—75.

A 570 : The pool ; Seven, Vol. 4, no. 4, 1944, 16—8.

A 571 : Resisting arrest ; Seven, Vol. 5, no. 2, 1944,
27—36.

A 572 : The resurrection of Reuben Cardigan ; ibid.
no. 1, 1944, 37—42.

A 573 : Saved ; ibid. Vol. 4, no. 3, 1943, 32—3.

A 574 : Turkey for five ; Bristol Writers and Artists
Association, Bristol Packet [No. 2, 1945],
45 *et seq.*

A 575 : Up-ladle at three ; Welsh short stories ; ed. by
G. Ewart Evans. 2nd ed. 1959, 212—8.
(Originally *in* Esquire [U.S.A.]).

A 576 : A visit to Dai's ; Seven, Vol. 6, no. 1 [1946],
13—20.

A 577 : Wil Saes ; Saturday saga. London, Progress
Publishing Co., 1946, 7—11.

Other Prose
A 578 : Summer long ago. Foreword by L. A. G.
Strong.
London ; Peter Nevill, 1954.
xi, [1], 204p. 21½cm. cloth.

A 579 : Another working day begins.
Seven, Vol. 3, no. 3, 1942, 10—3.
Welsh Review, Vol. III, no. 4, 1944, 290—3.

A 580 : Boyhood.
Wales, Vol. VI, no. 24, 1946, 115—9.

A 581 : Unwilling apprentice.
Welsh Review, Vol. V, no. 2, 1946, 129—33.

GOODWIN, Geraint

Novels
A 582 : Call back yesterday.
London ; Cape, 1935.
218p. 19cm. cloth.
Location : Partly in Wales.

A 583 : Come Michaelmas.
London ; Cape, 1939.
282p. 19cm. cloth.
Location : Welsh border country, Shropshire
and Montgomeryshire.

A 584 : The heyday in the blood : a novel.
London ; Cape, 1936.
[8], 9—287, [9]p. 19cm. cloth.
Location : Welsh border country : village of
"Tanygraig".
—Another ed. Penguin Books, 1954.
[6], 7—220, [4]p. 18cm. wrappers.

A 585 : Watch for the morning : a novel.
London ; Cape, 1938.
[14], 15—372p. 20cm. cloth.
Location : A Severn Valley town : Welsh
border country.

Stories
A 586 : The white farm, and other stories.
London ; Cape, 1937.
[6], 7—288, [8]p. 19cm. cloth.
Location : Wales and Shropshire.
Contents : The white farm—Saturday night—
The trial of Shoni Bach—Janet Ifans' donkey
—The auction—Into the dark—The picnic
—The old folk in the dead-houses—The
flying hours are gone—The young bull—
Come Michaelmas—The auld earth—The
old man leaves home—The coroner's
office—Late Spring.

A 587 : Ap Towyn ; Welsh Review, Vol. II, no. 4, 1939, 185—92.

A 588 : A Chelsea cameo : the record of a chance encounter ; Welsh Outlook, Vol. XIII, 1926, 159.

A 589 : Janet Ifans' donkey ; Welsh short stories ; ed. by G. Ewart Evans. 2nd ed., 1959, 52—70.

A 590 : The lost land ; Welsh Review, Vol. 1, no. 3, 1939, 122—30.

A 591 : The penny reading ; English story. Second series ; ed. by Woodrow and Susan Wyatt, 1941, 176—86.

A 592 : The shearing ; Welsh Review, Vol. III, no. 2, 1944, 85—102.

A 593 : A sitting of eggs ; Welsh short stories ; ed. by Gwyn Jones, 1956, 64—72. (Originally in *Lilliput*, 1941).

GRANDFIELD, Denis Edward

Verse
A 594 : Gower poems.
Hull ; The Guild Press, 1957.
39p. 22cm. wrappers.

A 595 : The Battlefield, Caswell ; Gower, Vol. 5, 1952, 40.

By the sea in winter ; ibid. Vol. 6, 1953, 10.

Oxwich at dusk ; ibid. Vol. 5, 1952, 40.

The trippers ; ibid. Vol. 6, 1953, 33.

A wet night ; ibid. 10.

Where ships lie ; ibid. 33.

GRAVES, Alfred Perceval

Verse
A 596 : Ballad of the old bachelor of Ty'n y Mynydd (from the Welsh of W. J. Gruffydd) ; Wales (J.H.E.), Vol. II, 1912, 218. Essays by Divers Hands, New series, Vol. VIII, 1928 (included in article, 81—105).

The ballad of the Welsh Buccaneers ; Welsh Outlook, Vol. IV, 1917, 135—7.
The black monk ; Pencader Poems, 1952, [4].

The dove ; Wales (J.H.E.), Vol. II, 1912, 147.

The high tide (after the Welsh of Elfed) ; ibid. 207.

Holiday hymn ; Welsh Outlook, Vol. XIII, 1926, 78.

The Men of Harlech (from the Welsh of Ceiriog) ; The Land of my Fathers. London, Hodder, 1915, 36—7.

Plas Gogerddan (from the Welsh of Ceiriog) ; ibid. 37.

GRENFELL-HILL, Jeffrey Du Cann

Verse
A 597 : New thoughts.
Ilfracombe ; Stockwell, 1963.
[2], 3—36p. 18½cm. wrappers.
(Includes one poem by Ieuan Roberts).

A 598 : A young man's thoughts.
Ilfracombe ; Stockwell, 1962.
24p. 28cm. wrappers.

GRIFFITH, G. J.

Drama
A 599 : Hannah comes round : a play in one act.
Cardiff ; Educational Publishing Co., [1919].
32p. 15cm. wrappers. (E.P.C. Welsh Drama Series, no. 18).
Scene : Welsh cottage, Spring 1918.
B.M. Cat. note : Series entry numbered as "27" and note follows : This play is wrongly numbered 18.

GRIFFITH, Jack

Stories
A 600 : Babel's offsprings ; The Dragon, Midsummer Term, 1933, 31—7.

A 601 : Captain ; ibid. Lent Term, 1933, 32—4.

A 602 : Dawn—a fragment ; ibid. Easter Term, 1932, 11.

A 603 : The debt ; ibid. Lent Term, 1932, 14—17.

A 604 : Gambler ; ibid. Summer Term, 1934, 26—33.

A 605 : Man ; ibid. Easter Term, 1932, 15—18.

A 606 : The ray ; ibid. Michaelmas Term, 1931, 7—10.

A 607 : Sacked ; Welsh Review, Vol. 1, no. 1, 1939, 27—32.
The Dragon, Vol. 61, no. 1, 1938, 13—15.

A 608 : "Something to be thankful for" ; The Dragon, Lent Term, 1934, 14—16.

A 609 : Sonata ; ibid. Michaelmas Term, 1931, 18—19.

Other Prose

A 610   : "Me" ; Wales, Vol. V, no. 7, 1945, 55—58.

A 611   : Stormy passage ; Welsh Review, Vol. 1,
no. 6, 1939, 322—329.

Verse

A 612   : Arrow wound ; The Dragon, Lent Term, 1933,
40—41.
The forsaken muse ; ibid. Lent Term, 1932, 27.
Jest ; ibid. Michaelmas Term, 1931, 24.
One stormy night ; ibid. Michaelmas Term,
1932, 35.
Swan song ; ibid. Michaelmas Term, 1933, 24.
Who loves the troubadour ; ibid. Easter
Term, 1932, 28—9.

Drama

A 613   : The artist and the crucifix : a play.
The Dragon, Midsummer Term, 1933, 62—3.

GRIFFITH, Llewelyn Wyn

Novels

A 614   : The way lies west.
London ; Dent, 1945.
[4], 5—252p. 18½cm. cloth.
Location : Farming community above Dolgelley, Merioneth : emigration to America.

A 615   : The wooden spoon.
London ; J. M. Dent, 1937.
[8], 9—318, [2], 8p. 18½cm. cloth.
Location : Lleyn Peninsula.

Stories

A 616   : Ifan Owen and the grey rider.
Welsh short stories ; ed. by Gwyn Jones, 1956,
72—84.

A 617   : The sea between.
Welsh Review, Vol. II, no. 2, 1939, 80—3.

Other Prose

A 618   : Spring of youth. Foreword by the Rt. Hon.
David Lloyd George, M.P.
London ; Constable, 1935.
viii, [2], 134p. 18½cm. cloth.

A 619   : Learning English. [Extract from *Spring of
Youth*].
They Look at Wales, 1941, 84—6.

A 620   : Welsh hymn tunes. [Extract from *Spring of
Youth*].
They Look at Wales, 1941, 101—3.

Verse

A 621   : The barren tree : poems.
Cardiff ; Penmark Press, [1947].
80p. 22cm. cloth.
—The barren tree ;
Welsh Review, Vol. III, no. 3, 1944, 173—82.

A 622   : Branwen.
London ; Dent, 1934.
vii, [1], 14p. 18½cm. cloth.
—*Extract* : "I have borne . . . silent at your
name, Branwen, Branwen".
Modern Welsh Poetry ; ed. by K. Rhys, 1944,
52—3.

A 623   : Aircraft at dawn ; Welsh Outlook, Vol.
XVIII, 1931, 149.

All Saints ; Modern Welsh Poetry ; ed. by
K. Rhys, 1944, 54.

Beauty ; Welsh Outlook, Vol. XVII, 1930,
290.

The Colours (November 11) ; *In* Smith, Jane
Adam, *compiler*, Poems of tomorrowt
London, 1935, 48.

February night ; Wales, No. 1, Summer 1937,
20.
Modern Welsh Poetry ; ed. by K. Rhys, 1944,
50—1.

"If there be time" ; Wales, No. 2, 1937, 70.
Modern Welsh Poetry ; ed. by K. Rhys,
1944, 52.

Light and shade ; Welsh Outlook, Vol. XVIII,
1931, 216.

Madam Rumour ; Wales, No. 1, Summer
1937, 19.
Modern Welsh Poetry ; ed. by K. Rhys, 1944,
51—2.

Mametz Wood ; Welsh Outlook, Vol. XVII,
1930, 296.

New Year's Eve ; Modern Weish Poetry, 1944,
50.
In Smith, Janet Adam, *compiler*, Poems of
tomorrow. London, 1935, 49.

Searchlights ; The British Annual of Literature, 1938, Vol. 1, 25.

Silver Jubilee ; Wales, New Series, I, 1943, 70.
Modern Welsh Poetry, 1944, 53—4.

War Memorial ; Welsh Outlook, Vol. XVII,
1930, 68.

GRIFFITH, Peter M.

Verse

A 624   : Apart ; Triad, by P. Griffith [*and others*], 1963,
15.

Barracks ; ibid. 21.

Y capel ; ibid. 18.

The cold road ; A-W.R., Vol. 11, no. 28, undated, 49. Triad, 1963, 16.

Felling trees ; A-W.R., Vol. 9, no. 24, undated 94. Triad, 1963, 15.

The gardener ; Poetry Wales, I, Spring 1965, 6.

Homage to R. S. Thomas ; Critical Qtly., Vol. 4, no. 4, 1962, 358. Triad, 1963, 27.

Icarus ; Triad, 1963, 22.

The iconoclasts ; Poetry Wales, Vol. 1, no. 2, Autumn 1965, 14—5.

The long seam ; Triad, 1963, 24—5.

Macsen wledig to the Welsh ; A-W.R., Vol. 9, no. 24, undated, 75.
Triad, 1963, 26.

Poem II ; Critical Qtly., Vol. 1, no. 2, 1959, 138.

Shepherd ; **ibid.** no. 1, 1959, 13.
Triad, 1963, 19.

Shores ; Critical Qtly., Vol. 1, no. 4, 1959, 301.

The small nation ; Poetry Wales, Vol. 1, Spring 1965, 5.

The stranger ; Critical Qtly., Vol. 1, no. 2, 1959, 105.
Triad, 1963, 16.

To another ; A-W.R., Vol. 11, no. 28, undated, 48.

Woman with child ; Triad, 1963, 23.

GRIFFITH, Sydney S.

Novel
A   625   : Little Calvary (Calvaria Fach) : a romance of Welsh life.
London, New York ; Melrose, 1924.
vii, [1], 278, [1]p.   19cm.   cloth.

GRIFFITHS, Bryn

Verse
A   626   : After the snow ; The London Welshman, Vol. 18, no. 4, 1963, 10.

Another season gone ; PEN 1965, 76.

Break in a day ; The London Welshman, Vol. 18, no. 2, 1963, 12.

Burnt grass ; ibid.

The bus stops ; ibid.

Day after rain ; ibid. Vol. 18, no. 7, 1963, 17.

Dying at Pallau ; YCP, 183.

I hear the season's voices ; The London Welshman, Vol. 18, no. 10, 1963, 11.

Lip service ; Transatlantic Review, No. 18, 1965, 83—4.

Morning voyage ; W. Mail, June 13, 1964, 5.

My shipwrecked Christmas ; The London Welshman, Vol. 18, no. 12, 1963, 6.

Night over Carn Ingli ; W. Mail, Sep. 26, 1964, 5.

A note for R. S. Thomas ; Poetry Wales, Vol. 1, no. 2, Autumn 1965, 23.

Soft rain ; The London Welshman, Vol. 18, no. 7, 1963, 15.

Winter at Harlech ; Poetry Wales, Vol. 1, Spring 1965, 4.

GRIFFITHS, Glyn

Drama
A   627   : Moon on the hill : a play in one act.
London ; French, 1955.
[4], 20, [2]p.   plan.   18½cm.   wrappers.
(French's Acting Edition, no. 823).
Scene : N. Wales hillside cottage.

A   628   : My hills, my home : a play in one act.
London ; French, [1954].
[4], 16, [2]p.   plan.   18½cm.   wrappers.
(French's Acting Edition, no. 852).
Scene : N. Wales farmhouse kitchen.
—*Also in* Best one-act plays of 1952—53.
Harrap, 1954, 31—46.

"GRIFFITHS, Ieuan", *pseud. [i.e. D. Mathew Williams]*

Drama
A   629   : Cat among the pigeons : farce in three acts.
Aberystwyth ; Gwasg Aberystwyth, 1952.
[7], 8—78p.   18½cm.   wrappers.
Welsh version entitled "Tarfu'r C'lomennod".

GRUFFYDD, Penmaen

Verse
A   630   : To Gwalia : a poem.
Carnarvon (sic) ; The Welsh Publishing Co., [1912].
16p.   18cm.   wrappers.

A 631 : Christmas and the nations ; Wales (J.H.E.), Vol. 2, 1912, 686.

Invocation ; ibid. Vol. 6, 1914, 105.

The shining host ; ibid. Vol. 2, 1912, 494—5.

Tom Ellis ; ibid. 591.

Wales for the world ; ibid. 426.

"GUINNESS, Owen", *pseud. [i.e. Guy R. Williams]*

Novel
A 632 : Doctor Tonrondo : a novel.
London ; Chapman & Hall, 1958.
[6], 7—353p. 18½cm. cloth.
Location : Partly in Wales : the "Upper Dilwyn Valley".

GWYNN, Cyril

Verse
A 633 : Gower yarns told in rhyme.
[Swansea ; publ. by the author, 1928].
59p. illus. port. 17½cm. wrappers.

HALES, A[lfred] G[reenwood]

Novel
A 634 : The falcon's eyrie : a romance of North Wales.
London ; Hodder & Stoughton, [1925].
[4], 5—320p. 18½cm. cloth.
Location : North Wales coastal area : Conway, Menai Straits.

HANLEY, James

Novels
A 635 : Don Quixote drowned.
London ; Macdonald, 1953.
x, 11—248p. 20cm. cloth.
pp. 101—248 : "*Anatomy of Llangyllwch*".

A 636 : The Welsh sonata : variations on a theme.
London ; Verschoyle, 1954.
[6], 7—216p. 21½cm. cloth.
Location : Village of "Cilgyn" and "Cynant".
Stories
A 637 : Black gold.
Wales, no. 2, August 1937, 38—40.

A 638 : The kingdom.
Adelphi, Vol. 31, no. 3, 1955, 280—9.

A 639 : Miss Williams.
Wales, New Series, no. 5, January 1959, 65-9.

A 640 : My village.
Wales, October 1958, 52—8.

HARRIS, Ernest Howard

Verse
A 641 : An exile's lute.
London ; Erskine Macdonald, 1919.
[10], 11—86p. 18½cm. cloth.

A 642 : The harp of hiraeth.
London ; Selwyn & Blount, 1922.
[6], 7—63p. 18½cm. wrappers.

A 643 : Singing seas.
London ; Selwyn & Blount, 1926.
[4], 5—59p. 18cm. wrappers.
Author's note : "Songs of Swansea and i[ts] peninsula".

A 644 : Song cycle at the Worm, and other poems o[f] Gower.
London ; De la More Press, 1934.
40p. 19cm. wrappers.

A 645 : Songs in shot-silk.
London ; Selwyn & Blount, [1924].
[6], 7—71p. 18cm. boards.

A 646 : A Swansea boy : poems, 1918—1958.
[London ; The Centaur Press, 1959].
[10], 11—72p. front. (port.) 17½cm wrappers.

A 647 : Fanfare for festival ; Y Ddinas, Vol. 12, no. 8 1958, 11.
Hanner dyn ; Wales (J.H.E.), Vol. 6, Apr[il] 1914, 112—3.

HARRIS, Miriam

Verse
A 648 : Poems [Vol. 1].
Cardiff ; Western Mail, *printers*, 1945.
[4], 5—48p. front. 18½cm. wrappers.

A 649 : Poems [Vol. 2].
Cardiff ; Western Mail, *printers*, 1947.
[4], 5—48p. front. (port.) 18½cm. wrappers

HARRIS-BURLAND, John Burland

Novels
A 650 : The disc.
London ; Greening, 1909.
318p.
Location : Partly set in the villages of "Garth" and "Trethol", Cardiganshire.
—Another ed. 3rd ed., London ; S. Paul [1912].
[6], 318p. 17½cm. boards.

A 651 : The temple of lies.
London ; Hutchinson, [1921].
[6], 7—253p. 16½cm. cloth.
Location : The village of "Trethol".

HAWKES, Terry

Verse

652 : Femme fatale ; The Lilting House ; comp. by
T. Hawkes, 1955, 20.

The jazz singer ; ibid. 22.

Morning (*sub-titled :* Like Tears) ; Dragons
and daffodils, 1960, 18.
Dock L., Vol. 7, no. 20, 1956, 11.

A poem ("To sing you up and down a page") ;
Dragons and daffodils, 1960, 20.

Pour l'élection de son sepulchre ; The Lilting
House, 1955, 19.

Some words for winter ; Dragons and daffodils,
1960, 19.

Sotto voce ; The Lilting House, 1955, 21.
Dock L., Vol. 6, no. 17, 1955, 18.

Tersa Rima (for Colin Petherick) ; Dragons
and daffodils, 1960, 19.

HAYCOCK, B. Myfanwy

Verse

653 : Fantasy, and other poems.
Newtown ; Welsh Outlook Press, [1937].
[4], 5—50p. illus. 24cm. boards.

654 : More poems.
Cardiff ; Western Mail & Echo, 1945.
[4], 5—40p. 20½cm. wrappers.

655 : Mountain over Paddington.
Cardiff ; Tudor Graphic Ltd., *printers*, 1964.
[4], 5—83p. 20½cm. wrappers.

656 : Poems.
Cardiff ; Western Mail & Echo, 1944.
[4], 5—40p. 21½cm. wrappers.

657 : [Extract from] June thoughts ; In Praise of
Wales ; comp. by Maxwell Fraser, 1950, 54.

Too much loveliness ; The Poetry Review,
Vol. 38, no. 3, 1947, 189.

HEINEMANN, Margot

Novel

658 : The adventurers.
London ; Lawrence & Wishart, 1960.
[8], 9—319p. 19½cm. cloth.
Location : Partly in Mid-Wales.

HELLINGS, Peter

Verse

659 : Firework music.
London ; Fortune Press, [1950].
[6], 7—70p. 19cm. boards.

A 660 : Bard ; Little Reviews Anthology, 1946, 164-5.

Beyond explanation ; Welsh Review, Vol.
VII, no. 4, 1948, 268.

Display ; Wales. No. 10. 1939, 272.

Enemies of forgetting : I, Flag Day, Jerusalem
1948—II, Drunk and disorderly—III, The
crucifixion of the moment—IV, The exiles
—V, Twelve bells ; Welsh Review, Vol.
VII, no. 4, 1948, 266—8.

[Extract from] Suite—Academic Festival ;
Poetry Book Magazine. Vol. 6, no. 5,
Fall 1954, 12—3.

Fairytales ; Modern Welsh Poetry ; ed. by
K. Rhys, 1944, 59.

Fired by a strange tongue ; More Poems from
the Forces ; ed. by K. Rhys, 1943, 123—5.

Five poems from Pennard ; Wales. Vol. V,
no. 8/9, 1945, 69—71.
Contents : Across Cefn Bryn—Swansea burning
—Heatherslade—The Castle—Song in
Hunt's Bay.

Five landscapes ; Welsh Review, Vol. VII,
no. 2, 1948, 110—2.
Contents : Aerial flowers—Harlot and hack—
Black sunset—Men of Kharkov and Kiev—
Red landscape.

From distant lands ; Modern Welsh Poetry ;
ed. by K. Rhys, 1944, 54—5.
More Poems from the Forces, 1943, 124—5.

Icarus : variations on a theme ; Dawn,
Cylchgrawn Myfyrwyr Coleg y Brifysgol,
Abertawe [Magazine of University College,
Swansea], Winter 1951.

Maid without tears ; Welsh Review, Vol. VI,
no. 3, 1947, 172—4.

Material for magic ; ibid. Vol. VII, no. 2,
1947, 112.

Picasso at Antibes ; PEN, 1954, 45.

Pictures at an exhibition ; Welsh Review,
Vol. IV, no. 3, 1945, 179—81.
Contents : Pit—Chapel—Girl—Peasant—Bard.

Poem ("Except for the hump-backed phant-
oms . . .") ; Life and Letters Today, Vol. 24,
no. 31, March 1940, 277.

Pyramid fires ; Rann. No. 19 (Welsh number), 1953, 15.

Rhapsody on a theme of Lorca ; Welsh
Review, Vol. VII, no. 4, 1948, 269.

Study : for Ezra Pound ; Modern Welsh Poetry ; ed. by K. Rhys, 1944, 57—8.

Suite—Academic Festival ; Dock L., Vol. 2, no. 5, 1951, 10—2.
Contents : 1, Congregation of the waters. 2, Entry of the pedagogues. 3, Honoured in Welsh. 4, Invocation to the Master-singer. 5, Dance of the apprentices.

Swansea Market ; Modern Welsh Poetry ; ed. by K. Rhys, 1944, 58—9.

Synthesis, above Swansea : stanzas I, II, III ; ibid. 55-7.

HEMINGWAY, Richard D'Oyly

Novel
A 661   : Land of my fathers.
London ; Melrose, 1920.
viii, [2], 323p. 17½cm. cloth.
Location : "Glanrafon".

HERBERT, Evelyn

Novels
A 662   : Anna Priestly : a novel.
London ; Cape, 1932.
[8], 9—334p. 19cm. cloth.
Location : (South Wales conjectured).

A 663   : The white peony.
London ; Cape, 1935.
[12], 13—314 + 8p. 19cm. cloth.
Location : North Monmouthshire between World War I and II.

"HEREFORD, John", *pseud. [i.e. H. L. V. Fletcher]*

Novel
A 664   : Shepherd's Tump.
London ; Hodder & Stoughton, 1947.
[4], 5—312p. 18½cm. cloth.
Location : Radnorshire : Claerwen Valley.

HESELTINE, Nigel

Stories
A 665   : Tales of the squirearchy : short stories.
Carmarthen, Dublin ; The Druid Press, 1946.
[6], 7—115p. 18cm. Illustrated boards.

A 666   : Break away if you can.
Penguin New Writing, no. 28, 9—19.

A 667   : Cam-Vaughan's shoot.
Wales, New Series, I, 1943, 33—7.

A 668   : A day's pleasure.
Penguin New Writing, no. 32, 28—46.

A 669   : Flaming tortoises : a story.
Wales, Vol. VI, no. 24, 1946, 25—42.
Welsh short stories ; ed. by G. Ewart Evan 2nd ed. 1959, 180—202.

A 670   : Gothic halls.
Wales, New Series, 3, January 1944, 34—8.

A 671   : Homecoming.
Celtic Story, Number One ; ed. by Ale Vaughan, 1946, 144—52.

A 672   : The lay reader.
Wales, No. 8/9, 1939, 227—31.

Verse
A 673   : The four-walled dream : poems.
London ; Fortune Press, n.d.
[6], 7—53p. 18½cm. cloth.
Includes some poems on Welsh themes.

A 674   : At first ; Modern Welsh Poetry ; ed. by K Rhys, 1944, 68.

Barter our northern darkness ; ibid. 70.

Denbigh Eisteddfod, 11th August 1939 ; ibid 66—7.

Epithalamion (for K.R.) ; ibid. 65.

The four-cornered tower, Llanybri ; ibid 65—6.

Gorse ; ibid. 68—9.

Hero of his village ; ibid. 67.

Recruiting Office ; Wales, New Series, 2 October 1943, 38.

[Six poems] ; Wales, No. 1, Summer 1937 10—3.

Solid cry ; ibid. No. 10, October 1939, 276—7

To a girl marrying a man with a wooden leg ibid. No. 11, 1939—49, 303.

Trapped man ; or, The freedom of smal nations ; Wales, New Series, 2, Octobe 1943, 37.

Wanderer's night-song ; Modern Welsh Poetry ; ed. by K. Rhys, 1944, 69.

HEWITT, Douglas

Novel
A 675   : Mountain rescue.
London ; Eyre & Spottiswoode, 1950.
[6], 7—251p. 18½cm. cloth.
Location : North Wales mountains.

HILL, John

Verse
A 676   : The balladry and lyrics of John Hill, Rhiwbina.
Ilfracombe ; Stockwell, 1962.
39p. 18cm. wrappers.

HOCKEY, Lawrence William

Verse
A 677   : The undying glory and other poems.
London ; Harmony Press, [1939].
64p. 19cm. cloth.

HOCKING, Silas Kitto

Novel
A 678   : A woman's love.
London ; Cassell, 1913.
viii, 370p. illus. 19cm. cloth.
Location : Set in Wales.

HOWARD-LLOYD, T.

Verse
A 679   : Sun on Merlin's pool : poems.
London ; Portsoken Press, printers, [1964].
vi, 22p. 18½cm. wrappers.
pp. v—vi : Foreword by Marguerite Caradoc
Evans (Oliver Sandys).

HOWELL, Florence

Drama
A 680   : Jane Wogan.
In Best one-act plays, 1934 ; ed. by J. W.
Marriott. London ; Harrap, 1934, 291—317.
Scene : A South Pembrokeshire village, 19th
century.
—*Also in* : The International One-Act Play
Theatre : Prize one-act plays. [1934].
Welsh version by Mary Hughes ; Aberystwyth,
Gwasg Aberystwyth, 1935.

HUGHES, Cledwyn

Novels
A 681   : After the holiday : a novel.
London ; Phoenix House, 1950.
[6], 7—224p. 18½cm. cloth.
Location : Seaside resort of "Llanmor".

A 682   : The civil stranger.
London ; Phoenix House, 1949.
[6], 7—192p. 18½cm. cloth.
Location : Village of "Cwm" and the town of
"Mwll".

A 683   : The different drummer.
London ; Pilot Press, 1947.
[6], 7—231p. 18½cm. cloth.

Bound with this work : The inn closes for
Christmas, pp. 145—231.

A 684   : Wennon.
London ; Pilot Press, 1948.
255p. 18½cm. cloth.
Location : The town and valley of "Cymaint".

Stories
A 685   : The black horse.
Pick of today's short stories, [No. 1], 1949,
139—48.

A 686   : The dance.
Pick of today's short stories, No. 3, 1952, 101-8.

A 687   : The first snow.
Welsh short stories ; ed. by G. Ewart Evans,
2nd ed., 1959, 203—11.

A 688   : The gramophone with a green horn.
Pick of today's short stories, No. 5, 1954,
101—18.

A 689   : The hedgehog.
Celtic Story, Number One ; ed. by Aled
Vaughan, 1946, 101—6.

A 690   : A master of the golden game.
World Prize Stories, 2nd ser. Odhams, [1956],
272—7.

A 691   : The miracle.
Life and Letters, Vol. 48, No. 103, March
1946, 190—6.
Best world short stories, 1947 ; ed. by J.
Gurnos and S. Norton, 84—90.

A 692   : Pritchard's bees.
English story. Seventh stories ; ed. by Woodrow Wyatt, 1947, 180—92.

A 693   : The unqualified.
Bugle Blast. 3rd Series, 1945, 37—45.

Other Prose
A 694   : The house in the cornfield. Illustrated by
Christopher Brooker.
London ; Werner Laurie, 1957.
[4], 5—252p. illus. 21½cm. cloth.

A 695   : Thoughts at Llangollen.
A.-W.R., Vol. 10, no. 25, undated, 38—40.

HUGHES, Cyril

Story
A 696   : The wanderings of Gwion Bach (a short fable
transmuted from the Welsh).
Welsh Review, Vol. VI, no. 2, 1947, 106—8.

Verse
A 697   : The literary swan, and other poems.
[Denbigh, Gee & Son, *printers*, 1965].
20p. 18cm. wrappers.
(Winning poems in a Bangor Poetry Comp-
etition. Foreword by R. S. Thomas).

A 698 : The agnostic; Outposts, no. 2 [1944], unpaged.

A ballad of capital punishment ; PEN 1957, 74—5.

The coming of Taliesin ; Outposts, no. 9, 1947, 7.

The eater of days ; Modern Reading, 16 ; ed. by R. Moore, 1947, 49.

Hiroshima ; For Those Who Are Alive ; ed. by H. Sergeant. Fortune P., 1946, 33—4.

The literary swan ; PEN 1955, 54—6.

Raids ; Prospect, no. 1. 1945, 3.

The seer ; ibid. no. 5. April 1946, 13.

Taliesin ; ibid. no. 3. May 1945, 12.

Ur and Tara and Segontium ; ibid. no. 10, Summer 1948, 29.

HUGHES, David

Novel
A 699 : A feeling in the air.
London ; Deutsch, 1957.
[6], 7—155p. 18¾cm. cloth.
Location : "Wender", Brecknock.

HUGHES, Edward William

Verse
A 700 : Poems.
Ilfracombe ; Stockwell, [1943].
[3], 4—15p. 18½cm. wrappers.

HUGHES, Eilian

Stories
A 701 : My island. Illustrated by Lady Stanley.
London ; Dent, 1901.
vii, [1], 208p. front. illus. 17cm. cloth.
Short stories set in Anglesey.

A 702 : The clever canon.
Wales (J.H.E.), Vol. V, Jan. 1914, 152—5.

A 703 : The pilgrimage of Betsan Ann.
Wales (J.H.E.), Vol. V, Feb. 1914, 229—33.

HUGHES, Isaac Craigfryn

Novels
A 704 : The Maid of Cefn Ydfa : an historical novel of the 18th century. [Preface to the first ed. dated 1881. This work was frequently reprinted, extending into the present century : e.g. the 28th ed. appeared in 1919 ; 30th ed. in 1927].
—30th ed. Cardiff ; Western Mail Ltd., 1927. 162p. wrappers.

A 705 : Merch o'r Scêr (English edition).
Ferndale ; D. Davies, 1902.
[5], 6—96p. 18cm. wrappers.
T.p. has note : "The present work has nothing to do with the celebrated romance by Mr R. D. Blackmore".
Location : Farmhouse of "Sker", parish of Pyle, Glam.

A 706 : The tragedy in the Gelli Wood.
Ferndale ; D. Davies, 1909.
[5], 6—79p. 18cm. wrappers.
Location : Rhondda Valley.

HUGHES, J. R. Lloyd

Stories
A 707 : Told by the cobbier of Llansionyn ;
I. The village confessional, The Welsh Outlook, Vol. 13, 1926, 162.
II. The cobbler as a detective, ibid. 193—4.
III. The parsons of the parish, 212.
IV. The tragedy of the smallholder, 249.
V. Religion and business, 274.
VI. The scientist in the pulpit, 300.
VII. The story of Myfanwy, 338.

HUGHES, John Wesley

Novel
A 708 : Vindicated : a story of Welsh life.
Wrexham ; Hughes, 1936.
[10], 11—249p. 18cm. cloth.
Location : "Caerwen".

HUGHES, Richard [Arthur Warren]

A 709 : Richard Hughes : an omnibus.
New York, London ; Harper, 1931.
xxxvii, 426p. front. (port.) 21½cm.
"Stories, poems and plays". (Library of Congress).

Novel
A 710 : The fox in the attic.
London ; Chatto & Windus, 1961.
352p. 19½cm. cloth.
—American ed. New York, Harper, [1962].
—Another ed. Harmondsworth, Penguin Books, 1961.
[11], 12—331[5]p. 18cm. wrappers. (Penguin no. 2069).
(Forms Vol. I of a projected trilogy or quartet entitled The Human Predicament).

Stories
A 711 : A moment of time.
London ; Chatto & Windus, 1926.
vii, [1], 243p. 18½cm. cloth.
Includes some stories of Welsh background.

A 712 : Justice.
Pick of today's short stories, no. 3, 1952, 109-14.

A 713 : A moment of time.
A Century of Writers, 1855—1955 ; comp. by D. M. Low and others, [1955], 489—91.

A 714 : Poor man's inn.
The "Evening Standard" book of best short stories. 2nd series, 1934, 154-67.

A 715 : The stranger.
Welsh short stories ; ed. by G. Ewart Evans. 2nd ed., 1959, 278—86.
Welsh short stories ; ed. by Gwyn Jones, 1956, 84—94.

Other Prose
A 716 : Wales through the looking-glass.
Listener, Vol. 45, May 24, 1951, 838—9.
(A talk broadcast in the B.B.C. Welsh Home Service).

Verse
A 717 : Confessio juvenis : collected poems.
London ; Chatto & Windus, 1926.
[4], 5—95p. 18½cm. cloth.
Bibliography, p. 95.

A 718 : Gipsy-night, and other poems.
Chicago ; W. Ransom, 1922.
[8], 9—65p. front. 22½cm. boards.
63 copies, signed by author and artist (P. Bianco), were issued. 30 for sale in America and 24 in England. Cardiff P.L. has copy no. 54.

A 719 : Felo de se ; Oxford Book of modern verse, 1892—1935 ; [comp.] by W. B. Yeats, O.U.P. 1947, 388.

Glaucopis ; ibid. 389—90.

The image ; ibid. 390.

Moonstruck ; Georgian Poetry, 1920—22 ; ed. by E. H. Marsh. London, 1922, 99—100.

Old Cat Care ; The Oxford Book of modern verse, 1892—1935 ; [comp.] by W. B. Yeats, O.U.P., 1947, 389.

Poets, painters, puddings ; Georgian Poetry, 1920—22 ; ed. by E. H. Marsh, London, 1922, 103.

The ruin ; Poems of Our Time, 1900—1962, Dent, 1959, 193—4. Poems of Our Time, 1900—1942, Dent, 1945, 193—4.
The Oxford Book of modern verse, 1892—1935 ; [comp.] by W. B. Yeats, O.U.P. 1947, 392—3.

The sermon ; The Oxford Book of modern verse, 1892—1935 ; [comp.] by W. B. Yeats, O.U.P., 1947, 387.

The singing furies ; Georgian Poetry, 1920—22 ; ed. by E. H. Marsh. London, 1922, 97—8.

Vagrancy ; ibid. 101—2.

The walking road ; The Oxford Book of modern verse, 1892—1935 ; [comp.] by W. B. Yeats, O.U.P., 1947, 390—1.

Winter ; ibid. 392.

Drama
A 720 : A comedy of good and evil : a play.
London ; Chatto & Windus, n.d.
[5], 40—141 p. 17cm. wrappers.
Scene : A kitchen in "Cylfant", Caerns.

A 721 : The sisters' tragedy : a play.
Carmarthen ; Druid Press, 1922.
[4], 5—35p. 17cm.
Location : A mansion in the Welsh hills.
—2nd ed. 1928.
—3rd ed. 1948.
—4th ed. 1949.
Another ed. Chatto & Windus, 1924.
—2nd ed., 1928.

A 722 : The sisters' tragedy, and three other plays.
London ; Heinemann, 1924.
vii, [3], 159p. 18½cm. cloth.
—Another ed. Chatto & Windus, 1928.
198p. 18cm. (Phoenix Library Service).
—Another ed. Chatto & Windus, 1956.
191p. 19½cm. cloth.
Contents : [Welsh scenes] : The sisters' tragedy —A comedy of good and evil—The man born to be hanged.
Also included : Danger.

A 723 : A rabbit and a leg : collected plays by Richard Hughes.
American edition.
New York ; A. A. Knopf, 1924.
vii, [2], 3—159p. 19½cm.
Contents : The sisters' tragedy—The man born to be hanged—A comedy of good and evil—A comedy of danger.

HUGHES, Thomas Rowland

Novels
A 724 : From hand to hand ; translated by Richard C. Ruck from the Welsh 'novel *O Law i Law*, with a foreword by Emlyn Williams. Line decorations by James Morris.
London ; Methuen, 1950.
vi, [4], 198p. illus. 18½cm. cloth.
Location : N. Wales slate-quarrying areas.
Also Cronies ; [an extract trans. by the author from *O Law i Law*]. Welsh Review, Vol. V, no. 1, 1946, 45—51.

A 725 : Out of their night : the Welsh novel *Chwalfa*
translated into English by Richard C.
Ruck.
Aberystwyth ; Gwasg Aberystwyth, 1954.
[9], 10—265p. 18cm. cloth.
Location : N. Wales slate-quarrying areas.

A 726 : William Jones, translated from the Welsh by
Richard C. Ruck.
Aberystwyth ; Gwasg Aberystwyth, 1953.
[9], 10—298p. 18½cm. cloth.
Location : North & South Wales.

Verse
A 727 : Wheels ; Welsh Review, Vol. II, no. 1, 1939,
13—4.

Drama
A 728 : The open road : a play of the Rebecca Riots
in Wales.
Cardiff ; Castle Book Company, 1945.
[4], 67p. 18½cm. wrappers.
Scene : A tavern a few miles outside Swansea.

HUMPHREYS, Emyr

Novels
A 729 : A change of heart : a comedy.
London ; Eyre & Spottiswoode, 1951.
[10], 239p. 18¾cm. cloth.
Location : Welsh university town of "Aber"
[Bangor].

A 730 : The little kingdom.
London ; Eyre & Spottiswoode, 1946.
[4], 5—221p. 18½cm. cloth.
Location : North East Wales : seaside town of
"Llanelyd".

A 731 : A man's estate.
London ; Eyre & Spottiswoode, 1955.
[10], 11—255p. 20cm. cloth.
Location : "Pennant", N. Wales.

A 732 : Outside the house of Baal.
London ; Eyre & Spottiswoode, 1965.
444p. 20cm. cloth.
Location : North and South Wales areas.

A 733 : A toy epic.
London ; Eyre & Spottiswoode, 1958.
[6], 7—158p. 18¾cm. cloth.
This work originally published in a Welsh
version entitled "Y Tri Llais". As "A Toy
Epic", awarded the Hawthornden Prize,
1959.
Extract from chapter 4, entitled "A death in
the street".
Wales. Nov. 1958, 21—5.

Story
A 734 : Mrs. Armitage.
Welsh short stories ; ed. by G. Ewart Evans,
2nd ed., 1959. 246—59.

Other Prose
A 735 : An imaginary encounter [between] Saunders
Lewis and Llywelyn ap Gruffydd.
Wales. Vol. IX, no. 31, 1949, 29—35.
(Written for broadcasting).

Verse
A 736 : The curate ; Wales. No. 10, 1939, 270.

The death of Gwilym de Breos ; trans. from
Siwan by Saunders Lewis.
A.-W.R., Vol. 10, no. 25, undated, 22.

A democratic vista ; Wales. New Series, 4,
1944, 87.

1536—1936 ; Wales. No. 6/7, 1939, 202.
Modern Welsh Poetry, 1944, 70.

Humble song ; Rann. No. 19 (Welsh no.),
1953, 9.

My great aunt ; Dock L., Vol. 7, no. 19,
1956, 8—9.

Myrddin's madness ; Poetry Book Magazine,
Vol. 6, no. 5, Fall 1954, 26—7.

A Nonconformist ; Modern Welsh Poetry ; ed.
by K. Rhys, 1944, 71—2.

Piecepomb for Vjayday ; Wales. Vol. VI,
no. 2, 1946, 6.

Rabbit ensemble ; Rann, No. 19 (Welsh no.),
1953, 14.

Sympathy explained ; Wales, No. 8/9, 1939,
226.
Modern Welsh Poetry, 1944, 71.

To John Gwilym Jones (Acting) ; Wales.
New Series, 3, 1944, 9—10.

Unloading hay ; Wales. No. 8/9, 1939, 231.
Modern Welsh Poetry, 1944, 70—1.

A young man considers his prospects ; Wales.
No. 6/7, 1939, 202—3.

HUMPHREYS, John Rees *and* HUMPHREYS, *Mrs.*

Verse
A 737 : Charmed moments, by Mr. & Mrs. J. R.
Humphreys.
Cardiff ; Western Mail and Echo, [1945].
140p. illus. 18cm. cloth.

HUWS, Edrica

Verse
A 738 : Congress of air and sea ; Wales, Vol. VII,
no. 26, 1947, 282.

A dimension of woman ; ibid. no. 25, 1947, 157.

The exiles ; ibid. no. 26, 1947, 285—6.

Lyric : 3 stanzas ; ibid. Vol. VIII, no. 30, 1948, 643.

The mind can never know ; Little Reviews Anthology, 1946, 166.

The mother ; Wales, Vol. VIII, no. 30, 1948, 641—2.

Poem to the paraclete ; ibid. Vol. VII, no. 26, 1947, 284.

A roll on the drum, Llanddyfnan ; ibid. no. 25, 1947, 158—60.

Sleep, my bed was his ; ibid. no. 26, 1947, 283—4.

Sonnet ; ibid. no. 25, 1947, 158.

INGLIS-JONES, Elizabeth

Novels
A 739   : Aunt Albinia.
London ; Faber, 1948.
[6], 7—303p. 18½cm. cloth.
Location : West Wales country mansions, and London.

A 740   : Crumbling pageant.
London ; Constable, 1932.
[8], 9—315, 5p. 19cm. cloth.
Location : "Morfa" and "Penllan", Cardiganshire.

A 741   : Pay thy pleasure.
London ; Faber, 1939.
[6], 7—334p. 18½cm. cloth.
Location : Partly in West Wales ("Forrest").

A 742   : Starved fields.
London ; Constable, 1929.
[6], 303p. 19cm. cloth.
Location : House of "Lluest, Dulas Valley", Cards.

JACOB, Violet [i.e., Violet Kennedy-Erskine]

Novels
A 743   : The history of Aythan Waring.
London ; Heinemann, 1908.
viii, 325p. 19½cm. cloth.
Location : Crickhowell, Brecon Beacons areas.

A 744   : Irresolute Catherine.
London ; Murray, 1909.
174p. 19cm. cloth.
Location : A Welsh farm.

A 745   : The sheep-stealers.
London ; Heinemann, 1902.
viii, [2], 3—341, [32]p. 18cm. cloth.
Location : Black Mountains : 19th century.
Other impressions : 1902 ; 1903 ; 1905.

JAMES, David Emrys   "Dewi Emrys"

Verse
A 746   : Rhymes of the road.
London ; Cecil Palmer, 1928.
viii, 56p. 19cm. cloth.
Title-page notes author as "David Emrys".

JAMES, Edwin Stanley

Verse
A 747   : The little land : poems of Anglesey. Illustrations by Margaret Nunn.
Liverpool ; Hugh Evans & Sons, printers, 1958.
v, [1], 7—28p. col. front. col. plates. 18cm. wrappers.

A 748   : Short measures.
Abingdon, Berks. ; Abbey Press, [1948].
56p. 17½cm. wrappers.

A 749   : The statue and other poems.
London ; Erskine Macdonald, 1921.
[7], 8—84p. 18½cm. cloth.
Includes three translations from the Welsh : The poet (D. Emrys James), Seeking a Fairer Heaven (Islwyn), Red and White (Wil Ifan).

A 750   : Moonrise ; Welsh Review. Vol. III, no. 4, 1944, 282.
The old order—Glasynys ; Wales. Vol. V, no. 8/9, 1945, 32.
Scattered ; translated from "Chwalu" by T. Gwynn Jones ; ibid. 7.
The slanting road ; Welsh Outlook, Vol. XIII, 1926, 260.
Ystrad Fflur : translated from the Welsh of T. Gwynn Jones ; Wales. Vol. V, no. 7, 1945, 17—9.

JAMES, Margot

Novel
A 751   : The Cardi comes home.
London ; Cape, 1956.
[6], 7—253p. 18½cm. cloth.
Location : Cardiganshire coastal village.

JENKINS, John   "Gwili"

Verse
A 752   : Poems.
[Cardiff ; publ. by the author, 1920].
xii, 104p. 19cm. cloth.

JOHNS, Rowland

Novel
A 753   : Mind you ; or ; Lewys Lad and his friend
            Shadrach.
            London ; Methuen, 1922.
            v, [1], 213, 8p. 19cm. cloth.
            Location : Village of "Bot".

JONES, Alun James   *(of Brecon)*

Verse
A 754   : Miscellaneous verse.
            Southend-on-Sea ; Citizen Publishing Co.,
            Ltd., 1964.
            7p. 18½cm. wrappers.

JONES, D. D.

Novel
A 755   : Silurians.
            London ; Stockwell, 1939.
            [6], 7—142p. 18cm. cloth.
            Location : "Nantwen Vale" : farming
            community.

Story
A 756   : Common lanes.
            Llandyssul ; Gomerian Press, 1941.
            [8], 9—118p. 18cm. cloth.

JONES, David [Michael]

A 757   : The anathemata : fragments of an attempted
            writing.
            London ; Faber, 1952.
            [4], 5—243p. plates. 22cm. cloth.
            —American ed. New York ; Chilmark Press,
            1963.

A 758   : Epoch and artist : selected writings by David
            Jones ; edited by Harman Grisewood.
            London ; Faber, 1959.
            [8], 9—320p. front. 22cm. cloth.
            Section I, pp. 25—82 consists of essays on
            Welsh topics.

A 759   : [The fatigue].
            A volume intended for private publication in
            1965 as a 70th birthday tribute to David
            Jones. Copy not seen.

A 760   : In parenthesis.
            London ; Faber, 1937. New York, Viking
            Press, [1961].
            xv, [7], 226p. front. illus. 22cm. cloth.
            Awarded the Hawthornden Prize for 1938.
            —Another ed.—Limited ed. of 70 signed
            and numbered copies, 50 only being for
            sale. NLW has copy no. 58, BM no. 52
            signed by the author & T. S. Eliot. Faber,
            1961.

xxi, 226p. front. plates. 22½cm. cloth.
            —Reissued by Faber, 1963. (Paperback
            edition). xv, [7], 224 [2]p. 21½cm. wrappers.

A 761   : [Extract] from the Anathemata : "Stands a
            lady . . . Restituis rem." ; Presenting Welsh
            poetry, 1959, 106—8.

            The five unmistakable marks ; Modern Welsh
            Poetry ; ed. by K. Rhys, 1944, 72—6.

            From Mabinog's Liturgy ; Poetry Book
            Magazine, Vol. 6, no. 5, Fall 1954, 15.

            The hunt ; Agenda, IV, no. 1, Apr/May,
            1965, 3—6.

            The tribune's visitation ; The Listener, May
            22, 1958, 843—5.

            Two passages from *In Parenthesis* : 1. "You can
            hear the silence of it . . . It's cushy enough".
            2. "And the place of their waiting . . . to
            wait for the hearers" ; The Faber book of
            modern verse ; ed. by M. Roberts. 3rd ed.
            rev., 1965, 301—5.

            The wall ; Landmarks and Voyages ; ed. by
            Vernon Watkins. Poetry Book Society,
            1957.

JONES, E. M.

Verse
A 762   : The collected poems of E. M. Jones.
            London ; Mitre Press, 1950.
            [6], 7—72p. 18½cm. cloth.
            Some poems on Welsh themes.

JONES, F. L. Wilson

Novel
A 763   : A Welsh nightingale.
            London ; Digby, Long, 1911.
            [7], 8—95p. 18½cm. wrappers.
            Bound with this work : pp. 71—95 : A would-be
            suffragette.

JONES, George

Verse
A 764   : Llandudno lays : a souvenir of Llandudno.
            London ; A. H. Stockwell, n.d.
            16p. illus. 18½cm. cloth.

JONES, George Edkins

Verse
A 765   : Away from noise : thoughts on beauty, truth
            and goodness.
            Gwernaffield, Mold, Flint. ; publ. by the
            author, 1942.
            viii, 62p. 15cm. cloth.

JONES, Glyn

Novels

A 766 : The island of apples.
London ; Dent, 1965.
American ed., John Day Co., New York, 1965.
[6], 7—256p. 19cm. cloth.
Location : The town of "Ystrad".

A 767 : The learning lark.
London ; Dent, 1960.
[4], 5—224p. 19cm. cloth.
Location : "Treniclas".

A 768 : The valley, the city, the village : a novel.
London ; Dent, 1956.
[6], 7—316p. 19cm. cloth.
Location : Merthyr Tydfil and Llanstephan.

Stories

A 769 : The blue bed, and other stories.
London ; Cape, 1937. New York, E. P.
Dutton, 1938.
[4], 5—245p. 19cm. cloth.
Contents : I was born in the Ystrad Valley—
The kiss—Knowledge—Wil Thomas—Eben
Isaac—Cadi Hughes—Eden tree—The blue
bed—Porth-y-rhyd.

A 770 : The water music, and other stories.
London ; G. Routledge & Sons, 1944.
162p. 18½cm. cloth.
Contents : The apple-tree—The saviour—The
wanderer—The four-loaded man—The
little grave—Explosion—An afternoon at
Ewa Shad's—Wat Pantathro—The last
will—Price-Parry—Bowen, Morgan and
Williams—The water music.

A 771 : An afternoon at Uncle Shad's ; Welsh Review,
Vol. 1, no. 1, 1939, 8—15.

A 772 : The appletree ; Life and Letters Today,
Vol. 24, no. 31, March, 1940, 288—98.

A 773 : Bowen, Morgan and Williams ; Penguin
Parade, no. 11 ; ed. by D. Kilham Roberts,
1945, 155—84.

A 774 : The boy in the bucket ; A-W.R., Vol. 12,
no. 30, 22—9.

A 775 : Explosion ; Life and Letters Today, Vol. 21,
no. 19, 1939, 70—7.

A 776 : The four-loaded man ; Wales, No. 3, 1937,
110—14.

A 777 : The golden pony ; Chance, No. 4, Autumn
1953, 11—22.

A 778 : It's not by his beak you can judge a woodcock ;
Stand, VII, 1954, 5—12.
Welsh short stories ; ed. by G. Ewart Evans,
2nd ed. 1959, 42—51.

A 779 : The Last-Will ; English story. Fourth series ;
ed. by Woodrow Wyatt, 1943, 159—73.

A 780 : Lias Lewis ; Welsh Review, Vol. V, no. 4,
1946, 233—45.

A 781 : Price-Parry ; Welsh Review, Vol. III, no. 4,
1944, 236—46.
Welsh short stories ; ed. by Gwyn Jones,
1956, 109—27.

A 782 : The wanderer ; Wales, New Series, 2, October
1943, 26—34.

A 783 : Wat Pantathro ; English story, Second
series ; ed. by Woodrow and Susan Wyatt,
1941, 74—87.
Stories of the 40s : Vol. I ; ed. by R. Moore &
W. Wyatt, 1945, 233—43.
Welsh short stories ; ed. by Gwyn Jones, 1956,
94—109.

Verse

A 784 : The dream of Jake Hopkins.
London ; Fortune Press, 1955.
[6], 7—44p. 19cm. cloth.
pp. 42—4 : Author's note on poetry and
radio.

A 785 : Poems.
London ; Fortune Press, [1940].
[4], 5—45p. 19cm. cloth.
Edges uncut.

A 786 : Ambush ; Wales, Vol. IV, no. 5, 1944, 8.

Beach ; Modern Welsh Poetry ; ed. by K.
Rhys, 1944, 79.

Choirs ; Wales, no. 3, 1937, 88—9.

Comrades ; ibid. Vol. 4, no. 5, 1944, 8—9.

Easter ; ibid. 10.
Grigson, Geoffrey, *comp.* Poetry of the
present.
London ; Phoenix House, 1949, 127.

Esyllt ; Modern Welsh Poetry ; ed. by K.
Rhys, 1944, 77—8.
The colour of saying : an anthology of verse
spoken by Dylan Thomas ; ed. by R. N.
Maud and A. T. Davies, 1963, 96.

The garden ; A-W.R., Vol. 9, no. 24, undated, 44.

Gull ; Twentieth Century Verse, No. 3, 1937
(pp. unnumbered).
Modern Welsh Poetry ; ed. by K. Rhys,
1944, 78.

High wind in the village ; Dragons and
daffodils : an anthology of verse, 1960, 25.

Ladybird ; PEN 1953, 136—7.

Le jaloux ; Rann, No. 19 (Welsh number), 1953, 12.

Merthyr ; Presenting Welsh Poetry, 1959, 115—8.

Morning ; A-W.R., Vol. 9, no. 24, undated, 43.
Dock L., Vol. 1, no. 2, 1950, 24.
PEN 1961, 56.

Nightmare ; Dragons and daffodils : an anthology of verse, 1960, 24.

Park ; Wales, No. 4, 1938, 154.
Modern Welsh Poetry ; ed. by K. Rhys, 1944, 77.

Poem "I kept neat my virginity . . ." ; Wales, No. 6/7, March 1939, 197.

Returning ; Outposts, No. 18, 1951, 6—7.

The ruin-world, *from* "Biography" ; Grigson, Geoffrey, *compiler.* Poetry of the present. London ; Phoenix House, 1949, 128.

Sande ; Modern Welsh Poetry ; ed. by K. Rhys, 1944, 79.
Dragons and Daffodils, 1960, 25.
Grigson, Geoffrey, *compiler.* Poetry of the present. London ; Phoenix House, 1949, 127.

Scene ; Wales, No. 1, Summer 1937, 7—8.
Grigson, Geoffrey, *compiler.* Poetry of the present, London ; Phoenix House, 1949, 128—9.

Shadow ; Twentieth Century Verse, No. 3, 1937. (pp. unnumbered).

The slum-world ; Wales, No. 11, 1939—40, 302.

Stars ; Dragons and Daffodils : an anthology of verse, 1960, 25.

Town ; Wales, No. 10, October 1939, 274.
Dragons and Daffodils : an anthology of verse, 1960, 22.

Tree ; Wales, No. 3, 1937, 87—8.

JONES, Gwilym Gwesyn

Verse
A 787   : The loom of love, and other poems : lyrics, songs, sonnets from Thornhill Top. Foreword by A. G. Prys-Jones.
Cardiff ; Western Mail & Echo, *printers*, [1953].
[2], 3—35p. 21½cm. wrappers.

JONES, Gwyn

Novels
A 788   : The flowers beneath the scythe.
London ; Dent, 1952.
[6], 7—254p. 18½cm. cloth.
Location : House of "Hafod", in "Happy Valley".

A 789   : The green island : a novel. Engravings by John Petts.
London ; The Golden Cockerel Press, 1946.
[4], 5—84p. front. illus. 25cm. cloth.
Scene : Pembrokeshire and a coastal island.
Limited ed. of 500 numbered copies, of which nos. 1—100 were specially bound. NLW has copy no. 469.

A 790   : Times like these.
London ; Gollancz, 1936.
[11], 12—319p. 18½cm. cloth.
Location : "Jenkinston" mining village, S. Wales valleys.

A 791   : The walk home : a novel.
London ; Dent, 1962.
[4], 5—205p. 19cm. cloth.
Location : N. & S. Wales areas, 19th century.

Stories
A 792   : The buttercup field, and other stories.
Cardiff ; Penmark Press, 1945.
[6], 138p. 18½cm. cloth.
—Another impression, 1946.
Contents : The pit—The buttercup field—A man after God's own heart—All we like sheep—Kittens—Shacki Thomas—Ora pro boscis—The dreamers—A night at Galonuchaf—Gwydion Mathrafal—The passionate people—Their bonds are loosed from above—Take us the little foxes.

A 793   : Shepherd's hey, and other stories.
London, New York ; Staples Press, 1953.
[10], 11—243p. 19¾cm. cloth.
Contents : Shepherd's hey—The brute creation—Old age—Copy—All on a summer's day—Two women—A death on Sisterland.

A 794   : The still waters, and other stories.
London ; Peter Davies, 1948.
[6], 188p. 18½cm. cloth.
Contents : The green island—The still waters—Bad blood—Shining morn—A white birthday—Four in a valley—The prisoners—Down in the forest something stirred—Guto Fewel—Goronwy's house of gold.

A 795   : All we like sheep.
English story. Fourth series ; ed. by Woodrow Wyatt, 1943, 59—65.

A 796   : At Beguildy.
English story. First series ; ed. by Woodrow and Susan Wyatt, 1941, 175—86.

A 797 : The brute creation.
    Welsh short stories ; ed. by Gwyn Jones, 1956, 140—51.

A 798 : The buttercup field.
    Welsh Review, Vol. II, no. 1, 1939, 15—22.

A 799 : Down in the forest something stirred.
    Little Reviews Anthology, 1949, 57—67.

A 800 : The dreamers.
    English story. Third series ; ed. by Woodrow Wyatt, 1942, 79—88.

A 801 : Goronwy's house of gold.
    Welsh short stories ; ed. by G. Ewart Evans, 2nd ed., 1959, 83—95.

A 802 : Gwydion Mathrafal.
    Penguin Parade, no. 11 ; ed. by D. Kilham Roberts, 1945, 7—17.

A 803 : If you want to know the time—take a lodger.
    The Dragon, Summer Term 1958 (Festival ed.), 46—50.

A 804 : Kittens.
    Welsh Review, Vol. III, no. 1, 1944, 42—8.
    Little Reviews Anthology, 1945, 58—65.

A 805 : A man after God's own heart.
    Welsh Review, Vol. 1, no. 4, 1939, 209—13.

A 806 : A night at Galon-uchaf.
    International short stories ; ed. by Denys Val Baker, New series, no. 1, 1944.
    Welsh short stories ; ed. by Gwyn Jones, 1956, 127—39.

A 807 : The passionate people.
    Stories of the 40s : Vol. I ; ed. by R. Moore & Woodrow Wyatt, 1945, 169—78.

A 808 : The pit.
    Penguin Parade, No. 9 ; ed. by D. Kilham Roberts, 1942, 107—26.

A 809 : Shepherd's hey.
    Adelphi, Vol. 28, no. 4, 1952, 682—71.

A 810 : The still waters.
    Welsh Review, Vol. VI, no. 1, 1947, 9—13.

A 811 : Take us the little foxes.
    A map of hearts ; ed. by Stefan Schimanski and Henry Treece.
    London ; L. Drummond, [1944], 111—9.

Other Prose
A 812 : A Prospect of Wales : an essay by G. J. with a series of water colours by Kenneth Rowntree.
    London ; Penguin Books, 1948.
    32, [20]p. illus. 18cm. boards.

Verse
A 813 : The blue day journey ; TLS, Dec. 2, 1955, 728.
    Hunter's moon ; Adelphi, Vol. 31, no. 2, 1955, 144—6.

JONES, Horace Charles

Stories
A 814 : Chief Petty Officer Kosco Ross.
    Wales, no. 45, 1959, 53—62.

A 815 : A high wind in Glamorgan.
    Adelphi, Vol. 29, no. 2, 1953, 130—4.

Verse
A 816 : The challenger : [poems].
    Merthyr Tydfil ; Merthyr Borough Council, 1963.
    [Copy not traced].

A 817 : Come take my hand ; Wales, no. 40, 1959, 17—8.
    Poet's epitaph ; Wales, Oct. 1958, 62.
    Table d'hôte ; ibid. no. 40, 1959, 16.
    The yellow rose of Spring ; ibid. no. 42/44, 1959, 62.

JONES, Idwal

Novels
A 818 : The splendid shilling : a novel.
    London ; Hodder & Stoughton, 1926.
    [6], 7—310, [8]p. 18½cm. cloth.
    —Another edition. New York ; Doubleday, Page, 1926.
    8, 332p. 19cm. cloth.
    (Endpapers decorated).
    Location : Partly set in Wales.

A 819 : Whistler's van.
    London ; Selwyn & Blount, [1936].
    [8], 9—256p, 32p. 18½cm. cloth.

JONES, Ivan Morgan Merlin

Novel
A 820 : The reclamation of Wales : a patriotic romance founded on facts.
    New York ; E. S. Gotham, 1912.
    192p. photos. 17cm. wrappers.
    Sequel to "Dear Old Wales" by T. O. Charles (q.v.).
    Location : "Llangwenllian".

JONES, Jack

Novels
A 821 : Bidden to the feast.
    London ; H. Hamilton, 1938.
    [8], 9—446p. 19½cm. cloth.

Location : Merthyr Tydfil, Glam.
—Reprinted in the Portway Series by C. Chivers, Ltd., 1965.
—American ed. New York, Putnam, 1938.

A 822 : Black Parade.
London ; Faber, 1935.
[8], 9—407p. 18½cm. cloth.
Location : Merthyr Tydfil, Glam.
—Another ed. H. Hamilton, 1948.
[4], 5—312p. 17½cm. cloth.
—Reprinted in the Portway Series by C. Chivers, Ltd., 1965.

A 823 : Choral symphony : a novel.
London ; H. Hamilton, 1955.
[6], 7—223p. 18½cm. cloth.
Location : Mining town of "Treshon" ("Johnstown").

A 824 : Come, night ; end, day ! or, The theatre that came to stay : a novel.
London ; H. Hamilton, 1956.
280p. 19½cm. cloth.
Location : "Hightown" and the "Queen's Theatre".
(Cardiff and the S. Wales valleys).

A 825 : Lily of the valley.
London ; H. Hamilton, 1952.
xi, [1], 210p. 18½cm. cloth.
Location : Partly South Wales ("Darren Valley").

A 826 : Lucky Lear.
London ; H. Hamilton, 1952.
[4], 5—224p. 18½cm. cloth.
Location : "Penrodyn" (mining valley) and other Welsh areas.
—Reprinted in the Portway Series by C. Chivers, Ltd., 1965.

A 827 : Off to Philadelphia in the morning.
London ; H. Hamilton, 1947.
[6], 7—372p. 18½cm. cloth.
Location : Merthyr Tydfil, Glam.
—Another impression. H. Hamilton, 1948.
—Another impression. Penguin Books, Ltd., 1951 (Vol. 863).
[6], 7—414, [3]p. 18cm. wrappers.
—An extract entitled "The Kingdoms of the Earth". In A Book of Wales, ed. by D. M. and E. M. Lloyd, 1953, 172—4.

A 828 : Rhondda roundabout.
London ; Faber, 1934.
[6], 7—351p. 18½cm. cloth.
—Another edition. H. Hamilton, 1949.
[4], 5—272p. 18½cm. cloth.
—Reprinted in the Portway Series by C. Chivers, Ltd., 1965.

A 829 : River out of Eden.
London ; H. Hamilton, 1951.
[8], 9—671p. 19½cm. cloth.

Location : Cardiff.
—Reprinted in the Portway Series by C. Chivers, Ltd. [undated].

A 830 : Some trust in chariots.
London ; H. Hamilton, 1948.
[6], 7—421p. 21cm. cloth.
Location : Glamorgan (farming and mining communities).

A 831 : Time and the business.
London ; H. Hamilton, 1953.
224p. 19½cm. cloth.

Prose
A 832 : Give me back my heart : final chapters in the autobiography of Jack Jones.
London ; H. Hamilton, 1950.
[8], 9—272p. 21½cm. cloth.

A 833 : Me and mine : further chapters in the autobiography of Jack Jones.
London ; H. Hamilton, 1946.
[8], 9—428p. 20½cm. cloth.

A 834 : Unfinished journey. Preface by Rt. Hon. David Lloyd George.
London ; H. Hamilton ; New York ; Oxford U.P., 1937.
[4], 5—318p. 21½cm. cloth.
—Another ed. H. Hamilton, 1938. Readers' Union edition. Collation as above.
An extract from Unfinished journey, entitled "Dowlais—Two generations".
A Book of Wales ; ed. by D. M. & E. M. Lloyd, 1953, 179—81.

A 835 : Collier boy of the gay 'nineties ; Welsh Review, Vol. 1, no. 2, 1939, 79—85.

A 836 : A gallery of grand chaps ; Welsh Review, Vol. III, no. 2, 1944, 130—5.

A 837 : Shoni in Shaftesbury Avenue ; Welsh Review, Vol. II, no. 1, 1939, 40—4.
(Describes the run of the author's play "Rhondda Roundabout" in the London theatre, 1939).

A 838 : A sinner and his saint ; Y Ddinas, Vol. 11, no. 6, Mar. 1957, 12 and 26.

Drama
A 839 : Land of my fathers : a play.
London ; Samuel French, 1937.
[4], 5—119, [5]p. plan. 18½cm. wrappers.
(French's Acting Editions, no. 71).
Scene : House in a mining town in "Heartbreak Valley" (Rhondda Valley).

A 840 : Rhondda roundabout : a play in three acts.
London ; H. Hamilton, 1939.
[8], 128p. 18½cm. cloth.
Scene : Rhondda Valley.
(NLW copy, signed by the author, contains pencilled alterations to pp. 127—8).

A 841 : Transatlantic episode : a comedy in a prologue and three acts.
London ; Samuel French, 1947.
[5], 6—102p. 18½cm. wrappers.
(French's Acting Edition, no. 167).
Scene : Mainly a Welsh miner's home.

JONES, Lewis

Novels
A 842 : Cwmardy : the story of a Welsh mining valley.
London ; Lawrence & Wishart, 1937.
x, 310p. 18½cm. cloth.
S. Wales mining community : c. 1890—1921.

A 843 : We live : the story of a Welsh mining valley.
Foreword by D. M. Garman.
London ; Lawrence & Wishart, 1939.
ix, [1], 334p. front. (port.) 18½cm. cloth.
Location : "Cwmardy", as in the volume of that title.

JONES, Margam

Novels
A 844 : Angels in Wales.
London ; John Long, 1914.
vii, [1], 9—320 + 20p. 19cm. cloth.
Location : Village of "Tredawel".

A 845 : The stars of the revival.
London ; John Long, 1910.
vii, [1], 9—318, 24p. 19cm. cloth.
Location : "Cwmhelig", Mid-Wales.

Verse
A 846 : The village lyre : a collection of short poems.
Aberdare ; H. Lloyd, *printer*, 1934.
[7], 8—50p. front. (port.) 18½cm. wrappers.

JONES, Melfin W.

Verse
A 847 : The dial hand.
London ; John Lane, 1932.
vi, [4], 84p. 19cm. cloth.
Includes some poems on Welsh themes.

A 848 : The hour glass : a collection of poems.
Wrecsam (sic) ; Hughes and Son, 1936.
108p. 18½cm. cloth.

A 849 : These things remain : poems.
London ; Staples Press, [1946].
44p. 27cm. cloth.

A 850 : The enchanted pool ; The Land of the Red Dragon [*i.e. 2nd ed. of The Welsh Gift Book*], 59.

The farewell of Owain Glyndwr ; The Welsh Gift Book, Llangollen, Gwynn Publ. Co., [1950], 61. Also in 2nd ed. [i.e. *The Land of the Red Dragon*], Cardiff, 1953, 63.

The Legend of Llyn Safaddan ; ibid. 54. Also in 2nd ed. 1953.

The new sword of song ; ibid. 61. Also in 2nd ed. 1953, 61.

[Stanzas, untitled] ; The Welsh Gift Book, Llangollen, Gwynn Publ. Co., [1950], [7], 33.
The Land of the Red Dragon, Cardiff, 1953, [vii].

The Welsh prisoner ; Welsh Outlook, Vol. 19, 1932, 293.

JONES, Percy Mansell

Prose
A 851 : Highland silences ; The Dragon, Nov. 1914, 13—4.

A 852 : The pavement artist ; Welsh Outlook, Vol. 10, 1923, 161—2.

A 853 : A poet at home ; The Dragon, May 1913, 185—8.

A 854 : Those other days ; ibid. March 1913, 130—3.

Verse
A 855 : Aberystwyth, 1915 ; Welsh Outlook, Vol. II, 1915, 464. The Dragon, Feb. 1916, 126.

All the difference , The Dragon, Feb. 1913, 76.

Audacity ; Welsh Outlook, Vol. 18, 1931, 187.

A ballad of ennui ; The Dragon, May 1914, 265.

Beyond ; ibid. Nov. 1914, 15—6.

Horizon ; Welsh Poets : compiled by A. G. Prys-Jones, 1917, 42—3.

Irradiations ; The Dragon, June 1919, 132.

Joy ride ; ibid. April 1919, [76].

The lifeboat ; ibid. May 1914, 280—1.

Lines suggested on reading a sports' programme ; ibid. May 1912, 268.

Memorials : I. For those gone from by the sea.
II. From among the dreamers.
III. Sea philosophy.
The Dragon, Dec. 1918, [12—13].

Monologue of a much-married man ; ibid. May 1912, [198].

Moon, night and dawn ; ibid. May 1914, 256.

Motif de legende ; ibid. Dec. 1916, 32.

Paysage macabre ; ibid. March 1917, 130.

The post-impressionist ; ibid. Dec. 1911, 77.

Quod (with an "o") ; ibid. Dec. 1911, 98.

Sea-sketches ; ibid. March 1912, 189.

Sonnet ; Welsh Poets : compiled by A. G. Prys-Jones, 1917, 42.

Sonnet to "The Dragon" ; The Dragon, Nov. 1911, 7.

The tokens ; ibid. June 1917, 158.

JONES, Thomas Gwynn

Verse
A 856   : Fairies ; Welsh Poets : compiled by A. G. Prys-Jones, 1917, 37—8.

Filigree ; The Dragon, April 1919, 75.

In England ; ibid. 74.

In Wales ; Welsh Outlook, Vol. V, 1918, 78—9.
The Dragon, June 1917, 164.

Life ; Welsh Outlook, Vol. II, 1915, 298. Welsh Poets : compiled by A. G. Prys-Jones, 1917, 39.

Passing ; The Dragon, April 1919, 75.

Remembrance ; trans. from "Atgof" by E. Prys.
Welsh Outlook, Vol. XI, 1924, 53.

Resignation ; Welsh Poets : compiled by A. G. Prys-Jones, 1917, 38.
Welsh Outlook, Vol. II, 1915, 298.

Waiting ; The Dragon, March 1917, 88.

The wanderer ; trans. from the Welsh by "Abon".
Welsh Outlook, Vol. XII, 1925, 224.

Ystrad Fflur ; trans. from the Welsh by A. Llywelyn-Williams.
Presenting Welsh Poetry, 1959, 61.

JONES, Thomas Henry

Story
A 857   : A day at the seaside.
Dock L., Vol. 5, no. 15, 1954, 7—12.

Verse
A 858   : The beast at the door.
London ; R. Hart-Davis, 1963.
[4], 5—76p. 20½cm. cloth.

A 859   : The enemy in the heart : poems, 1946—56.
London ; R. Hart-Davis, 1957.
[6], 7—80p. 20cm. cloth.

A 860   : Songs of a mad prince, and other poems.
London ; R. Hart-Davis, 1960.
[6], 7—71p. 20½cm. cloth.

A 861   : The Anglo-Welsh ; Poetry Book Magazine, Vol. 6, no. 5, 1954, 17.

The Anglo-Welsh (for Aneirin Talfan Davies) ; Dock L., Vol. 4, no. 11, 1953, 46.

The enemy in the heart ; Welsh Review, Vol. V, no. 3, 1946, 175.

Excuse (for Marlene) : A Review of English Literature, Vol. 1, no. 3, 1960, 18.

Grandparents ; PEN, 1958, 57.

In my returning ; Welsh Review, Vol. VI, no. 4, 1947, 272.

The persuasion of light ; Dock L., Vol. 2, no. 5, 1951, 36.

Poem "The Land that dreams of poems by my side" ; Poetry Qtly., Vol. II, no. 2, 1949, 82.

Small protest from a native ; The University of Wales Review, Summer 1965, 16.

Welsh pastoral elegy ; YCP, 185.

JONES, Tom Hughes

Stories
A 862   : John Wright's epitaph ; Welsh Outlook, Vol. XVIII, 1931, 215—6.

A 863   : Little tales : a series ; ibid. Vol. XII, 1925, 163—4 ; Vol. XIV, 1927, 292 ; Vol. XV, 1928, 23—4 ; 97 ; 346—7.

A 864   : Revenge ; ibid. Vol. XIX, 1932, 132—3.

A 865   : The thank offering ; ibid. Vol. XVI, 1929, 285—6.

A 866   : These three ; ibid. Vol. XVIII, 1931, 271—2.

A 867   : Victors ; ibid. 244.

Verse
A 868   : On listening to the Astronomer Royal, Feb. 21st.
The Dragon, April 1920, 204.

A wish ; ibid. 265.

JONES, Vernon

Verse
A 869   : Dic the Roadman ; Dock L., Vol. 7, no. 20, 1956, 38.

The guests ; ibid. Vol. 8, no. 22 [1958], 47.

Henry Jones ; A-W.R., Vol. 9, no. 23, undated, 11.

In memory of Caradoc Evans ; ibid. 10.

The old house ; Dock L., Vol. 7, no. 19, 1956, 9.

Such a morning ; A-W.R., Vol. 9, no. 23, undated, 9.

When night bejewelled rides the huddled farm ; Dock L., Vol. 6, no. 17, 1955. 9.

Whiterock Bay ; A-W.R., Vol. 9, no. 23, undated, 12.

JONES, Beatrice Louie

Verse
A 870   : Swansea Bay, and other poems.
Bishopston, Swansea ; publ. by the author, [1954].
vii, [1], 9—61p. 18cm. cloth.

KEATING, Joseph

Novels
A 871   : Flower of the dark.
London, New York ; Cassell, 1917.
viii, 9—347p. 18cm. cloth.
Location : "Bryn Bychan", Glamorgan mining village.

A 872   : The marriage contract : a novel.
London ; Hutchinson, 1914.
352, 32p. 19cm. cloth.
Location : Cynon Vale, Glamorgan.

A 873   : Maurice : a romance of light and darkness.
London ; Chatto & Windus, 1905.
vii, [1], 360, 32p. 18½cm. cloth.
Another ed. : London ; Hutchinson, 1912.
158p. 21cm. wrappers.
This edition has an alternative subtitle . . . "A romance of a Welsh coal mine".
Location : "Brynonen", S. Wales valley.

A 874   : Son of Judith : a tale of the Welsh mining valleys.
London ; G. Allen, 1900.
368p. 19cm. cloth.
—Another ed. London ; G. Newnes, 1912.

Stories
A 875   : Adventures in the dark.
Cardiff ; Western Mail, [1906].
[5], 6—122p. 21½cm. boards.
Leclaire notes : "Adventures of the dark" conjectured to be Cardiff Library's copy entitled "Short Stories", published Chapman & Hall, 1906.

Other Prose
A 876   : My struggle for life.
London ; Simpkin, Marshall, Hamilton, Kent, 1916.
xv, [1], 308p. 21½cm. cloth.

KENDRICK, *Sir* Thomas Downing

Novel
A 877   : Great love for Icarus. Illustrations by Ann Tout.
London ; Methuen, 1962.
192p. 21cm. cloth.
Location : Partly Llandudno area : refers to Robert Loraine, the aviator.

KENYON, Edith Caroline

Novels
A 878   : Jack's cousin Kate ; or, Among the mountains of Wild Wales. *New ed. revised.*
London ; W. Nicholson, n.d.
432p. 18cm. cloth.
Locations : Tal-y-llyn, Borth, etc.

A 879   : The winning of Gwenora.
London ; Holder & Hardingham, [1913].
[4], 320p. front. (port.) 18½cm. cloth.
Location : "Dyfrlan", in West Wales.

A 880   : The wooing of Mifanwy : a Welsh love story.
London ; Holden & Hardingham, n.d.
viii, 344, 12p. 18½cm. cloth.
Location : Machynlleth area.

KNIGHT, Leonard Alfred

Novels
A 881   : Deadman's bay.
London ; Sampson Low, Marston, [1930].
vii, [1], 280, 32p. map. 18½cm. cloth.
Location : Pembrokeshire.

A 882   : High treason.
London ; Gryphon Books, 1954.
[6], 7—191p. 18½cm. cloth.
Location : Pembrokeshire.

A 883   : Man hunt.
London ; Sampson Low, Marston, [1930].
vi, 282, 32p. 18½cm. cloth.
Location : South Wales.

A 884 : The morlo. Illustrated by Peter Scott.
London ; Gryphon Books, 1956.
[10], 11—62p. front. illus. col. plates.
19½cm. cloth.

A 885 : One way only.
London ; Gryphon Books, 1956.
[6], 7—240p. 18½cm. cloth.
Location : Pembrokeshire coast.

A 886 : The riddle of Nap's Hollow.
London ; Sampson Low, Marston, [1932].
viii, 312, 32p. 18½cm. cloth.
Location : Pembrokeshire and London.

A 887 : Valley of green shadows.
London ; Gryphon Books, 1955.
[6], 7—208p. 18½cm. cloth.
Location : "Madryn", a Welsh country house.

"LEE, Vernon" *pseud. [i.e. Violet Paget]*

Novel
A 888 : Penelope Brandling : a tale of the Welsh
coast in the eighteenth century.
London ; Fisher Unwin, 1903.
[10], 11—190p. 17cm. cloth. (Pseudonym
Library Series).

LEVY, Alban

Verse
A 889 : Nab Valley : poems.
London ; The Bodley Head, 1945.
[6], 7—47p. 16½cm. cloth.

A 890 : Frantic candles flame and flicker ; Wales,
New Series, I, 1943, 27—8. More Poems
from the Forces ; ed. by K. Rhys, 1943,
151—2.

"I have made a cloak of crying" ; Wales,
New Series, I, 1943, 26. More Poems from
the Forces ; ed. by K. Rhys, 1943, 150.

"Out of a dust . . ." ; Modern Welsh Poetry ;
ed. by K. Rhys, 1944, 82—3.

Since last I cried a year ago ; More Poems
from the Forces ; ed. by K. Rhys, 1943,
149—50.

The watchers ; Dragons and daffodils, 1960,
30—1.

LEWES, Evelyn

Story
A 891 : Dream folk and fancies.
Carmarthen ; Spurrell, [1926].
[8], 96p. 19cm. wrappers.

Short stories and miscellaneous essays.
—*Extract from the above :* "Watkin White
Lion" *in* Welsh Outlook, Vol. XII, 1925,
325—8.

LEWIS, Alun

Prose
A 892 : In the green tree . . . with a preface by A. L.
Rowse, a postscript by Gwyn Jones and a
sonnet by Vernon Watkins.
Drawing by John Petts.
London ; Allen & Unwin, 1949.
[6], 7—141p. front. (port.) 19½cm. cloth.
Includes four letters from India and six stories :
Night Journey—The raid—The earth is a
syllable—Ward "O" 3 (b)—The orange
grove—The reunion.

Stories
A 893 : The last inspection [and other stories].
London ; Allen & Unwin, 1942.
[8], 9—221p. 18½cm. cloth.
Contents : The last inspection—Flick—Private
Jones—Almost a gentleman—Farewell
binge—It's a long way to go (three stories)—
Lance-Jack—The wanderers—Picnic—The
lapse—Interruption—The Housekeeper—
Acting Captain—The Children—Ballerina
—Cold spell—Dusty hermitage—The
prisoners—They came.

A 894 : The children.
Tales of Innocence ; comp. by G. S. Green.
London, Faber, [1960], 251—260. (This
vol. first publ. Faber, 1950, as *First View*).

A 895 : Dwellers in the valley.
The Dragon, Summer Term, 1935, 22—4.

A 896 : The earth is a syllable.
Wyatt, Woodrow, *editor.* English story.
Fourth series, 1943, 174—8. London ;
Collins, 1943.

A 897 : The farewell binge.
Penguin New Writing, no. 5, 56—61.

A 898 : Grenadier.
Bugle Blast. 2nd Series, London, 1944, 161-80.

A 899 : "If such be Nature's holy plan".
The Dragon, Lent Term, 1934, 18—22.

A 900 : Interruption.
Wyatt, Woodrow *and* Wyatt, Susan, *eds.*
English story. First Series, 1941, 171—4.

A 901 : The motherland.
Modern reading, no. 6. London, [1943],
16—18.

A 902 : The orange grove.
Welsh short stories ; ed. by G. Ewart Evans.
2nd ed., 1959, 151—66.

A 903   : Private Jones.
Bugle Blast [No. 1] ; ed. by Jack Aistrop and Reginald Moore.
London, 1943, 135—156.

A 904   : The reunion.
Welsh Review, Vol. III, no. 2, 1944, 112—8.

A 905   : Squibs for the Guy.
The Dragon, Vol. 61, no. 1, 1938, 18—20.

A 906   : They came.
Wyatt, Woodrow *and* Wyatt, Susan, *eds.*
English story. Second series, 1941, 238—52.
Welsh short stories ; ed. by Gwyn Jones, 1956, 171—87.
Stories of the 'forties, Vol. 1 : ed. by R. Moore and Woodrow Wyatt, 1945, 47—59.

A 907   : The wanderers.
Welsh short stories ; ed. by Gwyn Jones, 1956, 151—70.
Welsh Review, Vol. II, no. 3, 1939, 128—39.

A 908   : Ward "O" 3 (b).
Penguin New Writing, no. 18 ; ed. by John Lehmann, 31—48.
Also in Pleasures of New Writing ; ed. by John Lehmann.

A 909   : The whirligig of fate.
The Dragon, Summer Term 1934, 40—3.

A 910   : Whit Monday.
The Dragon, Lent Term, 1935, 5—9.

Other Prose
A 911   : Letters from India : selected by G. Lewis and Gwyn Jones.
Cardiff ; Penmark Press, 1946.
98p. front. (facsim.) facsims. 18cm. cloth.
500 copies issued.
—Letters from India.
Welsh Review, Vol. IV, no. 2, 1945, 83—93.

A 912   : [Letter to his wife, Gweno, written from Burma, undated (1943—44)]. *In* Bacon, Wallace A. *and* Breen, Robert S.
Literature for interpretation. New York, Holt, Rinehart & Winston, 1961, 365—6.

A 913   : A sheaf of letters from Alun Lewis, 1941—1943.
First selection : "One modern poet at war".
Wales, Vol. VII, no. 28, 1948, 410—31.
(Letters from various addresses to Lynette Roberts and K. Rhys).

Verse
A 914   : Ha ! Ha ! among the trumpets : poems in transit . . . Foreword by Robert Graves.
London ; Allen & Unwin, 1945.
[12], 13—75p. front. (port.) 18½cm. cloth.

A 915   : Raiders' dawn, and other poems.
London ; Allen & Unwin, 1942.
[14], 15—93p. front. (port.) 18cm. boards.
—Another impression : [1943].

A 916   : Two poems : Raiders' dawn and Song of innocence.
Llanllechid ; Caseg Press, [1941].
Single Sheet. (Caseg Broadsheets, no. 1).

Verse

Note : Where a collection of poems forms a component part of an anthology, the titles are listed in the order in which they appear in the anthology.

A 917   : *In* Poems from the Forces ; ed. by K. Rhys, 1941.
All day it has rained ; 69—70.
The soldier ; 70—2.
On the Welsh mountains ; 72—3.
Christmas holidays ; 73—4.
Postscript for Gweno ; 74.

A 918   : *In* More Poems from the Forces ; ed. by K. Rhys, 1943.
The defeated : for Wales ; 153—4.
The poet ; 154.
Westminster Abbey ; 154—5.
Infantry ; 156.
Dawn on the East Coast ; 156—7.
Prelude and fugue ; 157—8.

A 919   : *In* Hamilton, Ian, *editor.* The poetry of war, 1939—45. London ; A. Ross, 1965.
Autumn, 1939 ; 8.
The sentry ; 13.
Rilke ; 26—7.
To Edward Thomas (on visiting the memorial stone above Steep in Hampshire) ; 28—9.
All day it has rained ; 35.
The public gardens ; 43—4.
Goodbye ; 60—1.
Dawn on the East Coast ; 68.
Sacco writes to his son ; 69—70.
Postscript : For Gweno ; 71.
Port of call : Brazil ; 77.
The Mahratta Ghats ; 78.
The jungle ; 79—82.
Song (on seeing dead bodies floating off the Cape) ; 105—6.
Westminster Abbey ; 125.
Corfe Castle ; 126.

A 920   : *In* Poetry in wartime ; ed. by M. J. Tambimuttu, 1942.
Christmas holiday ; 90.
Easter in Christmas ; 90—1.
Autumn, 1939 ; 91.
All day it has rained ; 91—2.
Fever ; 92—3.
To Edward Thomas ; 94—5.
Poetry in wartime ; 95—6.
Postscript for Gweno ; 97.

A 921   : *In* The colour of saying : an anthology of verse spoken by Dylan Thomas ; ed. by R. N. Maud and A. T. Davies, 1963.
In hospital, Poona (I) and (II) ; 107—9.
Song (on seeing dead bodies floating off the Cape) ; 109—11.

Sacco writes to his son ; 111—12.
The sentry ; 113.

A   922   : All day it has rained ; Palgrave, F. T., *ed.*
The Golden Treasury . . . 5th ed., O.U.P.,
1964, 543—4.
Little Reviews Anthology ; ed. by Denys
Val Baker, 1943, 66.

Celtic twilight ; Wales, New Series, I, 1943, 22.

Christmas holiday ; Presenting Welsh Poetry,
1959, 110.

The dancer ; Welsh Review, Vol. 1, no. 6,
1939, 313.

Dawn on the East Coast ; Faber book of
modern verse ; *ed.* by M. Roberts. New
ed., 1951, 404.
Modern Verse, 1900—1950 ; comp. by
Phyllis M. Jones. 2nd ed. enl. O.U.P.,
1955, 264.

The defeated : for Wales ; Modern Welsh
Poetry ; ed. by K. Rhys, 1944, 86—7.
Presenting Welsh Poetry, 1959, 109.

Encirclement ; Life and Letters Today, Vol.
36, no. 67, March 1943, 154—5.

Fever ; ibid. Vol. 24, no. 31, March 1940,
276—7.

From the Chinese ; The Dragon, Vol. 61,
no. 1, 1938, 18.

Goodbye ; Twentieth Century Love Poems :
Critical Qtly. Poetry Supplement, no. 4,
1964, 15.

Hubris ; The Dragon, Vol. 61, no. 1, 1938, 23.

Jason and Medea ; Reeves, James, *comp.*
The Cassell book of English poetry, 1965,
1001.

The ladybird wakes : a sonnet ; The Dragon,
Summer Term, 1934, 65.

The Mahratta Ghats ; Modern Verse,
1900—1950 ; comp. by Phyllis M. Jones.
2nd ed. enl. O.U.P., 1955, 262.

Mid-winter ; Modern Welsh Poetry ; ed. by
K. Rhys, 1944, 90—2.

The mountain over Aberdare ; ibid. 87—8.

The peasants ; The Faber book of modern
verse ; ed. by M. Roberts. New ed., 1951,
405.

The ploughman ; The Dragon, Vol. 61, no. 1,
1938, 20.

Poems from India ; Welsh Review, Vol. III,
no. 2, 1944, 103—11.

Postscript for Gweno ; Palgrave, F. T., *ed.*
The Golden Treasury . . . 5th ed. O.U.P.,
1964, 544—5.

Relics ; *In* Editor's choice : an anthology by
S. O'Sullivan, 1944, 26.

River Rhondda ; Modern Welsh Poetry ; ed.
by K. Rhys, 1944, 84.

The sentry ; ibid. 83.

The soldier (stanzas I—III) ; ibid. 88—90.

Song : oh, journeyman ; Modern Verse,
1900—1950 ; comp. by Phyllis M. Jones.
2nd ed. enl. O.U.P., 1955, 261.

Song (on seeing dead bodies . . .) ; Penguin
New Writing, no. 17, 167.

To a comrade in arms ; The Faber book of
twentieth-century verse ; ed. by J. Heath-
Stubbs and D. Wright, 1953, 218.

To Edward Thomas ; stanzas I—V ; Modern
Welsh Poetry ; ed. by K. Rhys, 1944, 84—6.

To one ; Wartime Harvest : an anthology ;
ed. by S. Schimanski and H. Treece, 1943,
57.
Kingdom Come, Vol. 3, no. 10, 1942, 30—1.

The unknown soldier ; Modern Verse,
1900—1950 ; comp. by Phyllis M. Jones.
2nd ed. enl. O.U.P., 1955, 263.

A Welsh night ; Wales, New Series, I, 1943, 21.

Westminster Abbey : ibid. 31.

LEWIS, Eiluned

Novels
A   923   : The captain's wife.
London ; Macmillan, 1943.
viii, 196p. 19cm. cloth.
Location : "St. Idris" (St. David's, Pembs.)

A   924   : Dew on the grass. Prefatory letter by Charles
Morgan.
London ; Lovat Dickson, 1934.
ix, [6], 16—222, [1]p. 18½cm. cloth.
Location : Welsh border country : Severn
Valley.
—New York ; Macmillan, 1934.
—Penguin Books, 1947. (No. 618).
185, [6]p. 18cm. wrappers.

Story
A   925   : The elastic-sided boots and the angel.
Welsh Outlook, Vol. XVI, 1929, 176—8.

Other Prose

A 926 : From the mountains ; Welsh Outlook, Vol. XV, 1928, 137.

Verse

A 927 : The birthright ; The Land of the Red Dragon [*i.e. 2nd ed. of The Welsh Gift Book*], 1953, [viii].
The funeral ; Welsh Outlook, Vol. XVIII, 1931, 207.
[Three stanzas, untitled] ; The Welsh Gift Book, Llangollen, Gwynn Publ. Co. [1950], 6.

LEWIS, Helen Prothero

Novels

A 928 : Ironwy and her lovers, by Helen Prothero Lewis (Mrs. James J. G. Pugh).
London ; Hutchinson, [1924].
[6], 7—286, [2], 48p. 18½cm. cloth.
Location : "Angoredig", near Welsh border.

A 929 : Love and the whirlwind : a novel, by Helen Prothero Lewis (Mrs. James J. G. Pugh).
London ; Hutchinson, 1916. (BM).
—Another edition. *2nd ed.*, 1916. (N.L.W. copy). 345, [3], 32p. 19cm. cloth.
Location : House of "Glyndyfrdwy", "Aber Valley".

LEWIS, Howell Elvet

Verse

A 930 : Hymns of hope and unity.
Cardiff ; Western Mail & Echo, Ltd., 1947.
[32]p. 18½cm. wrappers.

A 931 : Israel and other poems.
London ; Foyle's Welsh Press, 1930.
[6], 7—39p. front. illus. boards.

LEWIS, Ivor

Stories

A 932 : Home to their mountains.
Wales, Vol. VII, no. 26, 1947, 305—9.

A 933 : In the mist of life : a short story.
Wales, New Series, 4, 1944, 78—87.

Drama

A 934 : Iolo : a play in three acts.
Cardiff ; Educational Publishing Co., [1921].
[5], 7—64p. 15½cm. wrappers. (E.P.C. Welsh Drama Series, no. 50).
Scene : 12th century Welsh cottage.

LEWIS, John Saunders

Drama

A 935 : Amis and Amile ; trans. by H. Idris Bell from the Welsh version "Amlyn ac Amig".

Welsh Review, Vol. VII, no. 4, 1948, 232—55. (The original version written for broadcasting)

A 936 : The eve of Saint Joan : a comedy of Welsh life.
Newtown ; Welsh Outlook Press, [1920].
[5], 6—23p. 18½cm. wrappers.
Scene : Welsh farmhouse.

A 937 : Siwan ; trans. from the Welsh by Emyr Humphreys.
Plays of the Year ; ed. by J. C. Trewin. Vol. 21, 1959—60, 113—86.

Verse

A 938 : Cafe scene ; trans. from the Welsh by Gwyn Williams.
Presenting Welsh Poetry, 1959, 64—5.

The eagles depart ; trans. from the Welsh by D. M. Lloyd.
Poetry Book Magazine, Vol. 6, no. 5, Fall 1954, 4.

LEWIS, Miles

Novels

A 939 : Chapel : the story of a Welsh family.
London ; Heinemann, [1916].
vii, [1], 344, 16p. 18½cm. cloth.
Location : Village of "Porth", Vale of Glamorgan.

A 940 : The great attachment.
London ; Andrew Melrose, 1923.
320p. 18½cm. cloth.
Location : Parish of Dyffryn, Vale of Glamorgan.

LEWIS, Tegwen

Verse

A 941 : A singing mountain farm : poems.
Cowbridge, Glam. ; D. Brown & Sons, *printers*, [1955]. [24]p. 22cm. wrappers.
(Many of the poems previously publ. in *"The Western Mail"*).

A 942 : Summer noon.
Dock L., Vol. 4, no. 11, 1953, 7.

LEWIS-JAMES, Mary Janet

Drama

A 943 : The Return : a play in one act.
Cardiff ; Educational Publishing Co., 1921.
27p. 15cm. wrappers. (E.P.C. Welsh Drama Series, no. 47).
Scene : "Mountain Road Inn".

LITTLESTONE, Gilbert

Novel
A 944 : The psalm stone.
London ; Ward, Lock, 1913.
[5], 6—288p. front. 19cm. cloth.
Location : Valley of the "Eland", Radnor-
shire.

LLEWELLYN, Alun

Novel
A 945 : The deacon.
London ; G. Bell & Sons, 1934.
[8], 363p. 19cm. cloth.
Location : A Welsh village.

Story
A 946 : The severed self.
A-W.R., Vol. 15, no. 35, 1965, 30—41.

Verse
A 947 : The apples of Lincoln's Inn ; The Poetry
Review, Vol. 46, 1955, 14—5.

Artist ; The Poetry Review, Vol. 45, 1954,
18—20.

Bull ; ibid. Vol. 44, 1953, 310—1.

Galatea ; ibid. Vol. 47, 1956, 19.

The grave of Cronos ; ibid. Vol. 45, 1954,
138—9.

Heron ; Healing of the Nations ; ed. by Vera
Rich. A-W.R. Supplement, 1965, 23.

Strolling fiddler ; The Poetry Review, Vol. 52,
1961. 136—7.

Drama
A 948 : Ways to love : a comedy in one act.
London ; Samuel French, 1958.
[4], 29, [2]p. plan. 18½cm. wrappers.
(French's Acting Edition, no. 489).
Scene : A Radnorshire manor.

LLEWELLYN, Richard, *pseud. [i.e. Richard David Vivian
Llewellyn Lloyd]*

Novels
A 949 : How green was my valley.
London ; Michael Joseph, 1939.
651p. 20cm. cloth.
Location : South Wales mining areas, late
19th century.

—Another ed. Cheap ed. Joseph, 1949, 448p.

—Another ed. Penguin Books, 1951. (No. 800).
413, [3]p. 18cm. wrappers.

—Reprinted in the Ulverscroft Large Print
Series.
Anstey, Leics. ; Thorpe, [1965].
2 vols. 27cm. cloth.

Translated versions :
1948 : Denmark.
1949 : Norway. Czechoslovakia.
1950 : Holland. Greece.
1951 : Japan.
1954 : Israel, Finland, Sweden, Holland.
1955 : Germany, India, Yugoslavia.
1958 : Sweden.
1960 : France.
1963 : Yugoslavia.
(For publication details see the annual volumes
of the UNESCO Index Translationum).

A 950 : Sweet witch.
London ; Michael Joseph, 1955.
[4], 5—256p. 19½cm. cloth.
Illustrated endpapers.
Location : Coast of Pembrokeshire, February
1797.

—Another ed. Sweet witch. Illustrations by
Stuart Tresilian.
London, New York ; Longmans, Green
1959.
vii, [1], 280p. (Heritage of Literature
Series, Sect. A, no. 72).

—American ed. The Witch of Merthyn.
New York ; Doubleday, 1954.
253p. (Cavalcade Books).

A 951 : Up, into the singing mountain.
London ; Michael Joseph, 1963.
[6], 7—333p. 19½cm. cloth.
Maps on endpapers.
Location : Patagonia : the Welsh colony.

—Another ed. Penguin Books, 1966. (No
2456). [7], 8—313, [6]p. 18cm. wrappers

—American ed. New York ; Doubleday, 1960
378p. 22cm.

Translated versions :
1962 : Germany (2 versions).
1963 : Sweden.

"LLEWELYN, Michael Gareth" *pseud.   [i.e. Frederi
Evans]*

Novels
A 952 : The Aleppo Merchant.
London ; Murray, 1945.
vii, [1], 212p. 21½cm. cloth.
—Reprinted. 1946.
Location : A South Wales village : title is th
name of village inn.

A 953 : Angharad's Isle.
London ; Murray, 1944.
v, [1], 257p. 21½cm. cloth.
Location : A Glamorgan valley.

A 954 : To fame unknown.
London ; Murray, 1949.
[4], 5—316p. 18½cm. cloth.
Location : "Cwmyglo", a mining valley.

A 955 : White wheat : the story of Cefn Ydfa.
London ; Murray, 1947.
[4], 5—325p. 18½cm. cloth.
Location : Llangynwyd, Glam. Based on the
legend of Wil Hopcyn and the maid of Cefn
Ydfa.
—Another issue. 1950.
Translated version :
German : Das Tal von Glamorgan.
Zurich ; Diana Verlag, [1949].

Story
A 956 : Harvest home.
Y Ddinas. Vol. XII, no. 1, 1957, 15 and 22.

Other Prose
A 957 : Sand in the glass.
London ; Murray, 1943.
vi, 242p. front. 21½cm. cloth.
Childhood in a South Wales valley.

A 958 : Childhood Christmastide : memories of Welsh
Wales.
Holly Leaves, Vol. 204, 1957, 36—7.

LLOYD, Charles Ellis

Novels
A 959 : Love and the agitator.
London ; Century Press, 1911.
[9], 10—320p. 18½cm. cloth.
Location : Glamorgan mining valley of
"Abergarn".

A 960 : A master of dreams.
London ; Hodder & Stoughton, [1921].
[6], 7—317p. 18½cm. cloth.
Location : Vale of "Llanarmon", S. Wales.

A 961 : Scarlet Nest.
London ; Hodder & Stoughton, [1919].
[4], 5—367p. 18½cm. cloth.
Location : "Cynfael" village in "Cwm
Herlod", S. Wales.

LLOYD, J. H.

Novel
A 962 : Trevor of Nant Gwynant.
London ; Heath Cranton, 1927.
[4], 5—298p. 18½cm. cloth.
Location : Eryri, and other Welsh areas.
Early 15th century.

LLOYD, William Frederick

Drama
A 963 : The Welsh fasting girl, and other plays.
Swansea ; Thomas & Parry, *printers*, 1928.
[6], 7—156p. 15cm. cloth.
Contents : [with Welsh background] :
pp. 5—29 : The Welsh fasting girl.
pp. 71—99 : Cwm Farm.
pp. 101—126 : Gwyrth Cymru : (a Welsh
version of *The Welsh Fasting Girl*).
pp. 127—156 : Ffermwyr y Cwm.
—A new version of "The Welsh fasting girl"
publ. 1929 entitled "A Welsh Miracle".
Swansea, Thomas & Parry, 1929. [*Bound
with* An Incident].

LLOYD-WILLIAMS, Ellen

Stories
A 964 : The call of the river ; Welsh Outlook, Vol.
XII, 1924, 218—9.

A 965 : The fiddler ; ibid. Vol. XI, 1924, 44—6.

A 966 : Shân ; ibid. Vol. XII, 1925, 78.

A 967 : "When thou shalt be old—" ; ibid. Vol. XII,
1925, 329—30.

Verse
A 968 : Aeron Valley ; Welsh Outlook, Vol. X, 1923,
137.

The corpse-light ; Welsh Poets : compiled by
A. G. Prys-Jones, 1917, 46—7.

Dream-child ; ibid. 48.

The maid and the knight ; ibid. 44—5.

MACAULAY, Margaret

Novel
A 969 : The sentence absolute.
London ; Nisbet, 1914.
vii, [1], 312p. 18½cm. cloth.
Location : Seaport of "Aberyrfon".

MACAULAY, Rose

Novel
A 970 : The valley captives.
London ; Murray, 1911.
v, [1], 335, [8]p. 18½cm. cloth.
Location : "Llanfechan".

MACDONALD, Tom

Novels
A 971 : The black rabbit.
London ; Hurst & Blackett, [1948].
[4], 5—212p. 18½cm. cloth.
Location : Coastal village of "Gellywern".

A 972   : Gareth the ploughman.
London ; Thornton Butterworth, 1939.
416p. 18½cm. cloth.
Location : A Cardiganshire farm.

A 973   : How soon hath time.
London, New York, [etc.] ; Hurst & Blackett,
[1950].
[4], 5—256p. 18½cm. cloth.
Location : Wales ("Bwlch-y-Daran") and
Australia.

A 974   : The peak.
London ; Eyre & Spottiswoode, 1941.
314p. 19½cm. cloth.
Location : Cardiganshire background.

A 975   : The song of the valley.
London ; Hurst & Blackett, 1951.
[6], 7—256p. 18½cm. cloth.
Location : Village of "Porthangel", Cardiganshire.

MACHEN, Arthur [Llewellyn Jones] (1863—1947)
A comprehensive bibliography of the works of Arthur
Machen, including contributions to periodicals and
journalistic work, will be found in GOLDSTONE, Adrian
and SWEETSER, Wesley D. *A bibliography of Arthur
Machen. See* B 184. This complete bibliography
includes a large number of Machen's publications in
which it is not possible to discern a direct Anglo-Welsh
theme.

MACKWORTH, Cecily

Novel
A 976   : Spring's green shadow.
London ; MacGibbon & Kee, 1952.
[6], 202p. 18½cm. cloth.
Location : Partly in Wales ("Ponty-Gibby").

MADGE, Ernest   *of Morriston, Glam.*

Verse
A 977   : Vistas, and other poems.
Morriston ; Jones & Son, 1942.
[4], 5—48p. 18½cm. wrappers.

MAIDEN, Cecil

Novel
A 978   : Harp into battle.
New York ; Crowell, 1959.
[6], 281p. 20cm. cloth.
Location : 12th century Gwynedd.

MARKS, Jeannette

Novel
A 979   : The end of a song.
London ; G. P. Putnam's Sons, 1911.
[8], 9—224p. col. front. 18cm. cloth.
(The Mauve Library Series).
Location : A Welsh village.

Drama
A 980   : The merry, merry cuckoo, and other Welsh
plays.
New York, London ; Appleton, 1927.
x, [2], 226, [3]p. 18½cm. cloth.
Contents : The merry, merry cuckoo ; The
deacon's hat ; Welsh honeymoon ; A tress of
hair ; Love letters ; Steppin Westward ;
Look to the end.

A 981   : Three Welsh plays.
Boston, U.S.A. ; Little, Brown, 1917.
ix, [2], 87p. 18½cm. cloth.
Contents : The merry, merry cuckoo ; The
deacon's hat ; Welsh honeymoon.
—Another ed.   London ; Samuel French,
[1920].
ix, [2], 87p. 18½cm. wrappers.
(French's Acting Editions, no. 2497).

MARTIN, Clara

Novel
A 982   : Susan Jane.
London ; Arrowsmith, 1932.
[8], 9—319p. 18½cm. cloth.
Contents : Susan Jane [a novel], by S. Ferguson
and C. Martin. (Breconshire background).
Also short stories : The trucks—A vision of the
night—Credit—The wreath—Fleeing the devil
—The way to do it—The house of one night—
The palm—Jenny's wash-day.

MARTIN, David

Novel
A 983   : Tiger Bay.
London ; Martin & Reid, 1946.
118, [2]p. 18cm. wrappers.
Location : Cardiff dockland area.

MATHER, Zachary

Novel
A 984   : The wonderful story of Agnes and the white
dove : a tradition of Wales.
London ; A. Stockwell, [1903].
[9], 10—127, [1]p. 18cm. limp boards.

Story
A 985   : Tales from the Welsh hills.
London ; Elliot Stock, 1909.
vii, [1], 225p. 18½cm. cloth.

MATHEW, David

Novel
A 986   : The Prince of Wales's feathers.
London ; Collins, 1953.
[8], 9—223p. 19cm. cloth.
Location : "Port Caerleon" (South Wales).

MATHIAS, Roland

Stories

A   987   : The eleven men of Eppynt, and other stories.
[Pembroke Dock] ; Dock Leaves Press, 1956.
[6], 7—199p. 18½cm. cloth.

Contents : Take hold on Hell—Incident in Majorca—One bell tolling—Cassie Thomas—Block-system—Digression into miracle—The Rhine tugs—The neutral shore—A night for the curing—The palace—The eleven men of Eppynt—Agger makes Christmas—Ffynnon Fawr—Match.

A   988   : Block-system.
Dock L., Vol. I, no. 1, 1949, 12—20.

A   989   : Digression into miracle.
Wales, New Series, 4, Summer 1944, 23—9.

A   990   : The eleven men of Eppynt.
Dock L., Vol. 2, no. 5, 1951, 13—24.

A   991   : Ffynnon Fawr.
Dock L., Vol. 4, no. 10, 1953, 30—9.

A   992   : Joking with Arthur.
Seven, Vol. 4, no. 4, 1944, 13—5.

A   993   : Match.
Dock L., Vol. 7, no. 20, 1956, 13—20.

A   994   : A night for the curing.
Welsh short stories ; ed. by G. Ewart Evans. 2nd ed., 1959, 260—70.

A   995   : One bell tolling.
Wales, Vol. V, no. 8/9, 1945, 53—60.

A   996   : The only road open.
A-W.R., Vol. 14, no. 34, 1964-5, 105—9.

A   997   : The Palace.
Dock L., Vol. I, no. 2, 1950, 3—11.

A   998   : Study in hate.
Seven, Vol. 3, no. 3, 1942, 5—9.

Other Prose

A   999   : Take me over the border.
Y Ddinas, Vol. 16, no. 1, 1961, 8, 11, 12.

Verse

A   1000 : Break in harvest, and other poems.
London ; Routledge, 1946.
[4], 5—57p. 19cm. cloth.

A   1001 : Days enduring, and other poems.
Ilfracombe ; Stockwell, [1943].
[4], 5—64p. 18½cm. boards.

A   1002 : The flooded valley.
London ; Putnam, [1960].
[4], 32p. 21½cm. cloth.

A   1003 : The roses of Tretower. Illustrations by Eric Peyman.
[Pembroke Dock] ; Dock Leaves Press, 1952.
[8], 9—66p. 18½cm. cloth.

A   1004 : Afternoon in Water Street ; Outposts, no. 16, 1950. 4—5.

An age ; Dock L., Vol. 5, no. 15, 1954, 48.

Another dawn ; A-W.R., Vol. 13, no. 31, undated, 74.

Balloon over the Rhondda ; Modern Welsh Poetry ; ed. by K. Rhys, 1944, 92—4.

The bearers ; Welsh Review, Vol. III, no. 3, 1944, 186.

Break in harvest ; Wales, Vol. VII, no. 26, 1947, 280.

Building a house (in four movements) ; Dock L., Vol. 6, no. 16, 1955, 7—9.

Cascob ; The Dragon, Summer Term 1958, (Festival ed.), 8.

Chinon ; A-W.R., Vol. 12, no. 29, undated, 46.

Coed Anghared ; Rann, no. 19 (Welsh number), 1953, 16.

Conversation on Stackpole Head ; PEN 1955, 59.

Crossing into peace ; Welsh Review, Vol. IV, no. 4, 1945, 246.

Drover's song ; Wales, Vol. IV, no. 5, 1944, 27.

Enstone Rock ; Poetry London X ; ed. by Tambimuttu, 1944, 104—5.

The flooded valley ; Outposts, no. 12, 1948, 9.

Freshwater West revisited ; Poetry Wales, I, Spring 1965, 6.

Grace before work ; Wales, Vol. VII, no. 26, 1947, 281.

Judas Maccabeus ; Welsh Review, Vol. V, no. 3, 1946, 196—7.

A letter ; Dock L., Vol. I, no. 1, 1949, 9—10. Poetry Book Magazine, Vol. 6, no. 5, 1954, 23.

London Welshman ; Wales, New Series, 4, 1944, 62.

Lowbury Hill ; Welsh Review, Vol. V, no. 1, 1946, 30—1.

The lurking ancestor ; Outposts, no. 6, 1946, 9.

Morning : New Jerusalem ; Dock L., Vol. I, no. 1, 1949, 11—2.

The mountain ; Welsh Review, Vol. VI, no. 3, 1947, 190—2.

On the grave of Henry Vaughan at Llansaint-ffraed ; Wales, Vol. VII, no. 27, 1947, 334.

Orielton empty ; Dock L., Vol. 6, no. 17, 1955, 14.

O Tihuanaco ; Dock L., Vol. 1, no. 2, 1950, 48—50.

Pastorale ; Poetry London X ; ed. by Tambi-muttu, 1944, 103—4.

"Remember Charlie Stones, Carpenter" ; Dock L., Vol. I, no. 1, 1949, 10—1.

Riddle ; ibid. no. 3, 1950, 29. [This poem is illustrated with a full-page engraving by Eric Peyman].

Roses of Tretower ; Welsh Review, Vol. VII, no. 3, 1948, 166—71. [Illustrated with engravings by Michael Peyman].

Sarnesfield ; A-W.R., Vol. 14, no. 33, 1964, 57—8.

Scithwen Valley ; Healing of the Nations ; ed. by Vera Rich. A-W.R. Suppl., 1965, 37.

Seithon Valley ; Dock L., Vol. 6, no. 18, 1955, 22.

Solway ; Rann, no. 19 (Welsh number), 1953, 14.

Subite ; For Those Who Are Alive. Fortune P., 1946, 47—8.

A winter's day ; Dock L., Vol. I, no. 1, 1949, 11.

MERCHANT, E. Verley

Novel
A 1005 : Unto the hills : a novel dealing with farming and mining life in the hills of Wales. Cardiff ; Western Mail & Echo Ltd., 1944. [5], 6—230p. 18½cm. cloth.

MINOGUE, Valerie

Verse
A 1006 : Alas poor Yorick ; Wales, No. 40, 1959, 18.

In fog ; English, Vol. 13, no. 78, 1961, 245—6.

Llanelly ; Wales, Oct. 1958, 62.

Old stone of the world ; A-W.R., Vol. 9, no. 24 (undated), 118.

Sonnet ("It is a pride of moment . . ."); ibid. Vol. 11, no. 28 (undated), 41.

Talyllyn ; ibid. Vol. 9, no. 24 (undated), 112—3.

Thinking death ; ibid. Vol. 9, no. 24 (undated), 45.

To a lion in Regent's Park ; ibid. Vol. 10, no. 25 (undated), 72.

Venice ; ibid. Vol. 9, no. 23 (undated), 58—9.

Winter journey ; ibid. Vol. 10, no. 25 (undated), 96.

MITCHELL, Ronald Elwy

Novels
A 1007 : Deep waters. London ; Gollancz, 1937. [5], 6—286p. 18½cm. cloth. Location : The village of "Groes" (N. Wales).

A 1008 : Three men went to mow. London ; Museum Press, 1951. [6], 7—255p. 18½cm. cloth. Location : Village of "Pentrebychan".

Drama
Note : Many of the plays noted below have same setting, viz. the village of "Pentrebychan", North Wales.

A 1009 : At the Sitting Hen : a comedy in one act. London, New York ; Samuel French, 1957. [6], 30, [2]p. plan. 18½cm. wrappers. (French's Acting Edition, no. 514).

A 1010 : Better days : a play in one act. London, New York ; Samuel French, [1934]. 30p. 19cm. wrappers.

A 1011 : The goblin : a Welsh comedy in one act. London, New York ; Samuel French, 1934. 24p. 19cm. wrappers.

A 1012 : A handful of sheep : a comedy of North Wales in one act. London, New York ; Samuel French, 1935. 24, [2]p. plan. 19cm. wrappers. Scene : Bar of a Welsh inn. —Another ed. 1935. 20p. plan. 18½cm. wrappers. (French's Acting Edition, no. 1608).

A 1013 : Happy holiday : a comedy in one act. London ; Samuel French, 1957. [4], 28p. plan. 18½cm. wrappers. (French's Acting Edition, no. 441).

A 1014 : The Holy Dragon : a play in one act.
London, New York ; Samuel French, 1935.
22p. 18½cm. wrappers.
(French's Acting Edition, no. 1873).

A 1015 : A husband for breakfast : a comedy in a Welsh
setting.
London, New York ; Samuel French, 1937.
26, [2]p. plan. 18½cm. wrappers.
(French's Acting Edition, no. 1777).
—Also in Seven famous one-act plays. 2nd
series. Penguin Books, 1953, 119—43.
The best one-act plays of 1936.
Harrap, 1937, 179—201.

A 1016 : Long live Elias ! a comedy in one act.
London, New York ; Samuel French, 1957.
[6], 27, [2]p. plan. 18½cm. wrappers.
(French's Acting Edition, no. 518).

A 1017 : The meddler in miracles : a play in one act.
London ; Samuel French, 1936.
24p. plan. 18½cm. wrappers.
(French's Acting Edition, no. 2580).

A 1018 : The road to ruin : a comedy in one act.
London, New York ; Samuel French, 1959.
[4], 24, [2]p. plan. 18½cm. wrappers.
(French's Acting Edition, no. 1009).

A 1019 : A rogue in a bed : a comedy in a Welsh
setting of one act.
London ; Samuel French, 1936 (Acting ed.).
28, [2]p. plan. 18½cm. wrappers.
(French's Acting Edition, no. 2624).
—Also in The one-act theatre. Fourth book.
French, 1935, 49—70.

A 1020 : The Royal Inn.
Prize one-act plays, 1935.
Harrap, 1935, 9—28.

A 1021 : A singer in a cellar : a comedy in one act.
London, New York ; Samuel French, 1957.
[6], 25, [2]p. plan. 18½cm. wrappers.
(French's Acting Edition, no. 401).

A 1022 : The way to London : a Welsh play in one act.
London, New York ; Samuel French, 1935.
[6], 24, [2]p. plan. 19cm. wrappers.
Scene : A row of miners' dwellings.
—Also in The one-act theatre : the seventh
book.
London ; Samuel French, 1936, 67—85.

MONTGOMERY, Kathleen Letitia

Novel
A 1023 : The gate-openers.
London ; John Long, 1912.
vii, [1], 9—319p. 19cm. cloth.
Location : Carmarthenshire : Rebecca Riots.
—Another ed. 2nd ed. Undated.

MOOR, George

Verse
A 1024 : Poems from a Welsh mountain.
Ilfracombe ; Stockwell, 1949.
20p. 18½cm. wrappers.

MORAY, Ann

Novel
A 1025 : The rising of the lark.
London ; Dent, 1964.
[6], 374p. 19cm. cloth.
Location : "Bryn Llithrig" (Conway Valley).

MORGAN, Con

Stories
A 1026 : The black frost.
Life and Letters Today. Vol. 36, no. 67, 1943,
179—85.

A 1027 : Knock on the wall.
Life and Letters. Vol. 48, no. 103, 1946, 182-9.

A 1028 : The night of the fire.
Wales. Vol. VII, no. 26, 1947, 316—9.

A 1029 : Recollected in turmoil.
Welsh Review. Vol. VII, no. 3, 1948, 194—8.

A 1030 : Return of a stranger.
Wales. Vol. VIII, no. 29, 1948, 500—4.

A 1031 : Unquiet dwelling.
Celtic Story, Number One ; ed. by Aled
Vaughan, 1946, 136—9.

A 1032 : Winner takes both.
Wales. Vol. IX, no. 31, 1949, 54—7.

Verse
A 1033 : Poem "How shall we aid . . ." ; Wales, Vol.
VII, no. 25, 1947, 160.

Poem "My love is much concerned . . ." ;
Welsh Review, Vol. III, no. 3, 1944, 167.

Spring song ; Wales, Vol. VII, no. 25, 1947,
161.

MORGAN, David Derwenydd

Novels
A 1034 : Doctor Jim.
Caerfyrddin (Carmarthen) : "Seren Cymru"
and Cymric Times, 1936.
[4], 5—92p. 21cm. wrappers.
Wrapper : "An English novel with Welsh
characters".
Location : Mainly Carmarthen.

A   1035 : The tavern across the street.
London ; Temperance Publishing Co., 1915.
vi, 165p. port. 18½cm. wrappers.
Location : "Cambria", a mining town.

A   1036 : A Welsh doctor ; or, Wales' great reformer.
Lampeter ; Welsh Church Press Co., n.d.
[2], 185p. 18cm. wrappers.
Location : Towy Valley, Carms.

Drama
A   1037 : Wanted—a wife : a comedy in one act.
Carmarthen ; W. M. Evans, 193— ?
30, [2]p. 18cm. wrappers.
Scene : Welsh farmhouse.

MORGAN, Dyfnallt

Verse
A   1038 : The veil : an English version of the author's
poem "Y Llen".
Dock L., Vol. 4, no. 12, 1953, 45—50.

MORGAN, Elaine

Drama
A   1039 : The waiting-room : a play for women in one
act.
London ; French, 1958.
[4], 32, [2]p. 18cm. wrappers. (French's
Acting Edition, no. 1007).
Scene : Paddington Station : Welsh characters

MORGAN, Robert

Verse
A   1040 : Anniversary ; Poetry Wales, I, Spring 1965, 7.

Birth of a poet ; A-W.R., Vol. 13, no. 32, 1963,
58.

Blood donor ; Poetry Wales, I, no. 2, 1965, 17.

Farewell on a wet day ; PEN 1965, 116.

Gomer ; A-W.R., Vol. 15, no. 35, 1965,
111—2.

Pit borer ; Poetry Wales, Vol. 1, no. 2, 1965, 9.

Pit valley ; A-W.R., Vol. 13, no. 32, 1963, 58.

MORGAN, William John

Novel
A   1041 : The small world : a novel.
London ; Gollancz, 1956.
[6], 7—224p. 18cm. cloth.
Location : A Welsh university town.

Other Prose
A   1042 : Evans, Thomas and Lewis.
Twentieth Century, October 1956, 322—9.

A   1043 : An under-manager's journal.
Wales, Jan. 1959, 55—61.

MORGAN-RICHARDSON, Charles

Novel
A   1044 : Henry Vaughan : a story of Pembrokeshire.
London ; Thomas Burleigh, 1902.
[6], 319p. 18cm. cloth.
Author not named on title-page.

—Another ed. 2nd ed. 1902.
This ed. notes author as C. Morgan-Richardson.

NEPEAN, Edith

Novels
A   1045 : Bryn came to the valley : a love story.
London ; Stanley Paul, [1946].
[4], 5—144p. 18½cm. cloth.
Location : Farm of "Melyden", Snowdonia.

A   1046 : A bundle of myrrh : a romance of Wild Wales.
London ; Stanley Paul, 1925.
[7], 8—253p. 18½cm. cloth.
Location : Village of "Eden Arvon".

A   1047 : Cambria's fair daughter.
London ; Stanley Paul, [1923].
[6], 7—254p. 18½cm. cloth.
Location : "Llanfair" (Caernarvonshire ?)

A   1048 : Fading halos.
London ; S. Paul, n.d.
287, 32p. 18½cm. cloth.
Location : West Coast of Wales (in part).

A   1049 : Gwyneth of the Welsh hills.
London ; S. Paul, 1917.
[7], 8—320, 8p. 18½cm. cloth.
Location : "Llancoed", rural area.

A   1050 : Jewels in the dust : a Welsh novel.
London ; S. Paul, 1921.
vi, 7—255, 32p. 18½cm. cloth.
Location : "Crafnant".

A   1051 : Moonlight madness.
London ; S. Paul, 1926.
[6], 7—255, 40p. 18½cm. cloth.
Location : "Llanina", Snowdonia.

A   1052 : Perilous waters.
London, New York, [etc.] ; S. Paul, [1943].
[4], 5—176p. 18cm. cloth.
Location : "Abermor" and "Cwym Dyli".

A   1053 : Petals in the wind : a Welsh romance.
London ; S. Paul, 1922.
viii, 247p.   18½cm.   cloth.
Location : Snowdonia.

A   1054 : Sinners with wings !
London ; S. Paul, [1942].
[4], 5—224p.   18½cm.   cloth.
Location : "Coed Pella", slate quarrying
areas.

A   1055 : Starlight rapture.
London ; S. Paul, [1938].
256, 40p.   18½cm.   cloth.
Location : Snowdonia.

A   1056 : Sweetheart of the valley.
London ; S. Paul, 1927.
[6], 7—288, 8p.   18½cm.   cloth.
Location : Snowdonia.

A   1057 : Telephone at sunset.
London, Melbourne, [etc.] ; S. Paul, 1954.
[6], 7—192p.   18½cm.   cloth.
Location : Farm of "Merlin" [and London].

A   1058 : The valley of desire.
London ; S. Paul, 1924.
[8], 9—288p.   18½cm.   cloth.
—Another ed.   2nd ed.   1926.
Location : Bethesda and Snowdonia.

A   1059 : Welsh love.
London ; S. Paul, 1919.
[8], 9—288, [24]p.   19cm.   cloth.
Location : "Isbryn Quarries" and the village
of "Llancoed".

NEWBY, Percy Howard

Novels
A   1060 : The snow pasture.
London ; Cape, 1949.
[6], 7—224p.   19cm.   cloth.
Location : A Monmouthshire industrial valley.

A   1061 : The young May Moon.
London ; Cape, 1950.
[4], 5—288p.   19cm.   cloth.
Location : Partly Mid-Wales.

NIALL, Ian

Novel
A   1062 : A tiger walks.
London, Melbourne, [etc.] ; Heinemann, 1960.
[4], 289p.   18½cm.   cloth.
Location : Village of "Pentre Ddu".

NICHOLAS, Thomas Evan

Verse
A   1063 : The prison sonnets of T. E. Nicholas ;
translated from the Welsh by Daniel

Hughes, Dewi Emrys, Eric Davies [and]
Wil Ifan.
London ; W. Griffiths, 1948.
92p.   18½cm.   cloth.

NICHOLL, Theodore

Novel
A   1064 : The luck of wealth : a novel dealing with life
in the industrial towns of South Wales.
London ; Heath Cranton, 1926.
[10], 11—282p.   18½cm.   cloth.
Location : "Jacobston", S. Wales.

NIXON, David B.

Verse
A   1065 : For your pleasure : a collection of poems.
Maesteg, Glam. ; Messrs. Gibbs, *printers*,
[1965].
[22]p.   22cm.   wrappers.

NORRIS, Leslie

Verse
A   1066 : Poems.
London ; Falcon Press, [1946].
48p.   18½cm.   cloth.   (Resurgam Books).

A   1067 : At the grave of Dylan Thomas ; Outposts,
No. 35, 1957, 8, 14—5.

The ballad of Billy Rose ; PEN 1962, 93—4.

The bowl of roses (for Robert Gittings) ;
Outposts, No. 38, 1958, 1.

The Crucifixion ; Poetry London, X ; ed. by
Tambimuttu, 1944, 111.

The dove and the tree ; PEN 1955, 87—8.

Elegy for an old man found dead on a hill ;
PEN 1954, 86.

Elegy for Lyn James ; Poetry Wales, Vol. 1,
no. 2, 1965, 18.

The headland ; A-W.R., Vol. 15, no. 35, 1965,
26.

In Merthyr now ; Wales, Vol. VI, no. 2, 1946,
10.
Little Reviews Anthology, 1947—8, 165—6.

The poet (for Derrick Webley) ; Welsh
Review, Vol. IV, no. 3, 1945, 199.

Prologue for a prophet ; Outposts, No. 41,
1959, 8—9.

Retreat (for Alun Lewis, killed on active service, India, March 1944) ; Bugle Blast, 3rd Series, 1945, 145—6.

A sense of history ; PEN 1955, 87—8.

Siencyn ap Nicolas upon his death-bed ; A-W.R., Vol. 15, no. 35, 1965, 27—9.

NYE, Robert

Verse
A   1068 : Juvenilia 1.
Northwood, Middx. ; Scorpion Press, 1961. 66p. 21cm. cloth.

A   1069 : Juvenilia 2.
Lowestoft, Suffolk ; Scorpion Press, 1963. 65p. 21½cm. cloth.

A   1070 : Alan-a-Dale ; The London Magazine, Vol. 3, no. 5, 1956, 35.

Boyhood ; The London Magazine (N.S.), Vol. 2, no. 4, July 1962, 25—6.

The boys ; W. Mail Literary Review, March 13, 1965, 11.

The bungalow ; Outposts, No. 45, 1960, 18.

Darker ends ; W. Mail Literary Review, Dec. 5, 1964, 3. PEN 1965, 123.

Fishing ; Western Mail Literary Review, April 16, 1964.
Healing of the Nations ; ed. by Vera Rich, 1965, 11.

Incantation ; The London Magazine, Vol. 5, no. 1, 1958, 43.

Juvenilia [1 stanza : "There sits the boy Narcissus . . ."].
W. Mail Literary Review, July 17, 1964, 10.

Kingfisher ; The London Magazine, Vol. 2, no. 9, 1955, 47.

A loaf of bread ; W. Mail Literary Review, May 8, 1965, 11.

Narcissus ; English, Vol. 10, no. 59, 1955, [201].

A proper place ; Poetry Wales, Vol. 1, no. 2, 1965, 18.

Ropes ; ibid. Spring 1965, 8.

The same song ; The ' Observer ' : Weekend Review, May 24, 1964, 28.

Sounding six ; Poetry Wales, Vol. 1, Spring 1965, 8.

A time to dance ; The London Magazine, Vol. 5, no. 1, 1958, 44.

The voices ; ibid. Vol. 3, no. 5, 1956, 34—5.

O'BRIAN, Patrick

Novel
A   1071 : Three bear witness.
London ; Secker & Warburg, 1952. [4], 5—206p. 18½cm. cloth.
Location : Valley of "Cwm Bugail", N. Wales.

ONIONS, Oliver

Novels
A   1072 : Mushroom town.
London ; Hodder & Stoughton, 1915. viii, 316p. 18½cm. cloth.
Location : "Llanyglo".

A   1073 : A Penny for the harp.
London ; M. Joseph, 1952. [6], 7—272p. 18½cm. cloth.
Location : "Pentre", Morgannwg. Mediaeval.

A   1074 : Poor man's tapestry.
London ; M. Joseph, 1946. [11], 12—304p. 18½cm. cloth.
Location : Partly set in Marches of Mid-Wales.

OWEN, Alun

Drama
A   1075 : Three TV plays.
London ; Cape, 1961. [14], 15—152p. 19½cm. cloth.
Contents : Welsh location : After the funeral.
Other titles : No trains to Lime Street— Lena, Oh my Lena.

A   1076 : Dare to be a Daniel.
London ; Cassell, 1965. [8], 22p. 18cm. limp cloth.
(Eight Plays Series).
Scene : A school and a hotel in Wales.

A   1077 : A little winter love : a play in three acts.
London, New York ; Evans, 1964. [5], 6—68p. front. 21½cm. wrappers.
Scene : A small college in West Wales.

OWEN, D. Gareth

Novels
A   1078 : Black Brocade : an historical novel.
London, New York, [etc.] ; J. Long, [1950]. [6], 7—256p. 18cm. cloth.
Location : Valley of "Nant Alaw", North Wales.

A 1079 : Clouds across the moon.
London ; J. Long, 1947.
272p. 18½cm. cloth.

A 1080 : Come wind, come weather.
London, Melbourne, [etc.] ; J. Long, 1953.
[8], 9—224p. 18½cm. cloth.
Location : Moorland village of "Gernant".

A 1081 : The far end.
London, Melbourne, [etc.] ; J. Long, 1955.
[6], 7—192p. 18½cm. cloth.
Location : Near Welsh port of "Bangoed".

A 1082 : The place where we belong.
London ; J. Long, [1945].
[5], 7—192p. 18½cm. cloth.
Location : Moorland villages of "Gernant"
and "Glaslyn".

A 1083 : Spring in the air.
London, New York, [etc.] ; J. Long, [1946].
[6], 7—192p. 18½cm. cloth.
Location : "Caerystrad", Menai Straits.

OWEN, Richard David

Novel
A 1084 : Gwyneth of Eryri : a story of 1868.
Llanfairfechan ; W. E. Owen, 1932.
[9], 10—128p. 18cm. cloth.
Location : Village of "Llanygro".

PAINTER, Gertrude, *pseud.* [*i.e. Lady Carter*]

Novel
A 1085 : Tillage of the poor.
London ; Murray, 1926.
[9], 10—320p. 18½cm. cloth.
Location : Central Wales.

PARGETER, Edith

Novels
A 1086 : The green branch.
London, Melbourne, [etc.] ; Heinemann,
1962.
[4], 295p. 19½cm. cloth.
Location : Welsh borderland, 1228.

A 1087 : The heaven tree.
London, Melbourne, [etc.] ; Heinemann,
1960.
[6], 364p. 19½cm. cloth.
Location : Welsh Marches, 1200—1215.

A 1088 : The scarlet seed.
London, Melbourne, [etc.]; Heinemann, 1963.
[6], 291p. 19½cm. cloth.
Location : Welsh borders, mediaeval period.

PARKER, John   [Joseph Noel]

Novels
A 1089 : The alien land.
[7], 8—203p. 19½cm. cloth.
Location : South Wales.

A 1090 : Iron in the valleys.
London ; George Ronald, 1959.
[7], 8—221p. 19½cm. cloth.
Location : Merthyr Tydfil, 1830's—1840's.

Story
A 1091 : The boy, the dog and the mountain.
The London Welshman, Vol. 18, no. 6, 1963,
12—13.

PARRY, Elsie

Verse
A 1092 : Songs of a valley.
Newport, Mon. R. H. Johns, *printer* [1951].
[10], 11—43p. 17½cm. cloth.
NLW copy signed by the author, 21/5/51.

PARRY-WILLIAMS, Sir Thomas Herbert

Verse
A 1093 : Sonnets (1919—20).
[Privately printed], 1932.
[6], 7—47p. 19cm. wrappers.

A 1094 : The body ; trans. from the author's original
Welsh version. The Dragon, Dec. 1916, 11.

Christ at forty ; trans. from the author's
original Welsh version. ibid. May 1916,
225—6.

Christ at thirty ; ibid. Dec. 1917, 9—10.

Christmas 1916 ; ibid.   March 1917, 109.
Also Nov. 1928.

Clarach—a lyric ; ibid. Nov. 1909, 3.

The jokers ; ibid. Dec. 1918, [24].

The last drop ; ibid. March 1917, 130.

Murder ; ibid. April 1919, 78.

Palinode ; ibid. May 1910, 223.

Reasons ; ibid. March 1918, 68.

Response ; ibid. Dec. 1916, 12.

Sonnets, I, II ; ibid. Dec. 1918, [25].

Tears ; ibid. Dec. 1916, 11.

Thirty-three ; ibid. 12.

To a dog ; ibid. June 1917, 179.

Young death ; ibid. Nov. 1911, [12].

Prose
A 1095 : The pipes.
The Dragon, June 1923, 169—70.

A 1096 : Snowdonia.
The Dragon, May 1908, 228—30.

A 1097 : Swan-sonnets.
The Dragon, April 1919, 79—80.

A 1098 : Telegraph poles.
The Dragon, Dec. 1925, 18—20.

A 1099 : Topsy and turfy.
The Dragon, March 1926, 86—9.

PATTERSON, John Edward

Novel
A 1100 : The bridge of Llangasty.
London ; Digby, Long, 1900.
viii, 306, 16p. 19cm. cloth.
Location : Partly Welsh setting.

PHILLIPS, Douglas

Verse
A 1101 : Merlin's town, and other poems.
Carmarthen ; St. Peter's Press, 1965.
[4], 5—23p. 22cm. wrappers.

A 1102 : Bilingual ; W. Mail, Oct. 3, 1964, 5.

Day trip from Cardiff ; ibid. May 1, 1965, 8.

Death of Procris ; W. Mail Literary Review,
Dec. 5, 1964, 3.

Easter wedding ; Dragons and daffodils : an
anthology of verse, 1960, 38.

Errand boy ; W. Mail Literary Review,
April 16, 1964, 9.

For Elvira ; ibid. August 14, 1964, 3.

Gorse bushes ; ibid. Nov. 7, 1964, 9.

Green spring ; ibid. Mar. 13, 1965, 11.

I broke my soul ; ibid. July 17, 1964, 10.

Merlin's town ; Poetry Wales, Vol. 1, no. 2,
Autumn 1965, 19—20.

Merthyr Mayday ; Dragons and daffodils,
1960, 39.

Once I walked holy ; ibid. 38.

Out of the yellow sands ; ibid. 37.

Poem (for Nicholas and Dorothy Wadham) ;
Poetry Wales, Vol. 1, Spring 1965, 9.

Spring fever ; W. Mail, March 27, 1965, 7.

PHILLIPS, William Francis

Drama
A 1103 : The call : a play in one act.
London ; Drane, 1916.
[3], 4—36p. 18½cm. cloth.
Scene : Kitchen of a Welsh home.

A 1104 : The lost legacy : a play of Welsh domestic
life in one act.
Liverpool ; Hugh Evans & Sons, [1917].
[5], 6—24p. 15cm. wrappers.
Scene : Kitchen of a Welsh home.

PIERCE, Gwen

Drama
A 1105 : The eighth wonder of Wales : a one-act farce.
[Caerwys, Flint. ; G. Pierce, n.d.].
[5], 6—31p. 21½cm. wrappers.
Scene : A North Wales village.
Welsh version entitled : *Wythfed Rhyfeddod
Cymru.*

A 1106 : Magic at "The Dragon" : a one-act farce.
21 numbered leaves. Typescript.
[No imprint].
Scene : A hotel in the Welsh mountains.
Welsh version entitled "*Y Diafol yn Y Bedol*".

POPHAM, *Mrs.* Cecil

Novel
A 1107 : The two desires : an eisteddfod story.
London ; National Eisteddfod Association,
1908.
Also published serially in Wales (J.H.E.)
Vol. II, 1912, pp. 36—41 ; 110—16 ; 163—8 ;
214—8 ; 276—80.

Stories
A 1108 : Owen Owen : a tragedy of misunderstanding.
Wales (J.H.E.), Vol. IV, 1913 : May, 26—33 ;
June, 78—84 ; July, 165—9.

A 1109 : The ruling passion.
Wales (J.H.E.), Vol. 1, 1911, 155—6.

Verse
A 1110 : The land of hills ; trans. from the Welsh
"Gwlad y Bryniau" of T. Gwynn Jones.
Wales (J.H.E.), Vol. IV, 1913, June, 65—7 ;
August, 272—5 ; Oct., 361—2 ; Vol. V,
Jan. 1914, 133—5.

POWYS, John Cowper

Novels

A 1111 : Owen Glendower : an historical novel.
London ; John Lane, 1941.
[8], 952p. 20cm. cloth.
Location : Wales of the period 1408—1416.

A 1112 : Porius : a romance of the Dark Ages.
London ; Macdonald, 1951.
xix, 682p. 19½cm. cloth.
Location : Valley of Edeyrnion, N. Wales :
A.D. 499.

Other Prose

A 1113 : Autobiography.
London ; The Bodley Head, 1934.
[10], 652, [2]p. front. (port.) 21½cm. cloth.

A 1114 : Obstinate Cymric : essays, 1935—47.
Carmarthen ; Druid Press, 1947.
188p. 18½cm. cloth.
Includes some essays of literary interest.

A 1115 : Pair Dadeni ; or, "The Cauldron of Rebirth".
In Wales, Vol. VI, no. 2, 1946, 20—41.
—Limited collector's edition.
Llanybri, Carmarthen ; Druid Press, [1946].
24p. 21½cm. wrappers.
—Another impression. [Carmarthen], Druid
Press, [1946].
24p. 21½cm.
Verso of t.p. : "Reprinted from ' Wales ',
no. 22, Spring 1946".

Verse

A 1116 : The ailanthus.
A Review of English Literature. Vol. 4, no. 1,
1963.
[*First appeared* in The Dial : February 26,
1926].

The ridge ; ibid. 53—8.

Yr Wyddfa ; the tomb ; Poetry Book Magazine, Vol. 6, no. 5, Fall 1954, 29.
Dock L., Vol. 6, no. 17, 1955, 11.

PREECE, Peter

Story

A 1117 : The reward.
Dock L., Vol. 2, no. 5, 1951, 32—4.

Verse

A 1118 : The ringing stone.
[Pembroke Dock ; Dock Leaves, 1954].
8p. 20½cm. (Dock Leaves Pamphlets Series,
no. 3).

A 1119 : The altars of the sea ; The Lilting House,
comp. by T. Hawkes, 1955, 38.

Completion : A.-W.R., Vol. 9, no. 23, undated, 24.

Exile ; ibid. Vol. 12, no. 30, undated, 56.

From Wales to a stranger ; Poetry Book
Magazine, Vol. 6, no. 5, Fall 1954, 31.

The lyric of Fredwyn the Idiot ; London
Welshman, Vol. 18, no. 6, 1963, 8.

The naked flood ; The Lilting House, 1955, 36.

New Legend ; a poem for three voices ;
A.-W.R., Vol. 11, no. 27, undated, 26—32.

An old man's dream ; The Lilting House,
1955, 40.

On the death of Dylan Thomas ; Dock L.,
Vol. 5, no. 13, 1954, 29.

Paper-girl ; ibid. Vol. 7, no. 20, 1956, 39.

Potsherd ; A.-W.R., Vol. 12, no. 29, undated,
11.

The sea-bird's song ; Dock L., Vol. 5, no. 14,
1954, 11. The Lilting House, 1955, 39.

Solution ; A.-W.R., Vol. 9, no. 23, undated, 25.

Their burial ground ; The Lilting House,
1955, 37.

PRITCHARD, John

Verse

A 1120 : Easter poem ; Poems from the Forces, London
Routledge, 1941, 93—5.
Modern Welsh Poetry ; ed. by K. Rhys
1944, 102—3.

The green navies ; Wales, No. 4, 1938, 140
Wales, New Series, I, 1943, 20.
Modern Welsh Poetry ; ed. by K. Rhys
1944, 104.
More Poems from the Forces ; ed. by K.
Rhys, 1943, 207—8.

Poem ; Wales, No. 1, 1937, 9.

Poem ["In fear of death do not neglect small
bounty"] ;
Modern Welsh Poetry ; ed. by K. Rhys,
1944, 105.
Poems from the Forces, London, Routledge,
1941, 89—90.

Poem ["Is there virtue in the sweet
medium ?"] ;
Modern Welsh Poetry ; ed. by K. Rhys,
1944, 101.
More Poems from the Forces ; ed. by K.
Rhys, 1943, 207.

Poem ["October scavenger . . ."] ; Wales,
No. 3, 1937, 84.

Poem ["This brown vandal . . ."] ; Poems from the Forces, London, Routledge, 1941, 93.
Poem ["When birds and brittle leaves come down"] ;
Modern Welsh Poetry ; ed. by K. Rhys, 1944, 103—4.
Poems from the Forces, London, Routledge, 1941, 91—2.

Spring ; Poems from the Forces, London, Routledge, 1941, 90.

Spring excursion ; Wales, Vol. VII, no. 25, 1947, 161—2.

Swansea Bay ; Wales, No. 6/7, March 1939, 198.
Modern Welsh Poetry ; ed. by K. Rhys, 1944, 105—6.
More Poems from the Forces ; ed. by K. Rhys, 1943, 206—7.

The visitor ; Wales, No. 1, 1937, 23.

Winter ; Poems from the Forces, London, Routledge, 1941, 92.

Stories
A 1121 : The beloved.
Wales, no. 10, October 1939, 262—4.

A 1122 : King Pantygwydr.
Wales, no. 3, Autumn 1937, 100—7.

A 1123 : A woman's no.
Wales, Vol. VII, no. 26, 1947, 309—16.

PRITCHARD, Charles H.

Verse
A 1124 : Owen Glyndŵr, and other poems.
London ; A. Stockwell, 1908.
[5], 6—79p. 18cm. cloth.

PROSSER, Edward K.

Verse
A 1125 : Beauty ; A Book of Aberystwyth Verse ; ed. by Charles Davies and E. K. Prosser, [1926], 49.

Dead ; ibid. 46.

Despondency ; The Dragon, Feb. 1923, 92.

Lone thoughts ; ibid. Nov. 1923, 16.

Miracles of mind ; ibid. Dec. 1925, 20.

On discovering a bluebell in a thicket ; ibid. June 1923, 158.

San Francisco calling ; A Book of Aberystwyth Verse ; ed. by Charles Davies and E. K. Prosser, [1926], 48.

To imagination ; The Dragon, Feb. 1924, 141.

Town and country ; A Book of Aberystwyth Verse ; ed. by Charles Davies and E. K. Prosser, [1926], 47.

Wandering by twilight ; ibid. 45.

Written in the Reading Room of the National Library of Wales ; Welsh Outlook, Vol. XIII, 1926, 76.

PRYCE, Daisy Hugh [i.e. Margaret Jennette Hugh Pryce]

Novel
A 1126 : The ethics of Evan Wynne.
London ; Everett, [1913].
[6], 7—317, 6p. 18½cm. cloth.
Location : North Wales. Topics is Disestablishment of Church in Wales.

PRYCE, Gwendolen

Novels
A 1127 : John Jones, Curate.
London ; T. Fisher Unwin, 1901.
viii, 293, [3]p. 18½cm. cloth (Green Cloth Library).
T.p. illustrated with line-drawing and crest

A 1128 : A long shadow.
London, New York, [etc.] ; Cassell, 1912 (2nd imp.).
[8], 312, 4p. 19cm. cloth.
Location : Anglesey.

A 1129 : A son of Arvon.
London ; Fisher Unwin, 1906.
[4], 5—320p. 18½cm. cloth.
Location : Caernarvonshire.

PRYCE, Myfanwy

Novel
A 1130 : Parson's wives.
London ; Faber & Gwyer, 1926.
[6], 284p. 18½cm. cloth.
Locations : "Bryndinas", "Garth" and "Rhaidr".
Includes some verse.

PRYS-JONES, Arthur Glyn

Stories
A 1131 : The night we lost Aunt Emma.
London Welshman, Vol. 181, no. 7, July 1963 13, 14 and 17.

A   1132 : A winter's tale : night call.
Y Ddinas, Vol. 12, no. 3, Dec. 1957, 7 and 23.

Other Prose
A   1133 : My Christmas visitor.
Y Ddinas, Vol. 12, no. 5, 1958, 9.

Verse
A   1134 : Green places : poems of Wales.
Aberystwyth ; Gwasg Aberystwyth, 1948.
[11], 12—91p. 18cm. cloth.
Contents : Including four poems in Welsh.

A   1135 : Poems of Wales.
Oxford ; Blackwell, 1923.
[8], 64p. 18½cm. limp boards.
—Another ed. 2nd ed. 1924.
—Another impression. American imp. 1924.
—Another ed. 3rd ed. 1925.
Collation as 1st ed. Cloth binding.

A   1136 : At Trawsfynydd ; Welsh Outlook, Vol. XVI, 1929, 25.

Autumn storm : Glamorgan coast ; Glamorgan Historian, Vol. I ; ed. by Stewart Williams, Cowbridge, Glam. ; Brown, 1963, 67.

A ballad of Glyndŵr's rising ; Welsh Poets ; comp. by A. G. Prys-Jones, 1917, 55—6.

The ballad of Sir Owen ; Welsh Outlook, Vol. II, 1915, 316.

A ballad of victory ; ibid. Vol. V, 1918, 350.

The black pagans ; A-W.R., Vol. 14, no. 34, 1964—5, 45—6.

A day which endures not ; (adapted from the Welsh of Elidr Sais, 13th century) ; Poetry Wales, I, Spring, 1965, 10.

Deo gratias [a hymn] ; Y Ddinas, Vol. 12, no. 12, 1958, 17.

At Dinas Mawddwy ; Welsh Outlook, Vol. XII, 1925, 331.

An Eastern Garden ; ibid. Vol. XVII, 1930, 182.

Evening at St. Fagan's ; History on my doorstep ; ed. by Stewart Williams, 1959, 96.

Evening in Snowdonia ; Welsh Outlook, Vol. XVII, 1930, 36.

[*Extract from*] St. David's Cathedral ; Praise of Wales ; comp. by Maxwell Fraser, 1950, 41.

Fairy glen ; Welsh Outlook, Vol. V, 1918, 151.

For remembrance ; ibid. Vol. XV, 1928, 337.

Glamorgan coast ; History on my doorstep ; ed. by Stewart Williams, 1959, 76.
Dragons and daffodils, 1960, 40.

Green places ; Welsh Outlook, Vol. XV, 1928, 122.

Gwalchmai's delight [from the Welsh of Gwalchmai, a poet of the 12th century] ; Poetry Book Magazine, Vol. 6, no. 5, Fall 1954, 5.
Dock L., Vol. 3, no. 8, 1952, 12.

Henry Morgan's march on Panama ; A Book of Wales ; ed. by D. M. & E. M. Lloyd, 1953, 147—8.

A hymn for St. David's Day ; Welsh Outlook, Vol. XVII, 1930, 71.

Nativity ; ibid. Vol. XX, 1933, 345.

Madonna ; Welsh Poets : compiled by A. G. Prys-Jones, 1917, 56—8.

Merlin's Hill ; London Welshman, Vol. 16, no. 7, 1961, 13.

The mountains of Glamorgan ; Glamorgan Historian, Vol. I ; ed. by Stewart Williams. Cowbridge, Glam. ; Brown, 1963, 121. [Uncredited to the author] *in* They Look at Wales : an anthology of prose and verse, 1941, [21]. Welsh Outlook, Vol. II, 1915, 143.

October evening (in the Vale of Glamorgan) ; Glamorgan Historian, Vol. I ; ed. by Stewart Williams. Cowbridge, Glam. ; Brown, 1963, 88.

Olden princes ; Welsh Outlook, Vol. XII, 1925, 203.

On a Welsh mountain-top ; A-W.R., Vol. 10, no. 26, undated, 22.

Palestine, 1192—1917 ; Welsh Outlook, Vol. V, 1918, 96.

The passing of Owen Glyndŵr ; Wales (J.H.E.), Vol. IV, 1913, 360.

The ploughman and the poet (after Iolo Morganwg) ; History on my doorstep ; ed. by Stewart Williams, 1959, 43.

Poet down and out ; Wales, Vol. VI, no. 3, 1946, 21.

Puw the Ploughman ; A-W.R., Vol. 9, no. 23, undated, 35.

Queen Mab ; Welsh Outlook, Vol. IV, 1917, 291.

The rider ; ibid. Vol. V, 1918, 303.

Saint David ; ibid. Vol. XVI, 1929, 94.

St. Govan ; A Book of Wales ; ed. by D. M. & E. M. Lloyd, 1953, 52.

Salt marshes ; Western Mail, Nov. 13, 1965, 6.
Dragons and daffodils, 1960, 43.
PEN 1954, 97—8.
Rann, no. 19 (Welsh number), 1953, 17.

Shepherd poet ; Welsh Review, Vol. II, no. 3, 1939, 141.

Song ; Welsh Outlook, Vol. XV, 1928, 163.

Song at Easter-tide ; London Welshman, Vol. 18, no. 4, 1963, 10.

A song of Glyndŵr's Rising ; Welsh Outlook, Vol. IV, 1917, 221.

A song of the pilgrim road—St. Davids ; ibid. Vol. XV, 1928, 64.

A song of Wales ; ibid. Vol. IV, 1917, 174.

A song of the Welsh (St. David's Day, 1916) ; Welsh Poets : compiled by A. G. Prys-Jones, 1917, 53—5.

In south Glamorgan ; History on my doorstep ; ed. by Stewart Williams, 1959, 44.

Spring comes to Glamorgan ; ibid.   75.
Dragons and daffodils, 1960, 42.

There was a moot of waters ; Dock L., Vol. 6, no. 17, 1955, 19.

Time drifts slowly ; W. Mail, Jan. 2, 1965, 6.

Tree circle ; History on my doorstep ; ed. by Stewart Williams, 1959, 44.

Two triolets ; Welsh Outlook, Vol. II, 1915, 67.

Unrest ; ibid. Vol. XVI, 1929, 147.

The vanished people ; ibid. Vol. XII, 1925, 230.

Vigil ; ibid. Vol. XII, 1925, 203.

Vision ; ibid. Vol. XVII, 1930, 74.

Welsh manor garden ; History on my doorstep ; ed. by Stewart Williams, 1959, 28.

West Country ; Welsh Outlook, Vol. XII, 1926, 188.

When the long hours ; Wales, Vol. VI, no. 3, 1946, 17.

Where are you going ? ; Welsh Outlook, Vol. IV, 1917, 308.

A winter day (adapted from the Welsh of an anonymous 10th or 11th century poet) ; Y Ddinas, Vol. 12, no. 5, 1958, 14. Poetry Wales, I, Spring 1965, 11.

Winter woods in Wales—Carmarthenshire ; The London Welshman, Vol. 15, no. 6, 1960, 9.
Dragons and daffodils, 1960, 40.
Y Ddinas, Vol. 12, no. 2, 1957, 24.

PRYS-WILLIAMS, Marion

Novels
A 1137 : Blodwen.
London ; Simpkin, Marshall, Hamilton, Kent, [1916].
[4], 5—256p. 18½cm. cloth.
Location : N. Wales coast.

A 1138 : The call of a soul : a Welsh romance.
London ; Simpkin, Marshall, Hamilton, Kent, [1916].
288p. 18½cm. cloth.
Location : The farm of "Pen-y-Parc", and London.

Story
A 1139 : John's chair.
Wales (J.H.E.), Vol. I, 1911, 276—7.

Verse
A 1140 : Hearts of Wales.
Wales (J.H.E.), Vol. I, 1911, 264.

PUGH, Jonathan Argoed

Verse
A 1141 : "Einion Clyd" : a poem.
London ; Stockwell, [1937].
78p. 18cm. cloth.

"QUIN, Shirland", *pseud. [i.e. Enid Guest]*

Novel
A 1142 : Dark heritage.
London ; Harrap, 1931.
352p. 18½cm. cloth.

Drama
A 1143 : Elias and the mushrooms : a comedy in one act.
London ; Foyle's, 1928.
[3], 4—28p. 15cm. wrappers.
Scene : A North Wales farmhouse.

A 1144 : That which counts : a play in three acts.
London ; Foyle's, 1927.
108p. 15cm. wrappers.
Scene : Penmaenmawr, N. Wales.

RADCLIFFE, Garnett

Novel

A 1145 : The Great Orme terror.
London ; Thornton Butterworth, 1934.
254, [2]p. 18½cm. cloth.
Location : Llandudno, Caerns.

"RAINE, Allen", *pseud.* [*i.e. Anne Adalisa Puddicombe*]

Novels

A 1146 : By Berwen Banks : a novel.
London ; Hutchinson, 1899.
336p. cloth.
Location : "Caer Madoc" and "Abersethin",
Welsh coast.
—Another ed. Toronto ; W. J. Gage Co., 1899.

A 1147 : Garthowen : a story of a Welsh homestead.
London ; Hutchinson, n.d.
190p. 21cm.
—Another ed. 2nd ed.
Hutchinson, 1900.
381, [3]p. 18½cm. cloth.
—Another ed. Cheap ed.
Hutchinson, [1920].
286p. 16½cm. cloth.
(Some preliminary advertising pp. deficient
in NLW copy).

A 1148 : Hearts of Wales : an old romance.
London ; Hutchinson, 1905.
[4], 347, [1], 32p. 19cm. cloth.
—3rd ed. 1906.
Location : Wales in the period of the Glyndŵr
Rebellion.

A 1149 : Neither storehouse nor barn.
London ; Hutchinson, 1908.
316p.
Location : The village of "Llanidris".
—Another ed. Hutchinson, [1922].
[4], 276, [4]p. 17cm. cloth.
—Another ed. Hutchinson, n.d.
186p. 21cm. wrappers.
(Sixpenny Novels Series).
pp. 2 and 4 contain advertisements.

A 1150 : On the wings of the wind.
London ; Hutchinson, 1903.
vi, 344p. cloth.
Location : The town of "Tregarreg".
—Another ed. Hutchinson, [1930].
288p. 18½cm. cloth.
(Blue Star Library).

A 1151 : Queen of the Rushes : a tale of the Welsh
Revival.
London ; Hutchinson, 1907.
viii, 331, 32p. 18½cm. cloth.
Location : "Tregildas", sea coast.

A 1152 : Torn sails : a tale of a Welsh village.
London : Hutchinson, [1898].

359, [1]p. 18cm. cloth.
Location : Sail-factory in the Cardiganshire
seaside village of "Mwntseison".
—Another ed. Hutchinson, [1917].
[4], 320p. front. (port.) 16cm. cloth.
(Sevenpenny Novels Series).

A 1153 : Under the thatch.
London ; Hutchinson, 1910.
[4], 345, [2], 32p. 18½cm. cloth.
—Another ed. Hutchinson, 1912.
190p. wrappers.

A 1154 : A Welsh singer : a novel.
London ; Hutchinson, 1897.
viii, 367, [1]p. 18cm. cloth.
Scene is "Abersethin", Cardiganshire.
Published in Welsh version entitled *Myfanwy* ;
translated by Megan Morgan ; Aberystwyth, Cymdeithas Lyfrau Ceredigion,
1960.

A 1155 : A Welsh witch : a romance of rough places.
London ; Hutchinson, 1902.
viii, 431p. 18½cm. cloth.
Location : "Treswnd" on the Welsh coast.
—Another ed. 3rd ed. Hutchinson, 1902.

A 1156 : Where billows roll : a tale of the Welsh coast :
a novel.
London ; Hutchinson, 1909.
viii, 352p.
Location : Cardiganshire coast.
—Another ed. Hutchinson, [1924]. 270,
[14]p. 17½cm. cloth.
Welsh version, entitled *Lle Treigla'r Don* ;
translated by Megan Morgan ; Cymdeithas
Lyfrau Ceredigion, 1964.

Stories

A 1157 : All in a month, and other stories.
London ; Hutchinson, 1908.
v, [1], 279, [1], 32p. 19cm. cloth.

A 1158 : A life's chase.
Wales (J.H.E.), Vol. I, 1911, 351—5.

RAY, Jane

Novel

A 1159 : Mary into Mair.
London ; Mills & Boon, 1965.
187p. 18½cm. cloth.
Location : The market town of "Llanllon".

REES, Alun

Verse

A 1160 : My name is legend.
Southall, Middx. ; Scrip Magazine, 1962.
22p. 20½cm. Duplicated typescript.

A 1161 : Eros at the Tottenham Royal ; Poetry Wales, I,
Spring 1965, 12.

Glamorgan ; Healing of the Nations ; ed. by Vera Rich. A-W.R. Supplement, 1965, 9.

Release John Lucifer ! ; Poetry Wales, Vol. 1, no. 2, 1965, 21.

Still, starveling angel ; Poetry Wales, I, Spring 1965, 12.

REES, Enoch

Novels
A 1162 : The millers.
London ; Kobold Knight, [1941].
205p. 17½cm. cloth.
Location : "Allt Hir Valley" in West Wales.

A 1163 : To lighten their darkness.
London ; A. H. Stockwell, [1940].
207p. 18½cm. cloth.
Location : South Wales coal mining areas.

A 1164 : Whose sun is it ?
London ; Kobold Knight, [1941].
277p. 18cm. cloth.

Story
A 1165 : Death Ball, and other stories.
London ; Heath Cranton, 1943.
157p. 18½cm. cloth.

Verse
A 1166 : Song of the sand.
Ilfracombe ; A. H. Stockwell, [1942].
63p. 18cm. limp board cover.

REES, Goronwy

Novels
A 1167 : A bridge to divide them.
London ; Faber, 1937.
[8], 9—287p. 18½cm. cloth.
Location : Mining area of S. Wales.

A 1168 : The summer flood.
London ; Faber, 1932.
[8], 9—288p. 18½cm. cloth.
Location : Partly in the Lleyn Peninsula, N. Wales.

Story
A 1169 : The horsemen ; The London Magazine, (N.S.), Vol. 4, no. 1, 1964, 8—31.

Other Prose
A 1170 : A bundle of sensations : sketches in autobiography.
London ; Chatto & Windus, 1960.
[8], 9—240p. 21½cm. cloth.

Verse
A 1171 : A girl speaks ; Folios of New Writing, Spring 1940 ; ed. by J. Lehmann, 123.
The landscape fading ; Modern Welsh Poetry ; ed. by K. Rhys, 1944, 106—7.
The seasons' fool ; ibid. 107—8.

REES, Morwyth

Stories
A 1172 : The ferret ; Dock L., Vol. 1, no. 2, 1950, 40—3.

A 1173 : Tea for four ; ibid. Vol. 2, no. 5, 1951, 29—31.

A 1174 : The opportunist ; ibid. Vol. 1, no. 1, 1949, 22—5.

Verse
A 1175 : Abroad thoughts from home ; A-W.R., Vol. 10, no. 25 (undated), 67.

Ballad of Elidyr ; Dock L., Vol. 5, no. 14, 1954, 16—7.

Fallen feather ; ibid. Vol. 8, no. 22, 1958, 48.

Immutability ; ibid. Vol. 1, no. 2, 1950, 11.

Island ; Rann, No. 19 (Welsh no.), 1953, 11.

Magician in London ; Dock L., Vol. 3, no. 8, 1952, 20.

Mist ; ibid. Vol. 1, no. 3, 1950, 27.

Off-shore wind ; ibid. Vol. 3, no. 7, 1952, 11.

Old man's curse ; ibid. Vol. 1, no. 2, 1950, 11.

Precious stones ; ibid. Vol. 8, no. 21, 1957, 41.

REES, Thomas Hardy

Verse
A 1176 : Breezes from the Welsh hills, and other poems.
Caernarvon ; Herald Office, 1906.
[6], 7—78p. 19½cm. wrappers.

"REMENHAM, John" *pseud. [i.e. John Alexander Vlasto]*

Novel
A 1177 : Righteous Abel.
London ; Macdonald, [1943].
224p. 18½cm. cloth.
Location : A Mid-Wales rural valley.

"RHYS, Cadvan" *pseud. [i.e. David Delta Evans]*

Novel
A 1178 : Daniel Evelyn, heretic. Illustrations by Howard Hulme.
London ; Drane, 1913.
449p. front (plate) illus. pl. 18½cm. cloth.
Location : ". . . a . . . story of a Welsh village [Serthyd] and of the narrowness of Welsh Calvinism". *The Times*, 19 June, 1913.

RHYS, Edward Prosser

Verse

A 1179 : Memory ; trans. from the 1924 Crown Poem
"Atgof" by Hywel Davies.
[Pontypool, Mon. ; Publ. by the National
Eisteddfod Committee, 1924].
14p. 18½cm. wrappers.

A 1180 : Twenty-one ; trans. from the Welsh by J. T.
Jones. The Dragon, Vol. IX, 1922, 29.

RHYS, Ernest

Novels

A 1181 : The man at odds : a story of the Welsh coast
and the Severn sea.
London ; Hurst & Blackett, 1904.
viii, 316, [1]p. 19cm. cloth.

A 1182 : The whistling maid : a romance.
London ; Hutchinson, 1900.
viii, 341, [1]p. 18½cm. cloth.
Location : West Wales.

Story

A 1183 : The funeral of a poet (XIVth century).
The Celtic Year : [an annual]. [1900], 22—9.
(Reprinted from *Literature*).

Other Prose

A 1184 : Wales England wed : an autobiography.
London ; Dent, 1940.
x, 296p. front. (port.) illus. ports. 23cm.
cloth.

A 1185 : Black pilgrimage.
Welsh Review, Vol. II, no. 2, 1939, 91—7.

Verse

A 1186 : An autobiography ; Presenting Welsh Poetry,
1959, 101.
Poems of Our Time, 1900—1962, Dent,
1959, 71.
The Oxford book of English verse, 1250—
1918 ; comp. by Sir Arthur Quiller-
Couch, 1948, 1050.

The ballad of the buried sword ; Poems of
Wales, selected by Edmund D. Jones, 1914,
44—5.

The ballad of the homing man ; Welsh Poets :
comp. by A. G. Prys-Jones, 1917, 73—4.

Child lyrics : (*a*) The orange, (*b*) On a May
evening ; The British Annual of Literature,
1938, Vol. I, 12.

Clio ; Poems of Our Time, 1900—1962, Dent,
1959, 226.

The coming of Gwenhwyfar ; Welsh Poets :
comp. by A. G. Prys-Jones, 1917, 75.

Diana ; The Oxford Book of Victorian verse :
comp. by Arthur Quiller-Couch, 1948, 813.

The Field of Crogen ; trans. from the Welsh of
Ceiriog. The Land of My Fathers : a
Welsh gift book, London, Hodder, 1915,
35—6.

The Hall of Cynddylan (after Llywarch Hen) ;
The Land of My Fathers : a Welsh gift
book, 1915, 28—9.

The lament for Cynddylan (after Llywarch
Hen) ; Poems of Wales, selected by Edmund
D. Jones, 1914, 28.

The lament for Urien (from the Red Book of
Hergest) ; The Oxford book of modern
verse, 1892—1935, comp. by W. B. Yeats,
O.U.P., 1947, 52—3.

The lament of Llywarch Hen in his old age
(after Llywarch Hen) ; The Land of My
Fathers : a Welsh gift book. London,
Hodder, 1915, 51—2.

London ; Poems of Our Time, 1900—1962,
Dent, 1959, 285—6.

Lost in France : Jo's Requiem ; ibid. 95.

The miner ; trans. from the Welsh of Elfed ;
Praise of Wales, comp. by Maxwell Fraser,
1950, 52.

Music's remonstrance ; Welsh Outlook, Vol. 5,
March 1918, 75.

The old men ; Poems of Our Time, 1900—
1962, Dent, 1959, 206.

St. Marylebone ; Welsh Poets : comp. by A.
G. Prys-Jones, 1917, 71—2.

The song of the graves (from The Black Book
of Carmarthen) ; The Oxford book of
modern verse, 1892—1935 ; comp. by W. B.
Yeats. O.U.P., 1947, 50—2.

The song of the wind (after Taliesin) ; The
Land of My Fathers : a Welsh gift book.
London, Hodder, 1915, 27—8.

True love ; Poems of Our Time, 1900—1962,
Dent, 1959, 128.

RHYS, Keidrych, *pseud. [i.e. William Ronald Rees Jones]*

Verse

A 1187 : The Van Pool, and other poems.
London ; Routledge, 1942.
38p. 18½cm. cloth. (New Poets Series).

Verse   : single poems contributed to the same anthology are listed in the order in which they
appear in the anthology.

A 1188 : *In* Poems from the Forces, Routledge, 1941.
Garn Goch, 97.
Cinque Ports, 97—9.
Poem to Bill Empson, 99—100.
Section from The Van Pool : for my wife,
100—4.
Letter to my wife, 105—6.

A 1189 : *In* More Poems from the Forces ; ed. by K.
Rhys, 1943.
Alarm alarm, 233—4.
Death of a hurricane pilot, 235—9.
48 hours at Tenby, 232—3.
General Martel, 234—5.

A 1190 : *In* Twentieth Century Verse.
Building job, No. 3, 1937.
Poem for a neighbour, ibid.
Rip Van Winkle, ibid.

Landmark, no. 8, 1938.
Spin, ibid.

Triads during lambing season, no. 10, 1938,
40.
The last supper, ibid.

A 1191 : Air raid on East Coast ; Bugle Blast [No. 1] ;
1943, 104—7.

Bardic Crown ballad ; Wales, Vol. VIII, no.
29, 1948, 538—9.

Barddoniaeth (for J.D. and D.) ; Twentieth
Century Verse, no. 14, 1938, 126—7.

Chessmen associations ; NOW, no. 3, 1940, 5.
Little Reviews Anthology, 1943, 179.

Cartoon done in Something will be done
week ; Wales, no. 1, Summer 1937, 25—6.

The cock pheasant ; trans. from the Welsh
"Y Ceiliog Ffesant" of R. Williams Parry.
London Welshman, Vol. 16, no. 7, July
1961, 13.

Compassionate leave; Kingdom Come, Vol. 2,
no. 3, 1941, 84.

Coracle ; Welsh Review, Vol. 1, no. 6, 1939,
314.

Cross country ; Life and Letters Today,
Vol. 17, no. 9, 1937, 82.

Death-dance ; or Case History of the Lustrous
Navel ; Wales, no. 10, 1939, 270.

During lambing season ; Modern Welsh
Poetry ; ed. by K. Rhys, 1944, 109.

The emigrants ; LLT, Vol. 20, no. 16 [1939],
44—5.

Ephemerae for Bruska ; Wales, no. 6/7, 1939,
201.   Modern Welsh Poetry ; ed. by K.
Rhys, 1944, 108—9.

Epitaph ; Wales, Vol. VIII, no. 29, 1948, 531.

Fame ; Kingdom Come, Vol. 2, no. 1, 1940,
27.

The fire sermon ; or Bureaucracy burned ;
Wales, no. 2, 1937, 69.

Flashbacks ; Wales, New Series, 2, October
1943, 36.

Fortyeight hours at Tenby ; Poetry London,
no. 11, 1947, 19.

The fox ; trans. from the Welsh "Y Llwynog"
of R. Williams Parry ; London Welshman,
Vol. 16, no. 9, Sept. 1961, 11.

Fragment—The Prodigal speaks ; NOW,
no. 2, 1940, 5.

Fragments from the poem of asking ; Life &
Letters Today, Vol. 18, no. 12, 1938, 52—3.

For the late Lord Howard de Walden ; Wales,
Vol. VIII, no. 29, 1948, 532.

The good shepherd ; Life and Letters Today,
Vol. 19, no. 15, 1938, 54.

Incorruptible ; trans. from the Welsh of D.
Gwenallt Jones, Wales, Summer 1944, 33.

Interlude ; Modern Welsh Poetry ; ed. by K.
Rhys, 1944, 111—2.   Twentieth Century
Verse, no. 14, 1938, 126—7.

Laugharne pastoral ; Wales, no. 10, 1939,
274—5.
Penguin New Writing, no. 18, 170.
Y Ddinas, Vol. 15, no. 6, July 1960, 9.

Literary conservatives ; Wales, Vol. VIII,
no. 29, 1948, 533.

Llangadog Common ; Wales, New Series, 2,
October 1943, 35.

Manly and Elizabethan ; Kingdom Come,
Vol. 2, no. 3, 1941, 96.

On reading certain "Anglo-Welsh" literary
criticism ; Wales, Vol. VIII, no. 29, 1948,
533.

Poem of asking : for James Findlay Hendry ;
Poetry Scotland, no. 1, 1944 ; ed. by
Maurice Lindsay, 39.

Poem on being invalided out of the army ;
NOW, Vol. 5, [1945], 39.

Poem for a neighbour ; Modern Welsh Poetry ; ed. by K. Rhys, 1944, 111.

Ridiculous wrench ; NOW, No. 7, 1941, 25.

River Sawdde ; Modern Welsh Poetry, 1944, 110.

Room with a view ; Poetry Qtly., Vol. 6, no. 1, 1944, 9.

Sawdde ; Life and Letters Today, Vol. 24, no. 31, 1940, 278.

Sheep ; ibid. Vol. 21, no. 21, 1939, 58—9.
Bristol Packet. Bristol ; Bristol Writers' Assc., [1944], 38.
Modern Welsh Poetry ; ed. by K. Rhys, 1944, 110—1.

Shift ; Life and Letters Today, Vol. 23, no. 27, [1939], 197.

Socialites ; Wales, no. 1, Summer 1937, 27.

The soldier's plaint ; Poetry Scotland, no. 1, 1944, ed. by Maurice Lindsay, 38.

Special area ; LLT., Vol. 17, no. 9, 1937, 83.

Spell ; ibid. Vol. 22, no. 23, 1939, 57—8.

Spilling the beans ; ibid. Vol. 17, no. 9, 1937, 83.

Stone ; Wales, New Series, 2, October 1943, 35.

Tragic guilt ; Modern Welsh Poetry ; ed. by K. Rhys, 1944, 112—3.

Translations from the Welsh of R. Williams Parry : War Memorial ; His Father's son ; Soldier from Merioneth ; Wales, Summer 1944, 33.

Trichrug, North Carmarthen ; Seven, Vol. 6, no. 3, [1947], 60—1.

The Van Pool ; Wales, no. 10, 1939, 271.

The Van Pool : Trichrug ; Wales, no. 11, 1939—40, 292—3. Bristol Packet. Bristol ; Bristol Writers' Assc., [1944], 38—9.

Victoria leave train ; Wales, Vol. VIII, no. 29, 1948, 539—40.

Wales on the map ; LLT., Vol. 16, no. 7, 1937, 45—6.

Youth ; Modern Welsh Poetry ; ed. by K. Rhys, 1944, 112—3. LLT. Vol. 17, no. 10, 1937, 67.

RICHARDS, A. Edward

Stories
A 1192 : "The Admiralty regret . . ." ;
Wales, Vol. IV, no. 6, 1945, 40—6.
Little Reviews Anthology, 1946, 57—63.

A 1193 : Burial at sea.
Stories of the 40's, Vol. I ; ed. by R. Moore and Woodrow Wyatt, 1945, 143—6.

A 1194 : Home for good.
English story. Second series ; ed. by Woodrow and Susan Wyatt, 1941, 21—39.

A 1195 : Sacred ground.
Welsh Review, Vol. III, no. 3, 1944, 168—72.

A 1196 : Worthy is the Lamb.
Welsh Review, Vol. II, no. 4, 1939, 206—17.
Welsh short stories ; ed. by Gwyn Jones, 1956, 217—36.

RICHARDS, Alun

Novel
A 1197 : The elephant you gave me.
London ; Michael Joseph, 1963.
192p. 19½cm. cloth.
Stories
A 1198 : Everybody says it's for the best.
Wales, Nov. 1958, 56—9.

A 1199 : Love and hate and Matabele Hopkins (Cubicle J).
Wales, New Series, no. 5, 1959, 33—46.

A 1200 : Thy people : a fable.
Wales, Oct. 1958, 63—7.

RICHARDS, Ann

Novel
A 1201 : Gwen o' the Mill : [a serial novel].
Pt. I in Y Ddinas, Vol. 10, no. 11, 1956, pp. 3—4 and 10.
This work appeared in 31 monthly parts in Y Ddinas, with some intermissions, from August 1956 to its conclusion in Vol. 13, no. 9, June 1959, pp. 14—15.

RICHARDS, David Lloyd Seaborne

Novel
A 1202 : A romance of Prescelly.
Carmarthen ; W. Spurrell, [1927].
[5], 6—45, [1]p. 18½cm. wrappers.
Location : Prescelly Mountains, Pembs.

RICHARDS, Hedley

Novel
A 1203 : A Welsh princess.
London ; James Henderson, n.d.
80p. 18½cm. wrappers. (The "Budget"
Story Books Series).

ROBERTS, Arthur Owen

Drama

A 1204 : Cloud break.
In Three one-act plays.
Oxford ; Blackwell, 1925, 51—73.
(British Drama League Library Series, no. 12).

[Two further titles by this author noted : It
May Be This *and* Midsummer Morning.
No published copy traced].

ROBERTS, Barbara Dew

Novels
A 1205 : The Charlie trees : a Jacobite novel.
London ; Chatto & Windus, 1951.
vii, [1], 248p. 20cm. cloth.
Location : Partly in Wales.

A 1206 : The island feud : a novel.
London ; Chatto & Windus, 1947.
[4], 5—272p. 18½cm. cloth.
Location : Beaumaris and Anglesey.

A 1207 : Some trees stand.
London ; Chatto & Windus, 1945.
[6], 7—246p. 18½cm. cloth.
Location : "Trygarn" near "Porthafon".

A 1208 : Still glides the stream.
London ; Chatto & Windus, 1940.
vii, [1], 325p. 19cm. cloth.
Location : Caernarvonshire.

ROBERTS, Grace

Novel
A 1209 : Lowri.
Liverpool ; Brython Press, [1956].
[4], 5—306p. 18cm. cloth.
Location : The Vale of Clwyd, Denbs.
Stories
A 1210 : Idylls of Dyffryn Clwyd.
I : How Tomos Morgan entertained a
Cabinet Minister. Wales (J.H.E.),
Vol. VI, March 1914, 18—20.

II : How the "Diwygiad" came to Llanbych ;
ibid. April 1914, 103—5.

III : The folk-song lady ; ibid. May 1914,
153—6.

IV : The triumph of William Gruffydd ; ibid.
June 1914, 218—20.

V : Reconciliation ; ibid. July 1914, 265—8.

VI : The tinker's daughter ; ibid. August
1914, 321—4.

A 1211 : Little tales of Wales : The Ruling Passion.
Welsh Outlook. Vol. XIII, 1926, 247.

A 1212 : The return : a short story.
Y Ddinas. Vol. 13, no. 3, 1958, 6—7.

Other Prose
A 1213 : Sweets of my childhood.
Welsh Outlook. Vol. XIV, 1927, 80.

ROBERTS, Hugh Pierce

Novel
A 1214 : The Offa Minister : a story of Welsh life.
Cardiff ; Western Mail, 1914.
147p. 18cm. wrappers.
Location : An industrial district of N. Wales.

ROBERTS, Kate

Stories
A 1215 : A summer day and other stories ; [trans. from
the original Welsh versions]. Foreword by
Storm Jameson.
Cardiff ; Penmark Press, 1946.
[6], 7—121p. 18½cm. cloth.
Contents : Two storms—The wind—The loss—
The guilt—Old Age—A summer day—
Between two pieces of toffee—The letter—
Final payment—Sisters—The condemned—
Folded hands.

A 1216 : The condemned ; trans. by Dafydd Jenkins
from the Welsh version "Y Condemniedig".
Welsh Review. Vol. 1, no. 2, 1939, 72—8.

A 1217 : Old age ; trans. by Ll. Wyn Griffith from
"Henaint".
Welsh short stories ; ed. by Gwyn Jones, 1956,
236—43.
Welsh Review, Vol. III, no. 1, 1944, 21—5.

A 1218 : A summer day ; trans. by Dafydd Jenkins from
"Rhigolau Bywyd".
Welsh short stories ; ed. by G. Ewart Evans.
2nd ed. 1959, 36—41.

A 1219 : Two storms ; trans. by Dafydd Jenkins from
the Welsh "Dwy storm".
Welsh short stories ; ed. by Gwyn Jones, 1956,
243—52.
Welsh Review, Vol. IV, no. 2, 1945, 94—9.

A 1220 : The victory of Alaw Jim ; trans. by Walter
Dowding from "Buddugoliaeth Alaw Jim".
Life and Letters Today, Vol. 24, no. 31,
March 1940, 280—7.

ROBERTS, Lewis Miles

Verse
A 1221 : Some souvenirs of Wales.
Bangor ; Jarvis & Foster, 1903.
14p. illus. 19cm. wrappers.

ROBERTS, Lynette

Stories
A 1222 : An introduction to village dialect with seven
stories.
[London] ; Druid Press, [1944].
26p. 21½cm. wrappers.
Includes : Fox—Tiles—Steer—Graveyard—
Pub—Swansea raid—Fisherman.

Also in : Wales, New Series, 3, 1944, 64—71.
Fox—Tiles—Steer—Graveyard—Pub.
Verse
A 1223 : Gods with stainless ears : a heroic poem.
London ; Faber, 1951.
[10], 11—67p. 22cm. cloth.

[*Sections of this poem in* Modern Welsh Poetry ;
ed. by K. Rhys].

A 1224 : Poems.
London ; Faber, 1944.
[4], 5—54p. 22cm. cloth.
Some poems on Welsh themes.

A 1225 : Aircraft in flight ; Wales, no. 26, 1947, 319.

Blood and scarlet thorns ; Poetry in wartime ;
ed. by M. J. Tambimuttu, 1942, 133—4.

Broken voices ; Modern Welsh Poetry ; ed. by
K. Rhys, 1944, 118—9.

The circle of C ; ibid. 117—8.
Poetry in wartime, 1942, 130—1.

Dirge ; NOW, no. 2, 1940, 7.

Englyn ; Modern Welsh Poetry, 1944, 119.

Extract from "A Heroic Poem" ; ibid. 114—5.

Four poems ; Wales, Vol. IV, no. 5, 1944,
33—5.
Contents : Fifth of the Strata—Ecliptic blue—
Rhode Island Red—Rainshiver.

Four poems ; Wales, Vol. VIII, no. 30, 1948,
637—40.
Contents : Green madrigal—Saint Swithin's
Pool—Paulinus—Transgression.

The hypnotist ; Poetry (Chicago), Vol. 81,
no. 3, 1952, 164.

Lamentation ; Poetry in wartime ; ed. by M.
J. Tambimuttu, 1942, 132—3.
Modern Welsh Poetry ; ed. by K. Rhys,
1944, 115—6.

Love is an outlaw ; Poetry (Chicago), Vol. 81,
no. 3, 1952, 164.

Poem ("He alone could get me out of this") ;
The Penguin New Writing, no. 39, ed. by
J. Lehmann, 37.

Poem ("Let the man of darkness out") ; ibid.
38.

Poem ("I see 2 ears . . .") ; LLT., Vol. 22,
no. 24, 1939, 246.

Poem ("In steel white land . . .") ; Wales,
no. 11, 1939—40, 302.

Poem from Llanybri ; Poetry in wartime ;
ed. by M. J. Tambimuttu, 1942, 129—30.
Poetry Book Magazine, Vol. 6, no. 5,
Fall 1954, 30.
Modern Welsh Poetry ; ed. by K. Rhys,
1944, 116—7.

Poem without notes ; Wales, no. 6/7, 1939,
200—1.

The seasons ; Little Reviews Anthology,
1947—48, 157—8.
Modern Welsh Poetry ; ed. by K. Rhys,
1944, 119—20.

Song of praise ; Welsh Review, Vol. II, no. 3,
1939, 141.

Spring ; Poetry (Chicago), Vol. 82, no. 6,
1953, 322—3.

To a Welsh woman ; Welsh Review, Vol. 1,
no. 6, 1939, 313.

To Keidrych Rhys ; Wales, no. 10, 1939,
278—9.

To the priest of the middles ; Modern Welsh
Poetry ; ed. by K. Rhys, 1944, 113—4.

Two wine glasses ; Poetry (Chicago), Vol. 82,
no. 6 53, 19, 321.

Tygwyn ; ibid. 323.

These words I write on crinkled tin ; ibid.
Vol. 81, no. 3, 1952, 165—6.

Xaquixaguana ; Poetry in wartime ; ed. by
M. J. Tambimuttu, 1942, 131.

ROBERTS, Mary Elizabeth *"Mair Gwynedd"*

Novel
A 1226 : Dilys Morgan's thrilling adventures.
London ; Stockwell, [1926].
84p. front. (port.) 18½cm. cloth.
Drama
A 1227 : Shifting sands : a play in four acts.
Liverpool ; Hugh Evans & Son, [1937].
77ff. 16cm. wrappers.
Typescript.

ROBERTS, Rhian

Stories
A 1228 : The devil's blackberries.
Life and Letters Today. Vol. 36, no. 67, 1943,
164—70.

A 1229 : Keep up appearances.
Life and Letters. Vol. 48, no. 103, March
1946, 197—205.

A 1230 : The pattern.
Wales, Vol. VII, no. 25, 1947, 192—202.

ROBERTS, Sally

Verse
A 1231 : Daws Hill ; London Welshman, Vol. 18, no.
11, 1963, 13.

Decline in heroes—Alun Lewis and Hedd
Wyn ; ibid. no. 7, 1963, 9.

The dynasty (Westminster Abbey) ; ibid.
Vol. 17, no. 3, 1962, 13.

In exile ; ibid. 13.

Metamorphosis ; A-W.R., Vol. 12, no. 30,
undated, 30.

Mile Stone at the British Museum ; London
Welshman, Vol. 17, no. 9, 1962, 20.

Remembrance Day, Aberystwyth ; Poetry
Wales, Vol. 1, no. 2, 1965, 21.

A small tragedy ; YCP, 165—6.

The spinster to her charge ; London Welshman, Vol. 17, no. 9, 1962, 20.

Wreck of the Royal Charter ; ibid. Vol. 18,
no. 7, 1963, 5.

ROBERTSON, Graham

Novel
A 1232 : The individualist.
London ; George Ronald, 1960.
[6], 186p. 19½cm. cloth.
Location : Cardiff.

RUCK, Berta [*i.e. Amy Roberta Ruck, afterwards Mrs.
Oliver Onions*]

Novels
A 1233 : Intruder marriage : a new story.
London ; Hutchinson, [1945].
208p. 18½cm. cloth.
Location : Partly in Wales : coastal village.

A 1234 : The lap of luxury.
London, Toronto, [etc.] ; Cassell, 1931.
x, 318p. 18½cm. cloth.
Location : West Coast of Wales.

A 1235 : Out to marry money.
London ; Mills & Boon, 1940.
252p. 18½cm. cloth.
Location : Partly in Wales.

A 1236 : A star in love.
London ; Hodder & Stoughton, 1935.
314, [6]p. 19cm. cloth.
Location : Partly in Wales.

A 1237 : Surprise engagement.
London ; Hutchinson, [1947].
224p. 18½cm. cloth.
Location : Partly in Wales.

A 1238 : Tomboy in lace : a new story.
London ; Hutchinson, [1947].
264p. 18½cm. cloth.
Location : Partly in Wales.

SANDEMAN, Robert Gwynne

Verse
A 1239 : First poems.
Abergavenny ; Owen Bros., 1921.
[6], 48p. 18cm. wrappers.
Includes three poems in Welsh.

"SANDYS, Oliver", *pseud.*

For works by this author in the names of
"Oliver Sandys" and "Countess Barcynska",
see under EVANS, Marguerite Florence.

SAUNDERS, Roy

Novel
A 1240 : The drovers' highway.   Illustrated by the
author.
London ; Oldbourne, 1959.
[10], 11—190p. front. illus. 19½cm. cloth.
Location : Near Llandovery, Carms. Leads
up to Rebecca Riots, 1839.

SAUNDERSON, Irene

Novel
A 1241 : A Welsh heroine : a romance of colliery life.
London ; Lynwood, [preface 1910].
[4], 5—330p. front. 18cm. cloth.
Location : "Cwmglo".

"SCRUTATOR", *pseud.* [*i.e.*   ]

Novel
A 1242 : Caleb Jones, miner : a story of the South Wales
coalfield.
Merthyr Tydfil ; H. W. Southey, 1900.
226p. 18½cm. cloth.

SHIRLEY, Rae

Drama
A 1243 : Time the sad jester : a comedy in one act.
London ; Deane, 1954.
[3], 4—24p. 18½cm. wrappers.
Scene : A living-room : Welsh characters.

SLATER, Montagu

Drama
A 1244 : New way wins : the play from *Stay Down Miner.*
London ; Lawrence and Wishart, 1937.
viii, 70p. 18½cm. boards.
Scene : "Cwmllynfach" : mining area.

SMART, Arthur D.

Novel
A 1245 : The Chief of St. Donat's.
London ; John Ouseley, [1912].
291p. 18½cm. cloth.
Location : St. Donat's Castle, Glam.

SMITH, M[inna] Josephine

Novel
A 1246 : Llewellyn's Tower. Illustrations by Hildegard
Woodward.
New York ; The Macmillan Co., 1938.
[10], 170p. illus. 20cm. cloth.
Location : "Pen y Bryn", North Wales.

SNEYD-KYNNERSLEY, Edmund Mackenzie

Novel
A 1247 : Tom, Vron.
London, Edinburgh ; W. Blackwood, 1913.
vi, [3], 4—343p. 18½cm. cloth.
Location : "Llanpwll" (N. Wales).

SOMERSET, Raglan

Verse
A 1248 : The chieftain's ground : verses and translations grave and gay.
Usk, Mon. ; Four Ash Press, 1953.
[8], 37p. 20cm. wrappers.
Includes translations of poems by Wil Ifan
and Dilys Cadwaladr.

SPARROY, Wilfrid

Stories
A 1249 : The colliers of Windy Hill : crucial moments
in a Welsh village. *Cheap ed.*
London ; Elliot Stock, 1904.
viii, [2], 106p. 19cm. cloth.

SPRING, Howard

Prose
A 1250 : Heaven lies about us : a fragment of infancy.
London ; Constable, 1943.
viii, 108p. 19cm. cloth.
—Another ed. 2nd ed. 1956.

—Another ed. London ; Collins, 1956.
[6], 7—96p. col. front. illus. 21½cm. cloth.

A 1251 : In the meantime.
London ; Constable, 1942.
[5], 6—224p. front. port. 18½cm. cloth.
Illustrated endpapers.

—Another ed. 1947.
[6], 7—224p. 17½cm.

Drama
A 1252 : Jinny Morgan : a play in three acts.
London ; Evans, 1952.
94p. 21½cm. wrappers.
Scene set in a Rhondda Valley home.

Also in : Spring, H. Three plays. Collins,
1963, 13—106.

STEEL, Flora Annie

Novel
A 1253 : A sovereign remedy.
London ; Heinemann, 1906.
[4], 354, [2]p. 18½cm. cloth.

STEPHENS, Meic

Verse
A 1254 : Armor ; A-W.R., Vol. 11, no. 27, undated, **42.**
Triad, 1963, 40.

Cân y lloerig [Song of the madman] ; Triad,
1963, 39.

Children waiting ; ibid. 32.
The Dragon, Summer Term, 1958, (Festival ed.), 24.

Civic Centre, Cardiff ; Triad, by P. Griffith
[*and others*], 1963, 37.

The collier ; ibid. 33.
YCP, 186—7.

Cwm Rhondda ; Triad, 1963, 34—5.

Easter 1960 ; ibid. 41.
A-W.R., Vol. 11, no. 27, undated, 41.

Idris Davies, 1905—1953 ; Triad, 1963, 36.

I ferch [To a girl] ; ibid. 31.

Ker Ys (adapted from an old Breton song) ;
Poetry Wales, I, Spring 1965, 13.

Landscape with figures, Rhondda ; Wales,
no. 42/44, 1959, [80].

Nocturne ; Triad, 1963, 38.

Poems in her absence ; A-W.R., Vol. 14, no.
34, 1964-5, 8—9.

Ponies, Twynyrodyn ; Poetry Wales, Vol. 1,
no. 2, Autumn 1965, 22.
W. Mail, Nov. 6, 1965, 6.

STREET, Lucie
Novel
A 1255 : The wind on the Morfa.
London ; Hale, 1956.
192p. 18½cm. cloth.
Location : "The Morfa", North Wales.

STYLES, [Frank] Showell
Novels
A 1256 : Land from the sea.
London ; Faber, 1952.
262p. 20cm. cloth.
Location : Portmadoc, N. Wales.   The
construction of the reclamation dam of
W. H. Madocks.

A 1257 : The rising of the lark : a romance.
London, New York, [etc.] ; Selwyn & Blount,
[1946].
255p. 18½cm. cloth.
Based on the Welsh Jacobites and the 1745
Rebellion.

TABORI, Paul
Novel
A 1258 : The talking tree.
London ; Sampson Low, 1950.
246p. 18½cm. cloth.
Location : Partly located at "Teigerran",
Wales.

TAYLOR, Frederick
Drama
A 1259 : Tainted money : a Welsh comedy.
London ; Pitman, 1952.
[4], 35, [1]p. 18½cm. wrappers.

TAYLOR, Margaret Stewart
Novels
A 1260 : Another door opened.
London ; Hale, 1963.
192p. 19½cm. cloth.
Location : "Tremynach", a South Wales
industrial town.

A 1261 : The link was strong.
London ; Robert Hale, 1964.
[7], 8—191p. 19½cm. cloth.
Location : "Tremynach" (Merthyr Tydfil),
Glam.

TEGART, Kathleen Frances
Novel
A 1262 : Long vacation.
London ; Faber, 1936.
350p. 18½cm. cloth.
Location : Rural area of "Tresillet-y-Llant".

THOMAS, Alfred
Stories
A 1263 : In the land of the harp and feathers : a series
of Welsh village idylls. *New and revised
edition.*
Dolgelley ; W. Hughes & Son, 1910.
viii, 9—255p. 18½cm. wrappers.
Originally published London, H. R. Allenson,
1896.

THOMAS, Bertha
Stories
A 1264 : Picture tales from Welsh hills.
London ; T. Fisher Unwin, 1912.
251, [5]p. 19cm. cloth.

THOMAS, D. Brychan
Novel
A 1265 : The sensitive minister.
Carmarthen, Spurrell ; London, J. F. Spriggs,
1904.
viii, 316p. 18½cm. cloth.

THOMAS, Dylan Marlais

A bibliography of the works of Dylan Thomas, including his contributions to periodicals, will be found in J. A. ROLPH. *Dylan Thomas : a bibliography* (B 303). This notes the first publications, and the first appearances in book form, of the prose and poetic works of D.T. The entries below are therefore restricted to volumes of Anglo-Welsh interest published after the date of the Rolph bibliography (1956), together with a selection of the translated versions of D.T. Some locations are also shown for stories published during 1956, the year of the Rolph bibliography.

A 1266 : Letters to Vernon Watkins ; ed. with an introduction by Vernon Watkins.
London ; Dent & Faber, 1957.
[6], 7—145p. front. (port.) 22 cm. cloth.
—(American ed.) New York ; New Directions, 1957.
Includes poems by Dylan Thomas.

A 1267 : Miscellany : poems, stories, broadcasts.
London ; Dent, 1963.
vi, 118p. 18cm. wrappers.
(Aldine Paperback Series).

A 1268 : Miscellany Two : A visit to Grandpa's and other stories and poems.
London ; Dent, 1966.
v, 117p. 18cm. wrappers.
(Aldine Paperback Series).

A 1269 : Rebecca's daughters.
London ; Triton Publishing Company Ltd., 1965.
[6], 7—144p. 21½cm. cloth.
Note : An original story cast in the form of a screen play. Period is 1843 : Rebecca Rioters.

Translations :
A 1270 : [Poems] Gedichten ; vertaald door Henk Tikkemeijer.
Amsterdam, De Bonk, n.d.
31p. 19½cm. wrappers.
—2nd ed. Amsterdam, Broekman & De Meris, [1962].
33p. 19½cm. wrappers.

A 1271 : Prose e racconti.
Turin, Einaudi, 1961.
[8], 9—592p. 21½cm. cloth.
Italian translations of : Portrait of the Artist as a Young Dog—Adventures in the Skin Trade—The followers—A story—Under Milk Wood—The doctor and the devils—*Excerpts from* The World I Breathe *and* The Map of Love.

A 1272 : Pripovetke [short stories] ; trans. by Branka Petrovich. *2nd edition.*
Belgrade ; Prosveta, 1963.
Serbian version.

(*Portrait of the artist as a young dog*)
A 1273 : Als een jonge hond. Vertaald door H. Claus.
Rotterdam ; Donker, 1958.
[6], 7—166p. 18½cm. wrappers.

A 1274 : Az iró arcképe Kolyökkutya korából.
Budapest, Europa Konyvkiado, 1959.
[4], 5—201p. 16½cm. boards.

A 1275 : Porträtt av Konstnären som valp.
Stockholm ; Aldua/Bonniers, 1963.
[6], 7—141, [3]p. 18½cm. wrappers.

A 1276 : Taiteilijan Omakuva Penikkavuosilta.
Turku ; Kustannuslike Tajo, 1963.
[7], 8—176p. 21cm. cloth.

(*Under Milk Wood*)
A 1277 : Unter dem Milchwald : Dramatisches, erzählendes Lyrisches.
Reinbek bei Hamburg, Rowsht Verlag, 1958, 1960.
[6], 7—146, [12]p. 19cm. wrappers.
(Ro Ro Ro Paperbacks, no. 291).
(*Under Milk Wood* and extracts from *Quite Early One Morning* and *Deaths and Entrances*).

A 1278 : Unter dem Milchwald: ein Spiel für Stimmen.
Deutsche Nachdichtung von Erich Fried.
Heidelberg, Drei Brücken Verlag, 1954.
[4], 5—87p. 23cm. cloth.

Stories
A 1279 : The enemies.
Welsh short stories ; ed. by Gwyn Jones, 1956, 253—8.

A 1280 : Extraordinary little cough.
Tales of Innocence ; comp. by G. S. Green.
London, Faber, [1960], 236—47. [This vol. first publ. Faber, 1950 as *First View*].

A 1281 : The followers.
Smith, A. J. *and* Mason, W. H., *editors.* Short story study.
London, E. Arnold, 1961, 175—90 (with biographical notes on D.T.).

A 1282 : The orchards.
Welsh short stories ; ed. by G. Ewart Evans.
2nd ed., 1959, 113—22.

A 1283 : A story.
In Bacon, Wallace A., *and* Breen, R. S. Literature for interpretation. New York, Holt, Rinehart & Winston, 1961, 100—7.

A 1284 : A visit to Grandpa's.
Welsh short stories ; ed. by Gwyn Jones, 1956, 259—66.

Other Prose
A 1285 : I am going to read aloud : an introduction to a reading at the Massachusetts Institute of Technology, Boston, July 3, 1952.
London Magazine, Vol. 3, no. 9, 1956, 13—7.

A 1286 : A letter to Vernon Watkins. [Envelope dated April 20th, 1936, from Polgigga, Porthcurno, Penzance, Cornwall].
The London Magazine, Vol. 4, no. 9, 1957, 36—8.

Verse   : locations of more than one poem in the same anthology are listed in the order of their appearance in the anthology.

A 1287 : In Modern Verse in English ; ed. by David Cecil and A. Tate.
London, Eyre & Spottiswoode, 1958.
The force that through the green fuse drives the flower, 595.
Do not go gentle into that good night, 595—6.
After the funeral, 596—7.
Poem in October, 597—8.
Fern Hill, 600—1.
A refusal to mourn, 599—600.
And death shall have no dominion, 601—2.

A 1288 : In Modern Poetry, Vol. 7 ; ed. by Maynarp Mack and others. 2nd ed. 1961.
The force that through the green fuse . . ., 349—50.
And death shall have no dominion . . ., 351.
Fern Hill, 352—3.
Do not go gentle into that good night, 354.

A 1289 : In Faber book of modern verse. 3rd ed. rev., 1965.
The force that through . . ., 273.
Light breaks where no sun shines, 273—4.
After the funeral, 274—5.
A refusal to mourn the death, by fire, of a child in London, 276.
Poem in October, 276—8.

Verse : other locations
A 1290 : And death shall have no dominion ; Love for life ; comp. by John Hadfield, London, Book Society, 1961, 24.

The conversation of prayer ; In Palgrave, F.T. editor. The Golden Treasury . . . 5th ed. (with a new Fifth Book ed. by JohnPress). Oxford U.P., 1964, 540.

Do not go gentle into that good night ; In Blackburn, Thomas, comp. 45—60 : an anthology of English poetry. London, Putnam, 1960, 145—6.

Elegy ("Too proud to die") ; PEN 1956, 60—2 (with footnotes by Vernon Watkins).

Fern Hill ; In Palgrave, F.T. editor. The Golden Treasury . . . 5th ed. (with a new Fifth Book ed. by John Press), Oxford U.P., 1964, 542—3.

The force that through the green fuse drives the flower ; In Reeves, James, comp. The Cassell book of English poetry, 1965. No. 1002.

In memory of Ann Jones ; In Bacon, W.A. and Breen, R.S. Literature for interpretation. London, Holt, Rinehart, 1961, 274—5.

In my craft or sullen art ; In Palgrave, F.T. editor. The Golden Treasury . . . 5th ed., 1964, 541—2.

In the white giant's thigh ; In Blackburn, Thomas, comp. 45—60 : an anthology of English poetry, 1960, 146—8.

Jack of Christ ; W. Mail, July 30, 1960, 5. [First publication].

Over Sir John's Hill ; PEN 1952, 149—50.

Poem in October ; In Bacon, W. A. and Breen, R. S. Literature for interpretation, 1961, 272—4.

A refusal to mourn the death, by fire, of a child in London ;
In Palgrave, F.T. editor. The Golden Treasury . . . 5th ed., 1964, 540—1.
In Ball, W. J. and Thornley, G. C. The golden road to English literature. Book 4. London, Longmans, 1963, 115—6.

THOMAS, Evan Edward
Novel
A 1291 : Where eagles fly no bird sings.
Liverpool ; Brython Press, 1961.
210p. 18cm. cloth.
Wales in first half of the 20th century.

THOMAS, Gwyn
Novels
A 1292 : All things betray thee.
London ; Joseph, 1949.
[7], 8—318p. 18½cm. cloth.
Location : South Wales town of "Moonlea".
—American ed. Boston, U.S.A. ; Little, Brown, 1949. Entitled : *Leaves in the Wind.*

A 1293 : The alone to the alone.
London, Brussels ; Nicholson and Watson, 1947.
[6], 7—164p. 19cm. cloth.
Location : A mining village.
—American ed. Boston, U.S.A. ; Little, Brown, 1948. Entitled : *Venus and the Voters.*

A 1294 : A frost on my frolic.
London ; Gollancz, 1953.
[4], 5—285p. 18½cm. cloth.
Location : "Mynydd Coch".

A 1295 : Now lead us home.
London ; Gollancz, 1952.
[4], 5—256p. 18½cm. cloth.

A 1296 : A point of order : a novel.
London ; Gollancz, 1956.
[6], 7—224p. 18½cm. cloth.
Location: "Elmhill" and "Minerva Slopes".

A 1297 : The stranger at my side : a novel.
London ; Gollancz, 1954.
[4], 5—255. 18½cm. cloth.
Location : "Windy Way", S. Wales.

A 1298 : The dark philosophers : a novel.
In Triad one ; ed. by Jack Aistrop.
London ; Dobson, 1946, 81—193.
—Another ed. Boston ; Little, Brown, 1947.
[iv], 178p. 18½cm. cloth.

Translated version :
Pastor Emmanuel og Hans Kjaerlighet ;
trans. into Norwegian by Fredrik Wulfsberg.
Oslo ; Tiden, 1948.

A 1299 : The world cannot hear you : a comedy of
ancient desires.
London ; Gollancz, 1951.
[4], 5—288p. 18½cm. cloth.
Location : Village of "Meadow Prospect".

—American ed.   Boston, U.S.A. ; Little,
Brown, 1952.

Translated version :
Osi vagyak komediaja.
Budapest, Europa Konyrkiado, 1959.

Stories
A 1300 : Gazooka, and other stories.
London ; Gollancz, 1957.
[6], 7—200p. 18cm. cloth.

Contents : By that same door—O brother man
—As it was in the beginning—Not even then—
Gazooka—Little Fury—Where my dark
lover lies—The teacher—Tomorrow I shall
miss you less—The leaf that hurts the hand—
A team of shadows—Have you counted the
tooth marks ?—The pot of gold at Fear's End.

A 1301 : Ring Delirium 123 : [short stories].
London ; Gollancz, 1960.
[6], 7—192p. 19½cm. cloth.
[Some of the contents previously publ. in
PUNCH].

A 1302 : Where did I put my pity ? : folk tales from
the modern Welsh.
London ; Progress Publishing Co., 1946.
[6], 7—193p. 18½cm. limp board.

A 1303 : After you, Mr. Seigfeld.
The Dragon, Summer Term, 1958, 10—2.

A 1304 : And a spoonful of grief to taste.
Welsh short stories ; ed. by Gwyn Jones, 1956,
266—79.

A 1305 : The hands of Chris.
Saturday Saga. London, Progress Publishing
Co., 1946, 74—8.

A 1306 : I think, therefore I am thinking.
A-W.R., Vol. 10, no. 25, undated, 19—21.

A 1307 : The limp in my longing.
Modern Reading, no. 15 ; ed. by Reginald
Moore, London, Phoenix House, 1947,
131—8.

A 1308 : Little fury.
Pick of today's short stories, no. 5, 1954,
224—32.

A 1309 : My first upon the Stone.
New short stories, 1945—46 ; ed. by J. Singer.
Glasgow, Maclellan [1946], 148—58.

A 1310 : The pot of gold at Fear's End.
Modern Reading, no. 16 ; ed. by Reginald
Moore, London, Phoenix House, 1947,
98—107.
Little Reviews Anthology, 1949, 1—11.

A 1311 : The seeding twenties.
Pick of Today's short stories, no. 13, 1962,
186—93.

A 1312 : Thy need.
Welsh Review, Vol. VII, no. 2, 1948, 122—40.
Welsh short stories ; ed. by Gwyn Jones, 1956,
279—307.

A 1313 : Where my dark lover lies.
Welsh short stories ; ed. by G. Ewart Evans.
2nd ed., 1959, 131—40.

Other Prose
A 1314 : A hatful of humours ; edited by Brian Hamm-
ond [and] illustrated by Peter Rush.
London ; Schoolmaster Publishing Company,
1965.
[4], 5—164p. illus. 19½cm. wrappers.

A 1315 : A Welsh eye. Drawings by John Dd. Evans.
London ; Hutchinson, 1964.
[8], 9—176p. illus. 24cm. cloth.
Includes essays on literary themes. Chapter 6 :
A clutch of perished bards : W. H. Davies,
Dylan Thomas, Huw Menai.

A 1316 : Arrayed like one of these ; Pick of Punch, 1958,
108.

A 1317 : Beau ; ibid. 1963, 83—6.

A 1318 : Grace and gravy ; ibid. 1961, 106—9.

A 1319 : I dreamt that I dwelt ; ibid. 1963, 9—12.

A 1320 : If you want, I'll act it for you ; ibid. 1957, 167—71.

A 1321 : The longest evening ; Western Mail, Dec. 24, 1965, 6.

A 1322 : Night of the short thoughts ; Pick of Punch, 1959, 54—5.

A 1323 : Of all the saints ; ibid. 1955, 76—9.

A 1324 : Pass the can ; ibid. 1958, 88—91.

A 1325 : The speaking shade ; ibid. 1958, 60—1.

A 1326 : The treatment ; ibid. 1963, 41—3.

Drama

A 1327 : Jackie the Jumper.
Plays of the Year ; ed. by J. C. Trewin, Vol. 26, 1962—3, 209—97.

A 1328 : The keep : [a play in two acts].
London, Elek, 1962.
[12], 13—116p. 18½cm. cloth.
Scene : The Morton house in S. Wales, 1954.

—*Also in* Plays of the Year ; ed. by J. C. Trewin, Vol. 24, 1961, 119—232.

THOMAS, Henry Elwyn

Novels

A 1329 : The forerunner.
London ; Lynwood, 1910.
312p. front. 19cm. cloth.

—Another ed. *Cheap ed.*
Aberavon, Port Talbot ; Publ. for the Central Committee of . . . Evangelical Free Churches . . . by Rev. James Evans, [1913].
312, [4]p. 18cm. cloth.
Location : Breconshire and Carmarthenshire : mid-17th century.

A 1330 : Where Eden's tongue is spoken still.
London, H. R. Allenson ; Newport, Mon. ; G. Bell, n.d. [8], 200p. 19cm. cloth.

THOMAS, Howard

Novel

A 1331 : The singing hills.
Prospect, New York ; Prospect Books, 1964.
[iv], v—vii, [3], 274p. 20½cm. cloth.
Location : The Steuben Hills north of Utica, 1840's : Welsh settlers.

THOMAS, J. R.

Verse

A 1332 : Poems of the land and the sea.
Ammanford ; Jones and Mainwaring, *printers*, [1933].
44p. 18½cm. wrappers.

THOMAS, John

Novel

A 1333 : Lloyd of the Mill ; or, The first shall be last and the last first : a Welsh story, done into English, with some additions, by Mrs. O. Thomas.
London ; Elliot Stock, 1901.
vi, 312p. 19cm. cloth.
Location : The village of Nant.

From Welsh version : "Arthur Llwyd y Felin".

THOMAS, John Mansel

Stories

A 1334 : The big haul.
Gower, Vol. 15, 1962, 54—60.

A 1335 : Pickings.
Gower, Vol. 10, 1957, 26—30.

A 1336 : The primrose path.
Gower, Vol. 7, 1954, 19—24.

Drama

A 1337 : Barbed wire and bracken.
Morriston, Glam. ; Merlin Press, 1950.
76p. 18½cm. wrappers.
Scene : The "Rhoseithin Bay" Hotel, Welsh coast.

THOMAS, John Ormond

Verse

A 1338 : The angels in the air ; Poetry Qtly., Vol. 10, no. 1, 1948, 6.

Before the peace to be ; ibid. Vol. 5, no. 3, 1943, 110.

Birthday poem ; Welsh Review, Vol. III, no. 4, 1944, 252—5.

Bright candle, my soul ; Poetry Qtly., Vol. 5, no. 1, 1943, 25—6.

Epitaph for a shoemaker ; Gower, Vol. 15, 1962, 11.

Finding a fossil ; ibid. 34.

I, at the channel ; Poetry Qtly., Vol. 4, no. 3, 1942, 99.

Let us break down the barriers ; Modern Welsh Poetry; ed. by K. Rhys, 1944, 128—9.

Poem by air-graph : for Caradog Owen ; Poetry Scotland, no. 1, 1944 ; ed. by Maurice Lindsay, 41.

Poem in February ; Modern Welsh Poetry ; ed. by K. Rhys, 1944, 129—30. Poetry Qtly., Vol. 5, no. 1, 1943, 24.

[Poems] from "The Influences" ; Welsh Review, Vol. V, no. 3, 1946, 167—71.

Portrait of a shoemaker and my father ; Little Reviews Anthology, 1947—48 ; 159—60.

Procession ; Wales, New Series, I, 1943, 73.

Selections from "An Elegy for Alun Lewis". Stanzas 1—3 ; Wales, New Series, IV, 1944, 5—6.

Strange within the dividing ; Modern Welsh Poetry ; ed. by K. Rhys, 1944, 127—8.

Three R's ; Gower, Vol. 15, 1962, 60.

Windsor Forest fall ; Welsh Review, Vol. VII, no. 2, 93.

THOMAS, Luther

Novel
A   1339 : The deep of the earth.
London ; Macmillan, 1956.
[6], 314p.   19½cm.   cloth.
Location : Welsh mining areas.

THOMAS, Maude Morgan

Novel
A   1340 : Sing in the dark : a story of the Welsh in Pennsylvania. Illustrated by Clifford H. Schule.
Philadelphia ; John C. Winston, 1954.
xv, [1], 203p.   front. illus.   21½cm.   cloth.
(Land of The Free Series).

THOMAS, Muriel Morfydd

Drama
A   1341 : Dream folk and fairies, and other plays for St. David's Day.
London ; Foyle's, [1928].
[4], 5—80p.   15cm.   wrappers.

Contents : Dream and fairies—The spinning wheel—The saint by the roadside—The young brigand—The keeper of the chest—The house of March.

THOMAS, Murray

Novel
A   1342 : Buzzards pick the bones.
London, New York, [etc.] ; Longmans, Green, 1932.
[6], 327p.   19cm.   cloth.
Location : "Mynyth Moel" in the Cader Idris range of mountains.

THOMAS, Nathaniel

Novel
A   1343 : The Idol of Aberolwen : a Welsh story.
Carmarthen ; Spurrell, [1927].
119p.   18½cm.   wrappers.
Location : "Aberolwen", a Welsh coastal village.

THOMAS, Norman

Novel
A   1344 : Ask at the Unicorn.
London ; Weidenfeld & Nicolson, 1962.
222p.   19½cm.   cloth.
Location : The village of "Dyfneint".

THOMAS, R. M.

Novel
A   1345 : Trewern : a tale of the thirties.
London ; T. Fisher Unwin, 1901.
vi, 246p.   18½cm.   cloth.
Location : Trewern in "Merlinshire" (Carmarthenshire ?).
NLW copy signed by R. M. Thomas.

THOMAS, Ronald Stuart

Verse
A   1346 : An acre of land.
Newtown ; Montgomeryshire Printing Co., 1952.
[6], 7—38p.   21½cm.   wrappers.
—Another impression.   1952.

A   1347 : The bread of truth.
London ; R. Hart-Davis, 1963.
[4], 5—48p.   20½cm.   cloth.

A   1348 : The minister.
Newtown ;   Montgomeryshire   Printing Company, 1953.
[8], 9—24p.   21½cm.   limp boards.
Broadcast by the B.B.C., 18th September, 1952 in the series "Radio Odes".

A   1349 : Poetry for supper.
London ; R. Hart-Davis, 1958.
[6], 7—48p.   20½cm.   cloth.

A 1350 : Song at the year's turning : poems, 1942—
1954.
Introduction by John Betjeman.
London ; R. Hart-Davis, 1955.
[6], 7—115p. 20½cm. cloth.
Comprises 19 of the 37 poems publ. as "Stones
of the Field" ; 25 of the 31 poems publ. in
"An Acre of Land" ; "The Minister" as
broadcast ; 19 poems under separate title
of "Later Poems".

A 1351 : The stones of the field.
Carmarthen ; Druid Press, 1946.
[6], 7—48, [1]p. 18½cm. boards.

A 1352 : Tares : poems.
London ; R. Hart-Davis, 1961.
[6], 7—48p. 20½cm. cloth.

Verse   : contributions to anthologies. Locations of
more than one poem collected in the same
anthology are noted in the order in which
they appear in the anthology :

A 1353 : *In* Blackburn, Thomas, *comp.* 45—60 : an
anthology, Putnam, 1960.
Pisces, 149.
Saint Antony, 149.
Evans, 150.
Iago Prytherch, 151.

A 1354 : *In* Gillam, C. W. *ed.* Modern poems under-
stood. London, Harrap, 1965.
Too late, 41.
Hireling, 42.
The evacuee, 65—6.
Ninetieth birthday, 102.

A 1355 : *In* Poetry London X ; *ed.* by Tambimuttu,
1944.
Farm labourer, 174.
The strange Spring, 174.
A peasant, 175.
Homo sapiens, 1941, 175—6.
Evensong, 175.
Memories of Yeats whilst travelling to Holy-
head, 176.

A 1356 : *In* The Faber book of modern verse. 3rd ed.
rev., 1965.
Song for Gwydion, 320.
Death of a peasant, 320.
Evans, 321.
The country clergy, 321.

Verse   : other locations.
A 1357 : The belfry ; London Magazine (N.S.), Vol. 3,
no. 9, 1963, 13—4.

A blackbird singing ; Poetry 1960 : Critical
Qtly., Poetry Supplement, no. 1, 4.

Border blues ; Dock L., Vol. 4, no. 11, 1953,
8—11.

Ceridwen ; Transatlantic Review, No. 18,
1965, [78].

Children's song ; TLS, May 1, 1953, 288.

Confessions of an Anglo-Welshman ; Wales,
New Series, 2, Oct. 1943, 49.

Commission (for Raymond Garlick) ; Dock
L., Vol. 6, no. 17, 1955, 17.

Country church (Manafon) ; Wales, Vol. VI,
no. 3, 1946, 14.

The country clergy ; *In* Palgrave, F. T. *editor*,
The Golden Treasury . . . 5th ed. (with a
new Fifth Book ed. by John Press), Oxford
U.P., 1964, 537.

Cynddylan on a tractor ; Listening and
Writing ; (ed. by M. F. Doolan).
BBC Radio for Schools (Summer Term
1966, 39).
Poetry Book Magazine, Vol. 6, no. 5,
Fall 1954, 7.

Darlington ; Rann, no. 19 (Welsh number),
1953, 17—8.

Depopulation of the hills ; Dock L., Vol. 2,
no. 6, 1951, 23.

Eh ? ; PEN 1963, 123.

Evans ; PEN 1957, 117—8.

Exile; Critical Qtly., Vol. 6, no. 3, 1964, 212.

[Extract from] A Peasant : "Iago Prytherch
his name . . . to gob in the fire . . ." ; *In*
Ross, Alan. Poetry, 1945—50. London,
Longmans, for the British Council 1951,
38—9.

A Farmer ; Wales, New Series, 2, October,
1943, 48.

Frost ; ibid.

From home ; W. Mail, Aug. 20, 1960, 5.

Gideon Pugh ; Wales, Vol. IV, no. 6, 1945, 47.
(Author noted as S. R. Thomas).

Green categories ; TLS, April 27, 1956, 256.

The guests ; trans. from the Welsh of Dilys
Cadwaladr. Wales, Vol. VIII, no. 29, 1948,
541—3.

Hafod Lom ; W. Mail Literary Review,
April 16, 1964, 9.

Half-past five ; Transatlantic Review, No. 18,
1965, [78].

Here ; Poetry 1960 : Critical Qtly., Poetry Supplement, no. 1, 19.
In Palgrave, F. T. editor, The Golden Treasury . . . 5th ed., 1964, 537—8.

Hill farmer ; Wales, Vol. VIII, no. 29, 1948, 511.

The hill farmer speaks ; ibid. 536.

Hiraeth ; ibid. Vol. VI, no. 2, 1946, 7.

Iago Prytherch ; PEN 1957, 118.

In a country church ; TLS, Jan. 14, 1955, 21.

The labourer ; Wales, New Series, 2, October 1943, 48.

Lament for Prytherch ; Encounter, Vol. III, no. 1, 1954, 11.

Llanddewi Brefi ; Wales, Vol. VIII, no. 29, 1948, 521.

Lore ; Critical Qtly., Vol. 2, no. 4, 1960, 340.

Man and tree ; Wales, Vol. VI, no. 3, 1946, 13.

Meet the family ; PEN 1957, 117.

The Meeting ; English Poetry Now : Critical Qtly., Poetry Supplement, no. 3, 1962, 4—5.

Night and morning ; (trans. from the Welsh), Wales, Vol. VI, no. 2, 1946, 7.

Ninetieth birthday, Hill farm ; PEN 1961, 97,

Not so ; PEN 1962, 113—5.

The old language ; Wales, Vol. VI, no. 3, 1946, 13. Little Reviews Anthology, 1947—48, 163.

An old woman ; Wales, Vol. VIII, no. 30, 1948, 642.

On hearing a Welshman speak ; Dock L., Vol. 5, no. 14, 1954, 3.

Out of the hills ; Little Reviews Anthology, 1945, 175—6.
Wales, New Series, 3, January 1944, 11—2.

A peasant ; Modern Welsh Poetry ; ed. by K. Rhys, 1944, 130—1.
A Book of Wales ; ed. by D. M. & E. M. Lloyd, 1953, 151.

A person from Porlock ; PEN 1953, 88.

Propaganda ; Wales, New Series, 2, October 1943, 49.

The poet's address to the businessmen ; PEN 1960, 109.

The question ; Modern Welsh Poetry, 1944, 131.

Rhodri ; Healing of the Nations ; ed. by Vera Rich, A-W.R. Poetry Suppl., 1965, 8.

The Rising of Glyndŵr ; Wales, Vol. IV, no. 6, Winter 1944/45, 81.

Rose Cottage ; Critical Qtly., Vol. 6, no. 3, 1964, 213.

The scapegoat ; Outposts, no. 21, 1952, 7.

Sick visits ; Critical Qtly., Vol. 4, no. 2, 1962, 150. English Poetry Now : Critical Qtly., Poetry Suppl. no. 3, 1962, 4.

To the tourist ; Dock L., Vol. 3, no. 8, 1952, 4.

The tree ; Pencader Poems, 1952, [6—7].

Two figures ; TLS, April 1, 1960, 214.

Two versions of a theme ; Agenda, Vol. 4, no. 1, 1965, 18—9.

Wales ; Wales, Vol. VII, no. 26, 1947, 286.

A Welsh ballad singer ; Encounter, Vol. III, no. 6, 1954, 64.

Winter retreat ; Wales, Vol. IV, no. 5, 1944, 7.

Work to do ; Critical Qtly., Vol. 6, no. 3, 1964, 212.

THOMAS, Trevor Cyril

Story
A 1358 : Parson's orphan.
Pick of today's short stories, no. 7, 1956, 237—48.

Drama
A 1359 : Davy Jones's dinner : a Welsh comedy in one act.
London ; J. Garnet Miller, 1955.
[4], 5—31p. 18½cm. wrappers.
Location : A Welsh station signal-box.

—Also in : Best one-act plays of 1954—55. Harrap, 1956, 43—70.

A 1360 : Davy Jones's locker : a comedy of Welsh life in one act.
London ; J. Garnet Miller, 1956.
[5], 6—30p. 18½cm. wrappers.
Location : A Welsh railway signal-box.

"THORNE, Guy", *pseud. [i.e. Cyril Ranger Gull]*

Novel
A 1361 : Harder than steel.
London ; T. Werner Laurie, [1919].
[4], 217p. 18½cm. cloth.
Location : Partly at "Pendrylas", N. Wales.

TRAHERNE, Mrs. Arthur

Novel
A 1362 : The ghost of Tintern Abbey.
Clifton ; J. Baler, 1901.
vi, 313p. 19cm. cloth.
Location : Tintern Abbey, Mon.

TREFOR, Eirlys, *pseud. [Mrs. Eirlys Williams]*

Novel
A 1363 : Light cakes for tea.
London, Melbourne, [etc.] ; Hutchinson, 1958.
[6], 7—240p. 19½cm. cloth. (New Authors Limited).
Location : The village of "Cwm".
Stories
A 1364 : Mountain of Bronwen.
A.W. Review, Vol. 9, no. 23, undated, 68—77.

A 1365 : The promise.
Wales, Jan. 1959, 24—9.

TUCKER, Norman

Novels
A 1366 : Gay salute.
London, New York, [etc.] ; John Long, 1946.
192p. 18½cm. cloth.
Location : Partly North Wales : Jacobite Rebellion of 1745.

A 1367 : Minions of the moon.
London, New York, [etc.]; John Long, [1946].
208p. 18½cm. cloth.
Location : N. Wales during the Second Civil War : Sir John Owen : 1648.

A 1368 : No coward soul.
London, New York, [etc.] ; John Long, 1947.
255p. 18½cm. cloth.
Location : N. Wales coastal areas : Napoleonic War.

A 1369 : Restless we roam.
London, New York, [etc.]; John Long, [1950].
239p. 18½cm. cloth.
Location : Civil War in N. Wales : capture of Caernarvon and the siege of Denbigh Castle.

A 1370 : The Rising Gull.
London, New York, [etc.] ; John Long, 1952.
[4], 5—256p. 18½cm. cloth.
Location : Partly North Wales.

"TWM TEG", *pseud. [i.e. Colwyn Edward Vulliamy]*

Novel
A 1371 : Jones, a gentleman of Wales.
London ; Chapman & Hall, 1954.
[9], 10—232p. front. 20cm.
Location : "Lwmpsygraban".

VAL BAKER, Denys

Novel
A 1372 : The white rock.
London ; Sylvan Press, 1945.
[4], 5—196p. 18cm. cloth.
Location : N. Wales Coast, Snowdonia.
Stories
A 1373 : The mountain.
Dock Leaves, Vol. 2, no. 4, 1951, 13—7.

A 1374 : The woman on the couch.
Welsh Review, Vol. VI, no. 3, 1947, 177—84.

VALE, Edmund

Novels
A 1375 : Porth smuggler : a novel.
London, Edinburgh, [etc.] ; Nelson, 1926.
vii, 318p. 18cm. cloth.

A 1376 : The offing.
London, Toronto ; Dent, 1932.
[6], 308p. 18½cm. cloth.
Location : Valley of "Cwm Bychan".

VAUGHAN, Aled

Stories
A 1377 : The blarney gets the business : a short story.
Wales, no. 40, 1959, 34—9.

A 1378 : The feud.
Celtic Story, Number one ; ed. by A. Vaughan, 1946, 71—9.

A 1379 : The fever.
Gower, Vol. 15, 1962, 19—21. [Extract from a novel in progress].

A 1380 : Ifan Roberts' investment.
John O'London's Weekly, February 23, 1945, 205.
As The investment ; Welsh short stories ; ed. by G. Ewart Evans, 2nd ed. 1959, 141—50.

A 1381 : The white dove.
Welsh short stories ; ed. by Gwyn Jones, 1956. 308—12.
Stories and Afterthoughts ; selected by W. H. Mason, Oxford, Blackwell, 1965, 137—43.

VAUGHAN, Arthur Owen   *"Owen Rhoscomyl"*

Novel
A 1382 : Vronina : a tale of the Welsh mountains.
London ; Duckworth, 1907.
viii, 309, 20p. col. front. 18cm. cloth.

—Another impression. 1912.
310p. front. cloth.
Story
A 1383 : Mr. Tudor Carreg—and Norah.
Blackwood's Magazine, May 1911, 621—39.

VAUGHAN, Herbert Millingchamp

Prose
A 1384 : Nephelococcygia ; or, Letters from Paradise.
Carmarthen ; Spurrell, [1929].
vii, 1, 163p. 19cm. cloth.
Includes seven short stories, some on Welsh themes.

A 1385 : The last of the old squire (temp. 1750).
Welsh Outlook, Vol. II, 1915, 437—8.

A 1386 : "Luc Sais".
Welsh Outlook, Vol. V, 1918, 260—1.

A 1387 : Margaret Tŷ Coch.
Welsh Outlook, Vol. V, 1918, 228.

A 1388 : Martha Lewis.
Welsh Outlook, Vol. V, 1918, 356—7.

VAUGHAN, Hilda   [*afterwards Mrs. Charles Morgan*]

Novels
A 1389 : The battle to the weak.
London ; Heinemann, 1925.
[6], 7—288p. 18½cm. cloth.
Location : Welsh rural areas : "Llangantyn", etc.

—Another ed. New York & London ; Harper, n.d. [6], 7—288p. 19cm. cloth.
—Queensway Press, 1936. (Chevron Books, no. 17).

A 1390 : The candle and the light.
London ; Macmillan, 1954.
[6], 313p. 19cm. cloth.
Location : Welsh country town (Brecon conjectured).

A 1391 : The curtain rises.
London ; Gollancz, 1935.

[11], 12—463p. 19½cm. cloth.
Location : Partly in Wales (Radnorshire border areas).

—American ed. New York ; C. Scribner's Sons, 1935.

A 1392 : Harvest home.
London ; Gollancz, 1936.
[9], 10—288p. 18½cm. cloth.
Location : "Abercoran" and the house of "Hafod".
—Another ed. Cheap ed. 1938.

A 1393 : Her Father's house.
London ; Heinemann, 1930.
[10], 345p. 18½cm. cloth.
Location : Radnorshire.

A 1394 : Here are lovers.
London ; Heinemann, 1926.
viii, 325, 8p. 19cm. cloth.
Location : Welsh rural area : "Llangantyn", etc.

A 1395 : The invader.
London ; Heinemann, 1928.
[8], 336p. 18½cm. cloth.
Location : A farm, "Plas Newydd".

—Another ed. London & New York ; Harper, 1928. 339p.

A 1396 : Iron and gold.
London ; Macmillan, 1948.
vii, [1], 234p. 19cm. cloth.
Location : A Welsh hill farm.

—American ed. New York ; Duell, Sloane and Peace, 1942.
Published as : *The fair woman.*

A 1397 : Pardon and peace.
London ; Macmillan, 1945.
v, [1], 204p. 19cm. cloth.
Location : The Vale of "Clydath" and village of "Bryntawel".

A 1398 : The Soldier and the gentlewoman.
London ; Gollancz, 1932.
[10], 11—287p. 18½cm. cloth.
Location : Welsh rural estate : "Plas Einon".

—American ed. New York ; C. Scribner's Sons, 1932.

A 1399 : A thing of nought.   Decorations by Lee-Elliott.
London ; Lovat Dickson & Thompson, 1934.
[6], 7—51p. illus. boards.
Location : "Cwmbach Farm", border country.

—Another ed. Revised ed. London ; Percival Marshall, 1948. 55p. 22cm.

—American ed.   New York ; C. Scribner's Sons, 1935.

Other Prose
A 1400 : A Country childhood.
Lovat Dickson's Magazine, October 1934.

A 1401 : Far away, not long ago.
Lovat Dickson's Magazine, January, 1935.

Drama
A 1402 : She was too young, by Hilda Vaughan and Laurier Lister.
London ; Constable, 1938.
[6], 125p. illus. 18cm. wrappers.
Scene : Hall of a Welsh country house.

VAUGHAN, Richard, *pseud. [i.e. Ernest Lewis Thomas]*

Novels
A 1403 : All through the night.
London ; R. Hart-Davis, 1957.
[6], 7—130p. 19½cm. cloth.
Location : "Crognant", the Van Mountains.

Translated versions :
1958 ; Denmark, Germany.

A 1404 : Moulded in earth.
London ; J. Murray, 1951.
[6], 7—288p. 18½cm. cloth.
Location : "Trewern" (Carmarthenshire) farming community.

—Another ed. London ; Transworld Publishers, 1954.
283p. 16cm. wrappers. (Corgi Books, T48)
Translated versions :
1951 : Germany.
1961 : Netherlands.

A 1405 : Son of Justin.
London ; J. Murray, 1955.
[6], 7—200p. 18½cm. cloth.
Location : Van Mountains, farming community.

A 1406 : There is a river.
London ; R. Hart-Davis, 1961.
[8], 9—191p. 19½cm. cloth.
Location : Carmarthenshire.

A 1407 : Who rideth so wild.
London ; J. Murray, 1952.
[6], 7—283, [1]p. 18½cm. cloth.
Location : Dyfnant Valley, Van Mountains.

VERNON, David

Stories
A 1408 : The island, and other stories.
London ; Fortune Press, 1951.
[5], 6—131p. 18½cm. cloth.
Some stories on Welsh themes.

A 1409 : The chair.
Welsh Review, Vol. VII, no. 4, 1948, 282—4.

A 1410 : Wings.
Welsh Review, Vol. IV, no. 1, 1945, 13—9.

VULLIAMY, Colwyn Edward

Novel
A 1411 : The proud walkers.
London ; Chapman & Hall, 1955.
[9], 10—240p. 18½cm. cloth.
Location : "Llaneinioes" (S. Wales mining areas).

WALKER, *Mrs.* Hugh

Novel
A 1412 : With a great price : a Welsh story.
London ; Daniel O'Connor, 1921.
[8], 322p. 18cm. cloth.
Location : The village and parish of "Llaneirin", North Wales.

WALSH, J[ames] M[organ]

Novels
A 1413 : King of Tiger Bay.
London ; Collins, 1952.
192p. 18½cm. cloth.
Location : Cardiff dockland area.

A 1414 : Once in Tiger Bay.
London ; Collins, 1947.
256p. 18½cm. cloth.
Location : Cardiff dockland area.

WALTERS, Meurig

Verse
A 1415 : Age ; Welsh Review, Vol. II, no. 3, 1939, 142.

Rhondda ; Modern Welsh Poetry ; ed. by K. Rhys, 1944, 135.

Rhondda poems ; Wales, no. 4, March 1938, 150.
ibid. no. 10, October 1939, 273.

Seminary ; Modern Welsh Poetry ; ed. by K. Rhys, 1944, 136.

Two Rhondda poems ; Welsh Review, Vol. I, no. 2, 1939, 69.

Autumn song ; W. Mail, Oct. 31, 1964, 6.

WARD, Edith Marjorie

Novels
A 1416 : Isle of saints.
          London ; Methuen, 1943.
          [4], 219p. 18½cm. cloth.
          Location : Aberystwyth & North Cardigan-
          shire during early years of Second World
          War.

A 1417 : Voices in the wind.
          London ; Methuen, 1944.
          [4], 251p. 18½cm. cloth.
          Location : Partly Conway, N. Wales. Wartime

WARWICK, Pauline, *pseud. [i.e. Betty Evelyn Davies]*

Novels
A 1418 : Death of a sinner.
          London, Toronto, [etc.] ; Cassell, 1944.
          [4], 184p. 18cm. cloth.
          Location : The house of "Vron" and the
          "Llanwenno" area of S. Wales.

A 1419 : The Welsh widow.
          London, Toronto, [etc.] ; Cassell, 1948.
          352p. 18½cm. cloth.
          Location : A Welsh university town, "Rhyd-
          arthur".

WATKINS, Vernon [Phillips]

Verse
A 1420 : Affinities.
          London ; Faber, 1962.
          [6], 7—99p. 21½cm. cloth.

A 1421 : Ballad of the Mari Lwyd, and other poems.
          London ; Faber, 1941.
          [6], 7—92p. 22cm. cloth.
          —Another ed. 2nd. ed. Faber, 1947.

A 1422 : Cypress and acacia.
          London ; Faber, 1959.
          [6], 7—102p. 22cm. cloth.

A 1423 : The death bell : poems and ballads.
          London ; Faber, 1954.
          [8], 9—112p. 22cm. cloth.

A 1424 : The lady with the unicorn.
          London ; Faber, 1948.
          [8], 9—104p. 21½cm. cloth.

A 1425 : The lamp and the veil : poems by Vernon
          Watkins.
          London ; Faber, 1945.
          [4], 5—61p. 22cm. cloth.
          Edges uncut.

A 1426 : Selected poems.
          Norfolk, Conn., U.S.A. ; New Directions,
          1948.
          [8], 92p. 22cm. cloth.

Verse   : collections of poems included in the same
          volume are entered in the order in which
          they appear in the volume.

A 1427 : *In* Wales, no. 2, August, 1937.
          Empty hands, 61.
          The dancer in the leaves, 61.
          The turning of the leaves, 62.
          The sunbather, 63—4.
          Indolence, 64.

A 1428 : *In* Modern Welsh Poetry ; ed. by K. Rhys,
          1944.
          Llewelyn's chariot, 136—7.
          The sunbather, 137—8.
          The collier, 139—40.

A 1429 : *In* The colour of saying : an anthology of
          verse spoken by Dylan Thomas ; ed. by
          R. N. Maud and A. T. Davies, 1963.
          A lover's words, 152—3.
          The collier, 153—5.

A 1430 : *In* Modern verse in English, ed. by David
          Cecil & Allen Tate, London, 1958.
          The fire in the snow, 498—9.
          Ophelia, 499—500.
          The sunbather, 500—1.
          The feather, 501—2.

A 1431 : *In* The White Horseman ; ed. by J. F. Hendry
          and H. Treece. Routledge, 1941.
          Mana, 120—1.
          The mummy, 122—3.
          The keen shy flame, 124—5.
          In memory of Elizabeth Corbett Yeats, 126.
          After sunset, 127—32.

A 1432 : *In* The Faber book of modern verse ; ed. by
          M. Roberts. New ed., 1951.
          The turning of the leaves, 365—6.
          Music of colours—white blossom, 366—7.
          Foal, 368—9.
          A christening remembered, 369.

A 1433 : *In* The Faber book of twentieth-century verse ;
          ed. by J. Heath-Stubbs and D. Wright,
          Faber, 1953.
          The feather, 339—40.
          Indolence, 340.
          The collier, 340—2.
          The healing of the leper, 342—3.
          Zacchaeus in the leaves, 343—7.

A 1434 : *In* Poetry in Wartime ; ed. by M. J. Tambim-
          uttu, 1942.
          The shooting of Werfel, 181—2.
          The spoils of war, 183—4.
          Griefs of the sea, 184—5.
          Unveiling the statue, 186—90.

A 1435 : *In* Poetry of the present ; comp. by G. Grigson,
          1949.
          The collier, 221—2.
          Atlas on grass, 223.
          The dead words, 223.

A   1436 : *In* More Poems from the Forces ; ed. by K. Rhys, 1943.
Tempters, 304—6.
Griefs of the sea, 306—7.
The room of pity, 308.
Indolence, 309.

Verse   Other locations

A   1437 : All compact ; Review of English Literature Vol. 5, no. 4, 1964, 58.

Angelo's Adam ; Poetry 1960 : Critical Qtly. Poetry Supplement, [no. 1], 17.

A true picture restored : memories of Dylan Thomas ; The London Magazine, Vol. 1, no. 11, 1954, 40—3.

Autumn song ; Modern Verse, 1900—50 ; comp. by Phyllis M. Jones. 2nd ed. enl., Oxford U.P., 1955, 191—2.

The ballad of Culver's hole ; Gower, Vol. 5, 1952, 22—5.

Ballad of the Equinox ; Gower : journal of the Gower Society, Vol. 1, 1948, 8—9.
Presenting Welsh Poetry, 1959, 111—3.

Ballad of Hunt's Bay ; *In* Blackburn, Thomas, *comp*. 45—60 : an anthology. Putnam, 1960, 164—8.

Ballad of the rough sea ; LLT. Vol. 22, no. 25, 1939, 408—9.

Ballad of the Trial of Sodom ; Poetry (Chicago), Vol. 81, no. 5, 1953, 307—12. (Broadcast in B.B.C.'s "New Soundings").

Ballad of the two tapsters ; Little Reviews Anthology ; ed. by D. Val Baker, 1946, 87—9.
Focus One ; ed. by B. Rajan and A. Pearse. London, Dobson, 1945, 77—8.

Bishopston stream ; The London Magazine, Vol. 8, no. 1, 1961, 33.

Browning in Venice ; PEN 1960, 113—5.

Call it all names, but do not call it rest ; Poetry (Chicago), Vol. 81, no. 1, 1952, 83-4.
Outposts, no. 23, 1953, 1.

Camelot ; PEN 1957, 125—7.

The collier ; Wales, no. 6/7, March 1939, 205—6. Poetry Book Magazine, Vol. 6, no. 5, Fall 1954, 8—9.

The dead shag ; *In* Blackburn, Thomas, *comp*. 45—60 : an anthology, 1960, 162—3.
Botteghe Oscure, no. 9, 1952, 205—6.
PEN 1953, 61—2.

The dead words ; Modern Welsh Poetry ; ed. by K. Rhys, 1944, 140.

Demands of the muse ; Outposts, no. 45, 1960, 2—3.

Discoveries ; The Faber book of modern verse. 3rd ed. rev. Faber, 1965, 330—1.

Elegy on the heroine of childhood ; LLT, Vol. 22, no. 23, [1939], 55—7.

Epithalamion ; Botteghe Oscure, no. 9, 1952, 206—8. PEN 1953, 63—5.

The exacting ghost ; Encounter, Vol. 5, no. 6, 1955, 51. PEN 1956, 31—3.

Expectation of life ; Texas Qtly., Vol. 2, no. 2, 1959, 20—2.

Fidelities ; PEN 1963, 131.

First joy ; Focus One ; ed. by B. Rajan and A. Pearse. London, Dobson, 1945, 76.

The fossil ; TLS, Sep. 9, 1960, lxx.

From my loitering ; Modern Welsh Poetry ; ed. by K. Rhys, 1944, 143—4. Wales, no. 4, March 1938, 148.

Goleufryn ; Wales, New Series, I, 1943, 29-30.

Griefs of the sea ; Wales, no. 1, Summer 1937, 21.

The heron ; *In* Palgrave, F.T. *ed*. The Golden Treasury . . . 5th ed. (with a new Fifth Book, ed. by John Press), O.U.P., 1964, 506—7.

Hymn (for a Thanksgiving) ; Outposts, no. 11, 1948, 9.

In defence of sound ; Time and Tide, 13th Dec. 1958, 1526.

Ilston ; Gower, Vol. 5, 1952, 31.

The immortal in nature ; Outposts, no. 29, 1956, 1.

Lace-maker ; Partisan Review, Vol 20, no. 3, 1953, 298—9.

The last poems of Yeats ; LLT, Vol. 23, no. 27, 1939, 312—3.

Llewelyn's chariot ; LLT, Vol. 36, no. 67, March 1943, 151—2.

Llewelyn's spoon ; Wales, New Series, 3, January 1944, 74—5. Little Reviews Anthology, 1949, 145—7.

An LMNTRE alphabet ; Swift Annual, No. 8; ed. by Clifford Makins. Longacre P., 1961, 19.

Lover and girl ; Writing Today, 2 ; ed. by D. Val Baker, 1945, 68.

The mare ; The Faber book of modern verse. 3rd ed. rev. Faber, 1965, 331—2.

The mother and child ; Little Reviews Anthology ; ed. by Val Baker, Allen & Unwin, 1943, 120.

Moments ; The London Magazine, Vol. 2, no. 5, 1955, 18—9.

The mortal immortal ; The Poetry Review, Vol. 42, no. 3, 1951, 133—4.

Music of colours : the blossom scattered ; Outposts, no. 17, 1950, 2—3.

Music of colours—white blossom ; Poetry Qtly., Vol. 4, no. 3, 1942, 87—8.

New Year, 1965 ; The Listener, 73, Jan. 7, 1965, 22—3.

Ode ; Encounter, Vol. II, no. 6, June 1954, 34—5.

Ode at the spring equinox ; The London Magazine, Vol. 5, no. 4, 1958, 11—3.

Ode to Swansea ; Nimbus, Summer 1952.

On the death of Alun Lewis ; Little Reviews Anthology ; ed. by D. Val Baker, 1945, 93.

Orbits 1 : The Colosseum and the outer spaces.
2 : The revolution of the heart ; In Healing of the Nations ; ed. by Vera Rich, A-W.R. Suppl., 1965, 41—3. [Repr. from "The Hudson Review"].

Peace in the Welsh hills ; The London Magazine, Vol. 1, no. 2, 1954, 13—4.
PEN 1955, 99—100.
Palgrave, F.T., ed. The Golden Treasury . . . 5th ed. (with a new Fifth Book, ed. by John Press). Oxf. U.P., 1964, 507—9.

Phaedra ; The London Magazine (New Series), Vol. 1, no. 9, 1961, 8—10.

Poems for Llewelyn ; Life and Letters Today, Vol. 24, no. 31, March 1940, 278—9.

Poet and goldsmith ; The London Magazine, Vol. 1, no. 6, 1954, 13—4.

Portrait of a friend ; Life and Letters Today, Vol. 23, no. 27, [1939], 195—7.

The present ; The London Magazine, Vol. 8, no. 1, 1961, 32.

A question of time ; Partisan Review, Vol. 31, no. 3, 1964, 380—1.

The razor shell ; Gower, Vol. 15, 1962, 18.

Renaissance ; The Poetry Review, Vol. 42, no. 5, 1951, 248—9.

A reply to Roland Mathias ; Dock L., Vol. 2, no. 4, 1951, 4.

Resting places ; London Magazine (New Series), Vol. 1, no. 9, 1961, 10—11.

The return ; The London Magazine, Vol. 2, no. 5, 1955, 15—16.

Returning to Goleufryn ; Modern Welsh Poetry ; ed. by K. Rhys, 1944, 141—3.

Secrecy ; Botteghe Oscure (Quaderno XV) Rome, 1955, 93—4.

The sloe ; PEN 1956, 29.

The smoke of cities passed ; Critical Qtly., Vol. 1, no. 1, 1959, 72.

Song of the gravesdropper ; Outposts, no. 13, 1949, 6—7.

Sonnet : Innocent sleep ; Wales, Vol. VII, no. 26, 1947, 287.

Sonnet (on the Death of Alun Lewis) ; Wales, New Series, 4, 1944, 7.

Sonnet : pit-boy ; Wales, no. 10, October 1939, 272.

Swedenborg's Skull ; PEN 1958, 109—10.

Sycamore ; Modern Welsh Poetry ; ed. by K. Rhys, 1944, 141.

Taliesin in Gower ; Gower, Vol. 3, 1950, 24—5.

The three friends ; Rann, no. 19 (Welsh number), 1953, 10.

Touch with your fingers ; Botteghe Oscure, no. 18, 1956, 93—4.

The tributary seasons ; The Sunday Independent, Nov. 17, 1957, 10.
[This poem was awarded a first prize of £300 in the Guinness Poetry Awards, 1957].

Triton Time ; Wales, no. 1, Summer, 1937, 22.

True and false art ; Wales, Vol. IX, no. 31, 1949, 14.

Trust darkness ; The London Magazine, Vol. 2, no. 5, 1955, 16—8. PEN 1956, 29—31.

Two sources of life ; The London Magazine (N.S.), Vol. 1, no. 11, 1962, 22—3.

Vine ; PEN 1960, 112.
Time and Tide, Dec. 6, 1958, 1460.

Waterfalls ; W. Mail, Aug. 6, 1960, 7.

Westminster Bridge ; Wales, Vol. VI, no. 3, 1946, 18.
In Ross, Alan.   Poetry, 1945—1950. London, Longmans, 1951, 47.

Woodpecker and lyre-bird ; Poetry (Chicago), Vol. 81, no. 5, 1953, 305—6.

Yeats in Dublin ; LLT, Vol. 21, no. 20, 1939, 67—78.

Yeat's Tower ; Wales, no. 3, Autumn 1937, 86—7.

WATTS, Sidney G.

Verse
A   1438 : Some thoughts set down in quiet hours.
[No imprint].   Privately pr. for the author.
1935.   [8]p.   21cm.   wrappers.

A   1439 : Twilight reveries : calm and conflict.
Newport, Mon. ;   A. T. James, 1945.
84, [4]p.   port. 21cm.   cloth.

WEBB, Harri

Verse
A   1440 : Anial dir ; Wales, Vol. IX, no. 31, 1949, 52—3.

Big night ; Triad, by P. Griffith [and others] 1963, 45.

The boomerang in the parlour ; Poetry Wales, I, 1965, 14.

Carmarthen Coast ; Triad, 1963, 52—3.
Wales, Sep. 1958, [71].

Llys Ifor Hael (from the Welsh of Evan Evans, Ieuan Fardd) ; Triad ; 49.

Local boy makes good ; Triad, 1963, 47.

The nightingales ; ibid. 56.

Romantic peeps at remote peoples ; Poetry Wales, Vol. 1, no. 2, 1965, 23—4.

To Wales ; Triad, 1963, 57.

Towy idyll ; ibid. 50.

Triumphal entry ; ibid. 48.
Wales, Vol. IX, no. 31, 1949, 15.

Tŷ Ddewi : a prayer at St. David's ; Triad 1963, 54—5.

Valley winter ; ibid. 46.

Young fellow from Lleyn (trans. from the Welsh of William Jones, 1896—1961); ibid. 51.

WELLS, George

Novel
A   1441 : The Danecourt romance.
London ; A. H. Stockwell, [1923].
vi, [2], 9—267p.   18cm.   cloth.
Location : Partly in Wales.

WEST, Frederick William

Novel
A   1442 : A Welsh courtship.
London ; Jarrolds, [1931].
288, 32p.   18½cm.   cloth.
Location : Llandrillo-yn-Rhos, N. Wales.

"A WHISPER", pseud. [i.e.   ]

Novel
A   1443 : Ffynon the Sin-eater.
London ; Holden & Hardingham, [1914].
[6], 288, [4]p.   18½cm.   cloth.
Location : "Tanyrallt" and the village of "Llanbrenadog".

WHITE, Jon Ewbank Manchip

Verse
A   1444 : Dragon, and other poems.
London ; Fortune Press, 1943.
32p.   18cm.   cloth.
Includes some poems on Welsh themes.

WILLIAMS, Alis Mallt   "Y Ddau Wynne"

Novel
A   1445 : A maid of Cymru : a patriotic romance.
London, Simpkin Marshall ;   Carmarthen, Spurrell, n.d. 328p.   19cm.   cloth.
Location :   "Crawnant"   and   "Cynidr", Breconshire (?).
NLW has Llanover Library copy.

WILLIAMS, [David] Gwyn

Verse

A 1446 : Application for citizenship ; Personal land-scape : an anthology of exile. Editions Poetry Ltd., 1945, 110. (Indexed as 101).

Against women ; trans. from an anonymous 16th century Welsh poem "Araith ddychan i'r gwragedd". Welsh Review, Vol. VII, no. 1, 1948, 36—47.

The cock pheasant ; trans. from "Y Ceiliog Ffesant" of R. W. Parry ; Welsh Review, Vol. II, no. 2, 1939, 77.

The curlew ; trans. from "Y Gylfinhir" of R. W. Parry. ibid.

Death ; trans. from the Welsh "Hen benill-ion", Angau. Welsh Review, Vol. IV, no. 4, 1945, 284.

The fox ; trans. from the Welsh of R. W. Parry ; Presenting Welsh Poetry, 1959, 63.

Lines written in my forty-third year ; Welsh Review, Vol. VII, no. 1, 1948, 20.

Margam today ; PEN 1954, 101.

My elder tree at night ; Wales, Vol. VI, no. 3, 1946, 12.

Night on the bare mountain ; Welsh Review, Vol. VII, no. 1, 1948, 20.

Nine poems ; [trans. from the Welsh]. Welsh Review, Vol. V, no. 4, 1946, 246—57. Contents : Troilus and Cressida (from the Prologue)—In Praise of a Girl (I—V)—Dinogad's Petticoat—The Hall of Ifor Hael—Penillion.

The old men ; (trans. from the Welsh of G. J. Williams) ; Wales, Vol. VI, no. 3, 1946, 14.

Owens ; Welsh Review, Vol. VII, no. 1, 1948, 21.

The ploughman ; trans. from the 14th century Welsh of Iolo Goch. The London Magazine, Vol. 2, no. 7, 1955, 44—6.

Poem for Elspeth ; Welsh Review, Vol. VII, no. 1, 1948, 21.

The seagulls ; trans. from the Welsh of John Morris-Jones ; Presenting Welsh Poetry, 1959, 60.

Song for Carmarthen ; Wales, Vol. V, no. 7, 1945, 54.

To a sailor turned farmer ; Welsh Review, Vol. 1, no. 6, 1939, 315.

"Trefenter" ; ibid. Vol. IV, no. 4, 1945, 237.

The two meetings ; trans. from the Welsh of Nefydd Owen ; Wales, Vol. VI, no. 3, 1946, 12.

Welsh dancer ; Wales, New Series, 4, 1944, 16.

Words ; trans. from the Welsh of T. H. Parry-Williams ; Presenting Welsh Poetry, 1959, 68.

WILLIAMS, Edward Roland

Stories

A 1447 : Flotsam.
Welsh Outlook, Vol. XI, 1924, 75—7.

A 1448 : Jetsam, by Roland Williams.
London ; Collins, 1943.
51p. 18cm. wrappers.

A 1449 : The stranger.
The Dragon, Dec. 1914, 85—9.
Welsh Outlook, Vol. II, 1915, 62—4.

A 1450 : "West land, best land".
Welsh Outlook, Vol. I, 1914, 395—6.

Other Prose

A 1451 : Among the dunes.
Welsh Outlook, Vol. IV, Aug. 1917, 272—3.

A 1452 : Just ordinary old folk.
Welsh Outlook, Vol. V, 1918, 97.

A 1453 : "Menevia of the pilgrimages".
Welsh Outlook, Vol. II, 1915, 422—3.

A 1454 : Simple chronicles of a voyage.
Welsh Outlook, Vol. X, 1923, 190—1.

A 1455 : "Trefeli".
Welsh Outlook, Vol. XI, 1924, 215—6.

A 1456 : War economy on the heath.
Welsh Outlook, Vol. IV, June 1917, 215.

A 1457 : Wild Wales ! an essay.
Welsh Outlook, Vol. II, 1915, 311—2.

Verse

A 1458 : Clair de lune ; Welsh Outlook, Vol. V, January 1918, 17.

The end of the voyage ; In memoriam : G.G.R. died in France ; Welsh Outlook, Vol. IV, June 1917, 319—20.

Stage-struck ; The Dragon, March 1918, 67.

WILLIAMS, Elma Mary

Novels

A 1459 : Escape to death.
London, Melbourne, [etc.]; Ward Lock, 1961.
[6], 7—189, 3p. 18½cm. cloth.
Location : "Plas y Graig", Dovey Valley area.

A 1460 : The fifth lake.
London ; Wright & Brown, 1959.
188, [3] p. 18½cm.
Location : "Carn Llyn" and the "Tyfnant Valley" (Cards.)

A 1461 : The shaft of light.
London ; Wright & Brown, 1965.
175, [1]p. 18cm. cloth.
Location : "Bryn Glas", the Dovey Estuary.

A 1462 : Something of the world.
London ; Wright & Brown, 1960.
[4], 5—174, 2 p. 18cm. cloth.
Location : "Pant Bach", Dovey Valley area.

A 1463 : The valley.
London ; Wright & Brown, 1961.
[4], 5—192p. 18½cm. cloth.
Location : "Llyngros", North Wales.

WILLIAMS, [George] Emlyn

A 1464 : George : an early autobiography.
London ; H. Hamilton, 1961.
x, 461p. front (port.) illus. 20½cm. cloth.

—Another ed. New English Library, 1965.
384p. 18cm. Paperback. (Four Square Books).

Drama

A 1465 : The collected plays. Volume 1.
London, Melbourne, etc. ; Heinemann, 1961.
xxv, 470p. 19cm. cloth.
Includes [Welsh background] : The corn is green.
Other titles : Night must fall—He was born gay—The light of heart.

A 1466 : The corn is green, with two other plays, "The Wind of Heaven" and "The Druid's Rest".
London ; Pan Books, 1950.
[10], 11—255p. 17½cm. wrappers.

A 1467 : The corn is green : a comedy in three acts.
London, Toronto ; 1938.
[8], 125p. 18½cm. cloth.
Scene : Village of "Glansarno".

—Heinemann's Drama Library ed. 1956.
viii, 96p. boards.

—American eds. New York, Random House, 1941.
Dramatists' Play Service, 1945.

A 1468 : The corn is green.
In Cerf, B. A. *and* Cartnell, V. H., *eds.*
Sixteen famous British plays.
Garden City, U.S.A., 1942.
—Modern Library, 1943.

Abridged version *in* Mantle, Burns, ed. The best plays of 1940/41. U.S.A., Dodd.

A 1469 : The Druid's Rest : a comedy in three acts.
London ; Heinemann, 1944.
90p. 18½cm. cloth.
Scene : Village of "Tan-y-maes".

A 1470 : Trespass : a ghost story in six scenes.
London, Melbourne ; Heinemann, 1947.
—Heinemann Drama Library edition, 1954.
[6], 99p. 18½cm. boards.
Scene : "Llansoga" and "Crithin Castle" gatehouse.

A 1471 : Vigil.
The second book of one-act plays.
Heinemann, 1954. [pp. separately numbered].
Scene : Manor on the Welsh border.

A 1472 : The Wind of Heaven : a play in six scenes.
London, Heinemann, 1945.

—Heinemann's Drama Library edition, 1955.
vi, 79, [3]p. 18½cm. boards.
Scene : Village of "Blestin", 1856.

Welsh version by J. Ellis Williams, entitled "*Awel Gref*".

WILLIAMS, Herbert Lloyd

Verse

A 1473 : Too wet for the devil, and other poems.
Dulwich Village, S.E. 21 ; Outposts Publications, 1962.
12p. 21½cm. wrappers.

A 1474 : Autumn ways ; W. Mail Literary Review, Sep. 12, 1964, 2.

The carpenter ; ibid. April 16, 1964, 9.

The Castle choir ; ibid. Aug. 7, 1965, 9.

A celebration ; ibid. May 8, 1965, 11.

Dandelion days ; A-W.R., Vol. 12, no. 29, n.d. 62.

Daughter of the house ; ibid. Vol. 13, no. 32, 1963, 63.

Depopulation ; Poetry Wales, I, Spring 1965, 15.

Epitaph ; A-W.R., Vol. 12, no. 30, undated, 54—5.

The new tenants ; W. Mail, Nov. 13, 1965, 6.

Spring trophy ; ibid. May 30, 1964, 5.

The swallows ; ibid. Aug. 8, 1964, 5.

The tyro's path ; W. Mail Literary Review, August 14, 1964, 3.

The viewers ; A-W.R., Vol. 12, no. 29, n.d. 62.

Yorky ; ibid. Vol. 13, no. 31, undated, 35.

WILLIAMS, Huw Menai   *"Huw Menai"*

Prose

A 1475 : Humour of hard times.
Welsh Outlook, Vol. XV, 1928, 345—6.

A 1476 : That inferiority complex.
Welsh Outlook, Vol. XVIII, 1931, 82—3.

Verse

A 1477 : Back in the return, and other poems.
London ; Heinemann, 1933.
xii, 177p. 20½cm. cloth.

A 1478 : The passing of Guto, and other poems.
London ; Leonard & Virginia Woolf at The Hogarth Press, 1929.
99, [1]p. cloth. 19cm. (Hogarth Living Poets Series, no. 6).

The "Introduction" forms autobiographical account of poet's life & circumstances. Dated November 1928.

A 1479 : The simple vision : poems by Huw Menai, with a preface by John Cowper Powys.
London ; Chapman & Hall, 1945.
96p. 18½cm. cloth.

A 1480 : Through the upcast shaft. Introduction by Ellis Lloyd.
London ; Hodder & Stoughton, n.d.

—Another ed. 2nd ed. n.d.
93p. 13½cm. wrappers.

—Another ed. 3rd and enlarged ed. n.d.
xi, 94, [2]p. 18½cm. cloth.

A 1481 : As Time the sculptor ; Welsh Review, Vol. 1, no. 1, 1939, 17—18.

Back in the return ; Modern Welsh Poetry ; ed. by K. Rhys, 1944, 95—8.

The bench of stone ; Welsh Outlook, Vol. XV, 1928, 377.

Child song ; Dock L., Vol. 3, no. 7, 1952, 6.

Cwm Farm near Capel Curig ; Praise of Wales ; comp. by Maxwell Fraser, 1950, 12.
Modern Welsh Poetry ; ed. by K. Rhys, 1944, 94—5.

Earthworm ; The Poetry Review, Vol. 42, no. 1, 1951, 27.

Envied tree (about to be cut down) ; Wales, Vol. VII, no. 25, 1947, 155.

Extract from "Back in the return" [' Hungry, and penniless . . . of national rottenness '].
Modern Welsh Poetry ; ed. by K. Rhys, 1944, 98—9.

Five Poems : In the Vale of Glamorgan—During the raid—Stalingrad—The inexorable—When writing out "Reject" slips in a Royal Ordnance factory ; Wales, New Series, I, 1943, 51—2.

The flower border by the sea ; Dock L., Vol. 2, no. 6, 1951, 36.

Four sonnets.
  I : On hearing Keats's Ode to a Nightingale being read aloud by a young lady.
 II : The Weeder.
III : Maentwrog.
 IV : When listening to an argument between a scientist and a clergyman.
Dock L., Vol. 4, no. 11, 1953, 39—40.

Hiroshima ; Wales, Vol. VII, no. 25, 1947, 154.

Horizon ; The Poetry Review, Vol. 43, no. 3, 1952, 136.

Hunger ; The Poetry Review, Vol. 41, no. 3, 1950, 130.

I too when young ; (from my notebook) ; Wales, Vol. VI, no. 24, 1946, 22—3.
Poetry Book Magazine, Vol. 6, no. 5, Fall, 1954, 18—9.

In the Vale of Glamorgan ; Modern Welsh Poetry ; ed. by K. Rhys, 1944, 94.

I would have plucked a flower ; Welsh Outlook, Vol. XV, 1928, 365.

The inexorable ; Modern Welsh Poetry, 1944, 100.

J.C.P. [John Cowper Powys] ; Dock L., Vol. 7, no. 19, 1956, 29.

June (near Nevin, Caernarvonshire) ; Welsh Outlook, Vol. XVII, 1930, 262.

Large and small ; The Poetry Review, Vol. 41, no. 1, 1950, 6.

A moment's calm ; Listener, Jan. 26, 1950, 161.

Near Cwm Farm, Capel Curig ; Welsh Outlook, Vol. XVI, 1929, 9.

New poems : 1. Violin. 2. Night. 3. Storm ; Welsh Outlook, Vol. XIX, 1932, 203.

No strange ghost ; (From an old note-book) ; Wales, Vol. VII, no. 26, 1947, 288—9.

The old peasant in the billiard saloon ; Modern Welsh Poetry ; ed. by K. Rhys, 1944, 95.

The old thorn tree on our hillside ; Encounter, Vol. II, no. 6, 1954, 35.

On growing old ; Welsh Outlook, Vol. 20, May 1933, 127.

On seeing leaves falling on the clean-way ; Royal Ordnance Factory Magazine, 1944. Reproduced in entirety in J. C. Powys' preface to "*The Simple Vision*" (q.v.).

Prodigality ; Welsh Outlook, Vol. XVII, 1930, 334.

The skylark ; ibid. Vol. IV, Sept. 1917, 309.

Stalingrad ; Modern Welsh Poetry ; ed. by K. Rhys, 1944, 100.

The stars look down ; ibid. 99.

The swallow ; Welsh Outlook, Vol. IV, Aug. 1917, 274.

The unwritten page—A prayer for thick skin— 1931-1932—On changing counters ; ibid. Vol. XIX, 1932, 204.

War-time waiting ; ibid. Vol. V, January 1918, 8.

WILLIAMS, Ieuan Iwan

Novel

A 1482 : Red Robin.
London ; Methuen, 1946.
vi, 7—207p. front. illus. 18½cm. cloth.
Location : "Bryn Môr Farm", sea coast town of "Glanfor".

WILLIAMS, Islwyn

Novel

A 1483 : Dangerous waters.
London ; Gryphon Books, 1952.
224p. cloth.
Location : Parts of the action relate to Pembrokeshire.

WILLIAMS, Islwyn, *2nd of the name*

Stories

A 1484 : Adjudication.
Welsh Review, Vol. V, no. 2, 1946, 93—7.

A 1485 : "In fond remembrance".
Saturday saga. London, Progress Publishing Co., 1946. 43—6.

A 1486 : Will Thomas's cap.
Welsh Review, Vol. IV, no. 3, 1945, 161—5.
Welsh short stories ; ed. by Gwyn Jones, 1956. 322—30.
(English version of the author's original story, "Cap Wil Tomos").

WILLIAMS, John Ellis

Drama

A 1487 : The sheep of William Morgan.
London ; Samuel French, [1936].
96p. plan. 15½cm. wrappers. (Welsh Drama Series, no. 122).
Scene : A quarryman's cottage, N. Wales.

WILLIAMS, John Stuart

Verse

A 1488 : Last fall.
Dulwich Village ; Outposts Publications, 1962.
20p. 20½cm. wrappers.

A 1489 : A seat in the park ; Dragons and daffodils, 1960, 50.
Cherwell ; ibid. 51.
Tethered ; ibid.
End ; ibid.
Côte D'Azur ; ibid. 52.
In the sudden sun ; ibid. 52.
Infirmary blues ; ibid. 53.

A 1490 : The Rade, Toulon ; A-W.R., Vol. 10, no. 25, undated, 93.
Orange ; ibid. 95.
Theseus on Naxos ; ibid. Vol. 12, no. 30, undated, 35.
Last fall ; ibid. 36.
Dry autumn ; ibid. 36.
Gannets fishing ; ibid. Vol. 13, no. 32, 1963, 64.
En route ; ibid. 64.
Broken tower ; ibid. Vol. 14, no. 33, 1964, 46.
Skokholm ; ibid. 47.
Mozart in the spring ; ibid. Vol. 14, no. 34, 1964—5, 90.
Tree ; ibid. 91.
Orestes and Clytemnestra ; ibid. Vol. 15, no. 35, 1965, 86.

A 1491 : Theseus in Athens ; W. Mail Lit. Rev., July 10, 1965, 9.
Girl with violin ; ibid. Dec. 5, 1964, 3.
Outlaws ; ibid. Oct. 1, 1961.
Summer thunder ; ibid.
Troy ; ibid.
Windfall ; ibid. Nov. 7, 1964, 9.

A   1492 : Sea girl ; Wales, Sep. 1958, 12.
Forgotten summer ; ibid. 34.

A   1493 : Chrysanthemum ; Dock L., Vol. 7, no. 20,
1956, 21.
Night ; ibid.
Tame Tiger ; ibid. 22.
Moment ; ibid.

A   1494 : Commuter ; Poetry Wales, I, Spring 1965, 15.
Don't look now ; YCP, 187—8.
Exile ; English, Vol. 15, no. 87, 1964, 104.
Night scene ; Prospect, no. 7/8, Winter
1946—47, 14.
Sam Johnson in Paris ; London Welshman,
Vol. 20, 1965, Jul./August, 20.

WILLIAMS, John Toriel   *"Toriel"*

Verse
A   1495 : Coronation, and other poems.
Neath ; Neath & County Standard, Ltd.,
1913.
60p. wrappers.

A   1496 : [A collection of single sheet poems] : A 1915
winter song—The flood of war—When
will the War come to an end.
Seven Sisters, Glam. 1915.

A   1497 : Idols.
Cardiff ; Western Mail, 1921.
35p. 13½cm. wrappers.

A   1498 : Songs composed during the Great War.
Neath ; Neath & County Standard, 1914.
24p. wrappers.
—Another edition. 1915.

A   1499 : The white lily.
[Seven Sisters, Glam. ; publ. by the author,
1917].

WILLIAMS, Josephine Evans

Novel
A   1500 : Aberafon.
London ; John Long, 1911.
384p. 19cm. cloth.
Location : "Plas Pont-yr-afon", in a rural
area.

WILLIAMS, Leyshon

Drama
A   1501 : Seven-thirty prompt : a farce in one act.
Cardiff ; Castle Book Co., 1946.
[5], 6—31p. 18cm. wrappers.
Scene : A Welsh chapel vestry.

WILLIAMS, Raymond

Novels
A   1502 : Border country : a novel.
London ; Chatto & Windus, 1960.
351p. 19½cm. cloth.
Location : Village of "Glynmawr" and
"Gwenton", Welsh border country.
—Another edition. Harmondsworth, Penguin
Books, 1964.
334, [2]p. 18cm. wrappers.

A   1503 : Second generation : a novel.
London ; Chatto & Windus, 1964.
347p. 19½cm. cloth.
Location : Links with "Gwenton", a Welsh
border town. Mainly in English factory and
university city.

Story
A   1504 : Sack labourer.
English story. Third series ; ed. by Woodrow
Wyatt, 1942, 71—9.

WILLIAMS, Robert Coleman

Verse
A   1505 : Ladycross : poems.
Oxford ; Fantasy Press, 1962.
[2], 3—33, [2]p. 24cm. wrappers. (Fantasy
Poets Series).

WILLIAMS, Thomas Dewarden

Drama
A   1506 : The last of the Cambrian Princes : a trilogy.
Part I : The road to Aberconway.
Llandybie ; Llyfrau'r Dryw, 1960.
76p. 21½cm. wrappers.

Part II : Llandeilo and Moelydon.
Llandybie ; Llyfrau'r Dryw, 1964.
110p. 21½cm. wrappers.

WILLIAMS, Trevor

Novel
A   1507 : A nest among the stars.
London ; Hutchinson, [1936].
303, [48]p. 18½cm. cloth. (First Novel
Library, Nc 54).
Location : Slate-quarrying areas of N. Wales.

WILLIAMS, W.   *Rector of Freyshop*

Verse
A   1508 : A volume of poems (from "Wales Day by
Day").
Haverfordwest ; publ by the author, [1937].
[Printed Cardiff, Western Mail, 1937].
48p. 18½cm. wrappers.

WILLIAMS, William   *of Pontypool*

Verse
A   1509 : Songs of Siluria. Foreword by H. Elvet Lewis.
Cardiff ; Educational Publishing Co., 1916.
x, 153p. front. (port.) 18cm. cloth.

WILLIAMS, William Glynfab   *"Glynfab"*

Novel
A   1510 : The raven : a novel based upon the life and
times of Sir Rhys ab Thomas.
Carmarthen ; The "Journal" Co. Ltd., [1914].
36p. 24½cm. wrappers.

Drama
A   1511 : A nightmare : a comedy in one act.
Carmarthen ; W. M. Evans, [1931].
[5], 6—30p. wrappers.
Scene : "Mr. Pugh Jones' study".

WILLIAMS-BULKELEY, S.

Verse
A   1512 : Island songs and sketches.
London ; Stockwell, [1922].
31p. 18½cm. boards.

WILLIAMS-ELLIS, Amabel

Novel
A   1513 : The big firm.
London ; Collins, 1938.
398p. 20cm. cloth.
Location : Partly in Wales.

WILLIAMS-ELLIS, Amabel *and* **WILLIAMS-ELLIS,
Bertram Clough**

Novel
A   1514 : Headlong down the years : a tale of today.
Liverpool ; University Press, 1951.
[6], 7—118p. 21½cm. cloth.
Illustrated end-papers. Prologue and epilogue
by Richard Hughes.

WILLWYN, John

Verse
A   1515 : Poems of the Welsh border.
Oswestry ; T. Owen & Son, [1927].
[2], 3—30p. 17cm. wrappers.

WINSTANLEY, Lilian

Verse
A   1516 : The genius of Wales, and other poems.
Newtown ; Welsh Outlook Press, 1936.
[4], 5—46p. 24½cm. wrappers.

A   1517 : The praise of Wales.
Newtown ; Welsh Outlook Press, 1933.
38p. 25cm. wrappers.

A   1518 : The angel of Wales ; The Dragon, Lent Term,
1934, 30—1.

February ; ibid. March 1905, 161.

In memoriam : Rupert Brooke ; ibid. May
1916, 220.

Mountain music ; ibid. Summer Term, 1934,
61.

The new astronomy ; ibid. 60.

The open road ; ibid. Feb. 1911, 104—9.

Spring 1915 ; ibid. March 1915, [186].

The thrush in Cwm Woods ; ibid. Summer
Term, 1934, 59.

The voyage ; ibid. Dec. 1903, [53].

The Welsh in Palestine ; Welsh Outlook,
Vol. X, 1923, 277.

WINSTON, A.

Verse
A   1519 : Cambria, and other poems.   Foreword by
Principal William Edwards.
London ; Stockwell, [1923].
[6], 7—79p. plates. 18cm. cloth.

WOODCOCK, George

Verse
A   1520 : Ancestral tablet ; Life and Letters Today,
Vol. 23, no. 26, [1939], 69.

Landore ; Wales, No. 8/9, 1939, 239—40,
Modern Welsh Poetry ; ed. by K. Rhys.
1944, 144—5.

Merthyrmawr ; Modern Welsh Poetry ; ed.
by K. Rhys, 1944, 145—6.

Pentre ; Wales. New Series, I, 1943. 83.

Poem from Garn Llech ; Wales. Vol. IV,
no. 5, 1944, 50.

Sonnet ("Looking into the windows . . .") ;
Focus One ; ed. by B. Rajan and A. Pearse.
London, Dobson, 1945, 79.

Southerndown Beach ; Modern Welsh Poetry ;
ed. by K. Rhys, 1944, 146.

Steel Valley, 1938 ; ibid. 145.

Tree felling ; Focus One. London, Dobson, 1945, 79.

WOOLLAND, Henry

Novel
A   1521 : The Blue Mountain.
London ; Andre Deutsch, 1957.
[8], 9—188p. 18½cm. cloth.
Location : Partly in Caernarvonshire.

WRIGHT, John

Stories
A   1522 : Gone fishing.
Welsh short stories ; ed. by G. Ewart Evans
2nd ed., 1959, 242—5.

A   1523 : One Christmas.
A-W.R., Vol. 13, no. 31, undated, 28—34.

A   1524 : One summer evening.
Wales, Nov. 1958, 49—54.

"YORKE, Curtis," pseud. [i.e. Susan Richmond Lee]

Novel
A   1525 : Only Betty.
London ; J. Long, [1913].
[6], 7—318p. front. 15½cm. cloth.
Location : "Caenwar", Cards.

—Another ed. Popular ed. J. Long, 1923.
[4], 5—318, [1]p. 18½cm. cloth.

YOUNG, Francis Brett

Novel
A   1526 : The house under the water.
London ; Heinemann, 1932.
[viii], 691p. cloth.
Reprinted, 1932 ; 1933.

—Another ed. Severn ed., 1935.
Location : Radnorshire.

YOUNG-EVANS, John Bertram

Verse
A   1527 : Songs of the nymphs, and other poems.
Dolgelley ; The "Cymro" Office (E. W.
Evans), printers, 1919.
[3], 4—20p. 18cm. wrappers.

Section B : Bibliographical and Critical Works

I. ANGLO-WELSH LITERATURE IN GENERAL

Bibliographies and Indexes

B 1 : **CARDIFF.** *City. Public Libraries*

    Some contemporary Anglo-Welsh writers. Cardiff, City of Cardiff Public Libraries, [1951]. [4], 20p. 21½cm. wrappers.
(A catalogue to accompany an exhibition of the work of Anglo-Welsh writers, 1951. Contains biographical notes and bibliographies).

B 2 : **JENKINS, David Clay**

    An index to *The Welsh Review*.
Jnl. of the Welsh Bibliographical Society. Vol. IX, no. 4, 1965. pp. 188—210.

B 3 : **LECLAIRE, Lucien**

    A general analytical bibliography of the regional novelists of the British Isles, 1800—1950.
Paris, Société d'Édition "Les Belles Lettres", 1954.
[7], 399p. maps. 22½cm. wrappers.
(Collection d'Histoire et de Littérature Etrangères). p. 391 : Regional index of Anglo-Welsh writing.

Criticism and Commentary

B 4 : **ADAM, Gustav Felix**

    Three contemporary Anglo-Welsh novelists : Jack Jones, Rhys Davies and Hilda Vaughan.
Bern, A. Francke, n.d. (Preface dated Nov. 1948).
[4], 5—109p. 21½cm. wrappers.
Contains : pp. 13—29 : Wales and Anglo-Welsh literature : 31—48 : Jack Jones : 48—76 : Rhys Davies : 76—100 : Hilda Vaughan : 107—109 : Bibliographies of the three authors.

B 5 : **BOTTERILL, Denis**

    Three poets from Wales.
Life & Letters, Sept. 1948. pp. 252—260.
(Review article of (1) Evans, Margiad. Poems from obscurity : (2) Thomas, R. S. The stones of the field : (3) Griffith, Ll. Wyn. The barren tree).

B 6 : **CROSS, Peter G.**

    Llenyddiaeth Eingl-Gymreig. [Anglo-Welsh Literature]. Ffenics : [magazine of University College of N. Wales, Bangor]. Vol. 1, no. 4, 1963, pp. 73—77.

B 7 : **DAVIES, Aneirin Talfan**

    [Ar ymyl y ddalen].
Barn, Ionawr (Jan.) 1963, 68 : Chwefror (Feb.) 1963, 100—101.
(Welsh articles which refer in part to Vernon Watkins, Dylan Thomas, Rhys Davies, Caradoc Evans).

    A question of language.
The Welsh Anvil, V, [1953]. pp. 19—31.
(Anglo-Welsh writing, with particular reference to Dylan Thomas).

B 8 : **DAVIES, Evan**

    Welsh nationalism and the drama.
Welsh Outlook. Vol. 17, 1930. p. 222.
(Brief references to Anglo-Welsh plays).

B 9 : **DAVIES, Lewis**

    The Anglo-Cymric school of poets.
Welsh Outlook. Vol. 13, 1926. pp. 21—22.
L'école de poesie Anglo-Galloise ; traduit par M. Morgan Watkin.
La Renaissance d'Occident. Tome XVI, no. 2, Décembre 1925. Brussels, 1925. pp. 206—210.

    The soul of Wales : a plea for sane criticism.
Welsh Outlook. Vol. 9, 1922. pp. 169—72.
(Reviews the Anglo-Welsh contributions to the *Poetry Review* special number, March 1922).

B 10 : **EVANS, Benjamin Ifor**

    The collective genius of English literature : 1 : Wales.
The Author, Autumn 1949. pp. 7—9.

B 11 : **EVANS, Beriah Gwynfe**

    Wales and its novelists.
Wales (J.H.E.), Vol. 1, 1911. pp. 35—8 (with portrait of Allen Raine).

B 12 : **EVANS, George Ewart**

An emergent national literature.
Wales. New Series, 2, 1943. pp. 50—53.

[Introduction to] Welsh short stories. *2nd ed.*
London ; Faber, 1959. pp. 9—15.

B 13 : **EVANS, Illtud**

Words from Wales.
Blackfriars. March 1948. pp. 148—151.
(References to Anglo-Welsh writers).

B 14 : **GARLICK, Raymond**

An Anglo-Welsh accidence.
University of Wales Review. Summer 1965,
pp. 18—20.
(Reviews "accepted judgements" of Anglo-
Welsh literature, from historical viewpoint).

[Editorial]
Dock Leaves. Vol. 2, no. 6, 1951. pp. 1—7 (in
part).
(Considers the function and scope of Anglo-
Welsh writing of the 20th century).

[Editorial]
Dock Leaves. Vol. 4, no. 11, 1953, pp. 1—7.
(Traces historical background of Anglo-Welsh
literature, with references to Anglo-Irish
writing).

[Editorial]
A.W. Review. Vol. 9, no. 23, undated. pp. 3-8.
(Discusses Anglo-Welsh literature in general,
and in particular the lecture "The First
Forty Years" by Gwyn Jones, q.v.)

Poetry from Wales : an introduction.
Poetry Book Magazine. Vol. 6, no. 5, Fall 1954.
pp. 1—3.

Seventy Anglo-Welsh poets.
The Welsh Anvil. Vol. 6, 1954. pp. 76—84.

Welsh literature. 2. English.
New Catholic Encyclopedia. New York, St.
Louis, etc. McGraw-Hill, 1967. Vol. XIV,
p. 872.

B 15 : **GOODWIN, Geraint**

Thoughts on the Welsh novel.
Welsh Outlook. Vol. 17, 1930. pp. 72—74.

B 16 : **GRIFFITH, Llewelyn Wyn**

A note on "Anglo-Welsh".
Wales, New Series I, 1943. pp. 15—16.

The Welsh.
Harmondsworth, Middlesex ; Penguin Books,
1950.
pp. 102—115 : Welsh writers in English.

B 17 : **GRIFFITHS, Bryn**

What stirs the lyrical kick in the Welsh ?
' Western Mail ' Weekend Magazine, April 11,
1964. p. 5.
(Considers the position of Welsh poets writing
in English in 1964).

B 18 : **GRIFFITHS, Teifion**

The Welsh influence on modern English verse.
Y Ddinas. Vol. 10, no. 11, Aug. 1956. p. 19.
(Refers to Dylan Thomas, Alun Lewis and
W. H. Davies).

B 19 : **HART, Olive Ely**

The drama in modern Wales : a brief history of
Welsh playwriting from 1900 to the present
day.
Philadelphia, University of Pennsylvania, 1928.
96p. ports. 22½cm.
A Ph.D. thesis of the University of Pennsylvania,
1928. p. 90 : Partial list of Welsh plays.
pp. 94—6 : Bibliography.
(Library of Congress National Union Cat.).

B 20 : **JONES, Bobi** [*i.e. Robert Maynard Jones*]

The Anglo-Welsh.
Dock Leaves, Vol. 4, no. 10, 1953. pp. 23—28.

B 21 : **JONES, Glyn**

Slim volumes for a slim public.
Western Mail, July 23, 1960. p. 5.
(A general survey of A.W. writing, with
photographs of Glyn Jones, Huw Menai and
R. S. Thomas).

Three Anglo-Welsh prose writers.
Rann, No. 19 (Welsh no.), 1953. pp. [1]—5.
(Considers the prose work of Caradoc Evans,
Gwyn Thomas and Dylan Thomas).

B 22 : **JONES, Gwyn**

(*a*) Caradoc was the daddy of us all.
Western Mail, Aug. 20, 1960. p. 5.

(*b*) Forum needed for Welsh writers.
Western Mail, Aug. 27, 1960. p. 5.

The first forty years : some notes on Anglo-Welsh literature : the W. D. Thomas memorial lecture . . . 1957.
Cardiff, University of Wales Press, 1957.
28p.   21½cm.   wrappers.

Introduction to Welsh short stories.
Oxford University Press, 1956.   pp. ix—xv.

Language, style and the Anglo-Welsh.
Essays and Studies, 1953.   pp. 102—114.
(Considers the language and style of Dylan Thomas, Gwyn Thomas, Glyn Jones and Caradoc Evans).

The new Anglo-Welsh.
The Welsh Anvil, No. 1, 1949.   pp. 56—62.
(Comprises reviews of (1) Roland Mathias : Break in harvest. (2) R. S. Thomas : The stones of the field. (3) Gwyn Thomas : Where did I put my pity ? (4) Cledwyn Hughes : The inn closes for Christmas *and* The different drummer.   (5) George Ewart Evans : The voices of the children).

Notes on the Welsh short story writers.
Life & Letters Today, Sept. 1942, pp. 172—180, Mar. 1943, pp. 156—163.

B   23   : **JONES, Jack**

Nofelau'r Cymry Seisnig.   [Welsh article on Anglo-Welsh novel-writing].
Y Tir Newydd. Rhif (no.) 8, Mai (May) 1937, pp. 5—9.

B   24   : **JONES, Noel A.**

The Anglo-Welsh.
Dock Leaves, Vol. 4, no. 11, 1953.   pp. 20—26.

B   25   : **LECLAIRE, Lucien**

Le Roman regionaliste dans les Iles Britanniques, 1800—1950.
Paris ; Société d'Edition "Les Belles Lettres", 1954.
[9], 10—300p.   diagrs.   22½cm.   wrappers.
(Collection d'Histoire et de Littérature Etrangères).
pp. 265—275 : Bibliographie.

B   26   : **LEWIS, Evan Glyn**

Anglo-Welsh literature today.
Little Reviews Anthology, 1947—8 ; ed. by D. Val Baker.   pp. 125—137.

Some aspects of Anglo-Welsh literature.
Welsh Review, Vol. 5, no. 3, 1946.   pp. 176-186.

B   27   : **LEWIS, Frank R.**

Some great Welsh novelists of today.
The Dragon.   Michaelmas Term, 1933.
pp. 22—23.

B   28   : **LEWIS, Ivor**

The people and the latent wish (with a note on some Welsh writers as a cross-section).
Wales.   Vol. V, no. 8/9.   December 1945.
pp. 46—52.

Writers' countries.
Wales.   Vol. VI, no. 24.   1946.   pp. 74—79.
(Considers territorial background of certain Anglo-Welsh writers).

B   29   : **LEWIS, [John] Saunders**

"Is there an Anglo-Welsh literature ?" being the Annual Lecture delivered to the [Cardiff] Branch [of the Guild of Graduates of the University of Wales] on December 10th, 1938.
[Cardiff, The University Registry, 1939].
Imprint in Welsh : Swyddfa Gofrestru [sic], Parc Cathays, Caerdydd.
[3], 4—14p.   21½cm.   wrappers.

B   30   : **LLOYD, D. Tecwyn**

Dail y pren pwdr.   [Welsh article].
Barn, Rhagfyr (Dec.) 1962.   pp. 36 and 59.
[Discusses the language and idiom of Anglo-Welsh writers].

Rhyw ac Angst (Sex and ' Angst ').
Barn.   Chwefror (Feb.) 1963.   pp. 104—5.
(Welsh article referring in part to the novels of Alexander Cordell).

Yr Eingl-Gymry [The Anglo-Welsh].
Barn.   Mawrth (Mar.) 1963.   p. 141.
(A letter in reply to Davies, Aneirin Talfan, q.v. Reply by A. T. Davies in Barn, Ebrill (Apr.) 1963.   p. 168).

B   31   : **MERCHANT, William Moelwyn**

The relevance of the Anglo-Welsh.
Wales.   New Series, I, 1943.   pp. 17—19.

B   32   : **POWYS, John Cowper**

Welsh culture.
Welsh Review.   Vol. 1, no. 5, 1939.   pp. 255—262.
(Reviews the argument for and against the school of ' Anglo-Welsh ' writing).

B 33 : PRYS-JONES, Arthur Glyn

Anglo-Welsh poetry.
Dock Leaves, Vol. 2, no. 5, 1951. pp. 5—9.
(*Reprinted from :* The British Weekly).

B 34 : PRUISCHUTZ, Hildegard

Sensualismus als Stilelement in der modernen
anglo-walisischen Prosadichtung : Inaugural
Dissertation der Philosophischen Fakultät der
Friedrich-Alexander-Universität.
Munich ; Mikrokopie G.m.b.H., [1955].
[2], 3—167p. 20½cm. wrappers.
Photocopied typescript.   pp. 164—166 :
Bibliography of critical works consulted.
(Sensualism as a stylistic factor in Anglo-Welsh
prose fiction).

B 35 : REES, Ioan Bowen

Wales and the Anglo-Welsh.
The Welsh Anvil, No. IV, [1952]. pp. 20—31.

B 36 : RHYS, Keidrych   [*i.e. William Ronald Rees Jones*]
[The Anglo-Welsh].
Editorial notes (in part), Wales. New Series, 2.
Oct. 1943. pp. 6—8.

Anglo-Welsh verse.
The London Welshman. Vol. 16, no. 1, Jan.
1961. p. 18.
Consists of reviews of (1) Dragons and daffodils,
ed. by J. Stuart Williams and Richard
Milner ; (2) Formal poems, by Anthony
Conran ; (3) Land of song, by Charles Jones.

Contemporary Welsh literature (ii).
The British Annual of Literature, 1946. Vol. 3.
pp. 17—22.
(Reviews development of Anglo-Welsh writing).

Letter from Wales.
Twentieth Century Verse.   No. 18, 1939.
pp. 58—61.
(Considers purpose and scope of Anglo-Welsh
writing along with a survey of writing in the
Welsh language in 1939).

B 37 : RICHARDS, Alun

The Never-never land.
Wales. No. 45. October 1959. pp. 27—29.

B 38 : ROBERTS, Glyn

Welsh school of writers [in English].
Bookman. August 1933. pp. 248—9.

B 39 : ROWE, Dilys

The significance of the Welsh short story
writers.
Wales. Vol. V, no. 8/9, 1945. pp. 96—100.

Some variations on a main theme.
Wales. Vol. IV, no. 6, 1945. pp. 9—12.
(Discusses a number of Anglo-Welsh novels and
novelists).

Thoughts on the tenth anniversary of ' Wales '.
Wales. Vol. VII, no. 28, 1948. pp. 442—451.
(Discusses Anglo-Welsh writing and writers).

B 40 : THOMAS, Dylan

The poets of Swansea.
The Herald of Wales : January 9, 23, Feb. 20,
March 19, April 23, June 25, 1932.

B 41 : THOMAS, Ronald Stuart

Llenyddiaeth Eingl-Gymreig.
Y Fflam. Rhif (No.) 11, Awst (Aug.) 1952.
pp. 7—9.
(Welsh article on Anglo-Welsh writing in
general).

B 42 : TIMES LITERARY SUPPLEMENT

Anglo-Welsh attitudes.
TLS, June 1st, 1956. p. 328.
(Reviews *Welsh Short Stories*, ed. by Gwyn Jones.
Oxford U.P., 1956, and comments in general
on Anglo-Welsh literature).

The two literatures of Wales.
TLS, Aug. 5, 1955 (Supplement p. xii).

The Welsh Dragon.
TLS, Aug. 29, 1952. p. xxxi.
(Surveys both Welsh vernacular and Anglo-
Welsh writing of the mid-century period).

B 43 : VAUGHAN, Herbert Millingchamp

Wales and the historical novel.
Welsh Outlook. Vol. 18, 1931. [pp. 247—8].

B 44 : WADE-EVANS, Arthur Wade

"Anglo-Welsh".
Wales. Vol. VI, no. 3, 1946. pp. 29—39.

B 45 : WAY, Brian

Anglo-Welsh writing.
Adult Education, Vol. 32, no. 4, 1960. pp.
290—3.

B 46 : **WEBB, Harri**

New Anglo-Welsh poets.
Western Mail Literary Review, July 10, 1965.
p. 10.

B 47 : **WILLIAMS, Huw Menai**

[An adjudication at the 1930 Welsh National
Eisteddfod, Llanelly, on a competition for a
volume of original poetry in English,
written by a Welshman, or one of Welsh
descent].
Welsh Outlook. Vol. 17, 1930. pp. 235—243.

B 48 : **WILLIAMS, Michael**

Welsh voices in the short story.
(*a*) Welsh Review, Vol. VI, no. 4, 1947,
pp. 290—8.
(*b*) Little Reviews Anthology ; ed. by D. Val
Baker, 1949. pp. 103—116.

B 49 : **WILLIAMS, Waldo**

Anglo-Welsh and Welsh.
Dock Leaves, Vol. 4, no. 12, 1953. pp. 31—35.

B 50 : **WILSON, Adrian**

Fiction of Wales.
Welsh Outlook. Vol. V, July 1918. pp.
215—216.

B 51 : **WILSON, Eunice**

These I have loved.
Y Ddinas. Vol. 6, no. 1, 1951. p. 11.
Comprises review article of T. Rowland
Hughes' *From Hand to Hand* and Thomas
Firbank's *I Bought a Mountain*.

II. ANGLO-WELSH LITERATURE :
INDIVIDUAL AUTHORS

Arranged under the names of individual authors as
subject-headings, this section contains references to
critical, bibliographical and biographical sources. Further
references to authors prominent in the general sphere of
English literature will be found in the *Annual Bibliography of
English Language and Literature* (Modern Humanities
Research Association, latest issue, Vol. XL, 1965).

ABSE, Dannie

B 52 : Poet in the family.
The Listener, 69. 21 March, 1963. pp. 501—3.

AMIS, Kingsley

B 53 : Bergonzi, Bernard
Kingsley Amis.
London Magazine, 3 Jan. 1964. pp. 50—65.

B 54 : Bergonzi, Bernard
Reputations—IX : Kingsley Amis.
London Magazine. Vol. 3, no. 10, January,
1964. pp. 50—65.

B 55 : Brophy, Brigid
Just Jim.
Sunday Times Colour Magazine. Jan. 26, 1964.
pp. 11—13.
[Analyses structure and technique of *Lucky Jim*
and other Amis novels].

B 56 : Colville, Derek
The sane new world of Kingsley Amis.
Bucknell Review, Vol. 9, 1960. pp. 46—57.

B 57 : Conquest, Robert
Christian symbolism in "Lucky Jim".
Critical Quarterly. Vol. 7, no. 1, 1965.
pp. 87—92.

B 58 : Gindin, James
Postwar British fiction.
London ; Cambridge U.P., 1962.
pp. 34—50 : Kingsley Amis' funny novels.

B 59 : Hilty, Peter
Kingsley Amis and mid-century humor.
Discourse, Jan. 1960. pp. 26—8 ; 37—45.

B 60 : Lodge, David
The modern, the contemporary, and the
importance of being Amis.
Critical Quarterly. Vol. 5, no. 4, 1963.
pp. 335—354.
(Includes critical assessments of the Amis
novels).

B 61 : Parker, R. B.
Farce and society : the range of Kingsley Amis.
Wisconsin Studies in Contemporary Literature.
Fall, 1961. pp. 27—28.

BELL, Sir Harold Idris

B 62 : Reply to ' Wales ' Questionnaire.
Wales, Vol. VI, no. 3, 1946. p. 24.

CONRAN, Anthony

B 63 : The English poet in Wales, I. The alien corn.
Anglo-Welsh Review, Vol. 10, no. 25, undated.
pp. 28—35.

The English poet in Wales, II. Boys of summer
in their ruin.
Anglo-Welsh Review, Vol. 10, no. 26, undated.
pp. 11—21.

COOMBES, B. L.

B 64 : Reply to ' Wales ' Questionnaire.
Wales. Vol. VI, no. 3, 1946. pp. 25—26.

CRONIN, Archibald Joseph

B 65 : Frederick, John T.
A. J. Cronin.
College English. Vol. III, 1941. pp. 121—9.

DAVIES, Idris

B 66 : Collins, William John Townsend
Idris Davies of Rhymney.
Monmouthshire Writers.   Newport, Mon.,
R. H. Johns, 1945. pp. 147—150.
(Includes extracts from *The Angry Summer*,
Tonypandy and *Gwalia Deserta*).

B 67 : Jenkins, Islwyn
Idris Davies : a poet of Rhymney.
Anglo-Welsh Review.   Vol. 9, no. 23, 1958.
pp. 13—21.

B 68 : Jones, Glyn
Idris Davies : the man and the poet.
Y Ddinas. Vol. 13, no. 9, 1959. pp. 10—11.

B 69 : ' Poetry and Drama Magazine '.
Idris Davies (1905—53).
(A special number of the Poetry and Drama
Magazine, Vol. 9, no. 2, 1957).

DAVIES, Rhys

B 70 : [Autobiographical notes].
Wales, Sept. 1958, p. 7 (with portrait).

B 71 : [Bibliography].
Wales. No. 3, Autumn 1937. p. 133.
(No. 2 in series of "Bibliographies of modern
Welsh authors").

B 72 : Replies to ' Wales ' Questionnaire.
Wales. Vol. VI, no. 2, 1946. pp. 18—19.
(Considers the writer's own attitude to Anglo-
Welsh writing).

B 73 : Gawsworth, John, *pseud.* (*i.e. Terence Ian Fytton
Armstrong*)
Ten contemporaries : notes toward their
definitive bibliography. London ; Benn, 1932.
pp. 44—52 : Bibliography of the works of Rhys
Davies, prefaced by an essay by R.D.
(pp. 41—3).

B 74 : Mégroz, Rodolph Louis
Rhys Davies : a critical sketch.
London ; Foyle, 1932.
xiii, [1], 50p. 18½cm. cloth.

B 75 : Rees, David
Rhys Davies : professional author.
Wales, no. 6, 1959. pp. 70—3.

DAVIES, William Henry

B 76 : (Anon)
The apotheosis of W. H. Davies.
Shaded lights on men and books ; essays
selected from ' Peace of mind ' and
' Serenity '.
London, Melrose, 1922. pp. 88—94.

B 77 : Bibliography.
Wales. No. 10, 1939. pp. 289—290.
(No. 6 in series of "Bibliographies of Modern
Welsh Authors").

B 78 : Bibliographies of modern authors : 3 : W. H.
Davies.
London Mercury, Nov. 1927, pp. 76—80 ;
Jan. 1928, pp. 301—4 ; Apr. 1928, pp. 684—8.

B 79 : Church, Richard
Eight for immortality.
London, New York ; Dent, 1941.
pp. 1—12 : *W. H. Davies* (with frontispiece
portrait).

B 80 : Collins, William John Townsend
W. H. Davies, "The Tramp Poet".
Monmouthshire Writers. Newport, Mon.,
R. H. Johns, 1945. pp. 94—99 (with photo-
graph).
(Includes extract from ' Fancy ' : the poem
' Days that have been ' and ' The lodging
house fire ').

B 81 : De La Mare, Walter
W. H. Davies.
Private View. Faber, 1953. pp. 134—137.
(Reprinted from Times Literary Supplement,
June 8, 1916).

B 82 : Evans, Caradoc
W. H. Davies.
Welsh Review.   Vol. III, no. 3, 1944. pp.
183—186.
(Men and Women Series, no. 2).

B 83 : Gardiner, Wrey
The poems of W. H. Davies, 1940.
Poetry Quarterly. Vol. 2, no. 2, 1940. pp. 50-51.

B 84 : Gibbon, Monk
A great poet : [W. H. Davies].
Then and Now : a selection . . . from the first
fifty numbers of "Now and Then", 1921—35.
London, Cape, 1935. pp. 55—58 (1934).

B 85 : Hockey, Lawrence W.
Edward Thomas and W. H. Davies : [record
of a friendship].
Welsh Review. Vol. 7, no. 2, 1948. pp. 81—91.

Irving and W. H. Davies.
TLS, Feb. 5, 1944, p. 67.

W. H. Davies and his family.
Welsh Review. Vol. V, no. 3, 1946. pp. 191—5.

B 86 : John, Francis
Sidelights on the super-tramp.
Western Mail (Weekend Magazine), Jan. 21,
1961. p. 1.

B 87 : Knight, Laura
W. H. Davies.
Cornhill Magazine, Vol. 174, No. 1042,
Winter 1964/65.
pp. 282—292 (with photograph).
(Reminiscences of a visit by Davies to the
Cornwall home of the Knights in 1922).

B 88 : Lock, D. R.
The poetry of Mr. W. H. Davies.
Holborn Review, Oct. 1927. pp. 483—90.

B 89 : Looker, S. J.
Man and super-tramp : W. H. Davies, his life
and work.
Bookman's Journal. Vol. 16, 1928. pp. 363—70.

B 90 : Moult, Thomas.
[An appreciation].
Bookman, Nov. 1921. pp. 85—88 [with four
portraits].

B 91 : Obituary articles : (1) Journey's end of the
tramp poet.
Western Mail, Sep. 27, 1940 (with editorial
comment), p. 4.
TLS : Oct. 5, 1940. p. 508.
Times : Sept. 27, 1940. p. 7.

B 92 : Owen, David
The super-tramp in London.
Y Ddinas. Vol. 5, no. 3, 1950. pp. 4, 6.

B 93 : Parry-Williams, Sir Thomas Herbert
W. H. Davies—the super tramp.
The Dragon, Mar. 1917. pp. 89—96 ; continued
in June 1917, pp. 150—7.

B 94 : Sitwell, Sir Osbert
A character of the late W. H. Davies.
Horizon. Vol. 34, no. 59. pp. 2—12 ; Vol. 34,
no. 60, pp. 81—91.

B 95 : Sitwell, Sir Osbert
Irving and W. H. Davies : a letter [in reply to
L. W. Hockey].
TLS, Feb. 12, 1944. p. 79.
[L. W. Hockey writes in TLS, Feb. 5, 1944.
p. 67].

B 96 : Sitwell, Sir Osbert
Noble essences . . . being . . . the fifth and last
volume of Left Hand, Right Hand ! an autobiography.

London, Macmillan, 1950.
pp. 207—244 : W. H. Davies.

B 97 : Stonesifer, Richard James
W. H. Davies : a critical biography.
London ; Cape, 1963.
[6], 7—256p. 22cm. cloth.
pp. 13—152 : Biographical : pp. 155—232 :
Critical : pp. 233—4 : Chronology of
Davies's works.

B 98 : Stonesifer, Richard James
W. H. Davies : a critical biography.
Ann Arbor, Michigan ; University Microfilms,
1953.
(University Microfilms Publications, no. 5304).

B 99 : Stonesifer, Richard James
W. H. Davies and his Disney world.
Approach, No. 44, Summer 1962. pp. 3—10.
Analyses Davies's "creation of a haunting and
dream-like world which is of nature, but not
nature . . .''
(Twentieth Century Literature).

B 100 : Sturgeon, Mary C.
Studies of contemporary poets.
London, Harrap, 1916.
pp. 53—71 ; William H. Davies.

B 101 : Swann, John H.
The poetry of W. H. Davies.
The Papers of the Manchester Literary Club,
Vol. 52, 1926. pp. 54—63 (with bibliography).

B 102 : Williams, Charles
Poetry at present.
Oxford ; Clarendon Press, 1930.
pp. 70—82 : W. H. Davies.

B 103 : Williams, E[dward] Roland
The poetry of W. H. Davies.
Welsh Outlook. Vol. 5, Oct. 1918. pp. 304—306.

B 104 : Williams, Huw Menai
Simplicity in poetry : a critical note on W. H.
Davies.
Wales. New Series, 2. Oct. 1943. pp. 42—47.

B 105 : Wilson, George F.
A bibliography of W. H. Davies.
Bookman's Journal, March 1922. p. 202 ;
April, p. 29 ; May, p. 59.
(Bibliographies of Modern Authors, No. 17).

DAVIES, William Thomas Pennar

B 106 : Davies, W. T. P.
Reply to ' Wales ' Questionnaire.
Wales. Vol. VI, no. 3, 1946. p. 26.

EDWARDS, Dorothy

B 107 : Jones, S. Beryl
Dorothy Edwards as a writer of short stories.
Welsh Review, Vol. 7, no. 3, 1948, pp. 184—93.

B 108 : Watkins, H. M.
[An appreciation of Dorothy Edwards].
Wales, Vol. 6, 1946. pp. 43—50.

ETHERIDGE, Ken

B 109 : Etheridge, Ken
Towards a Cymric theatre.
Life & Letters Today. Vol. 17, no. 9, 1937.
pp. 142—5.
(Discusses production of the author's Anglo-
Welsh plays).

EVANS, [David] Caradoc

B 110 : [A bibliography]
Wales, No. 2, Aug. 1937. p. 78.

B 111 : Evans, Caradoc
Self-portrait.
Wales. (New Series), 3. Jan.—Mar. 1944.
pp. 83—5.

B 112 : Evans, D. L.
Caradoc Evans' boyhood days.
Wales. Vol. VII, no. 27, 1947. pp. 381—382.

B 113 : John, Ivor B.
The exploitation of bestiality.
Welsh Outlook. Vol. 4, March 1917. pp. 114-5.
(Assessment of "Capel Sion" and the work of
Caradoc Evans).

B 114 : John, Ivor B.
My People !
Welsh Outlook. Vol. III, 1916. pp. 83—84.

B 115 : Jones, Gwyn
Caradoc Evans.
Welsh Review. Vol. IV, no. 1, 1945. pp. 24—28.

B 116 : Marriott, R. B.
Caradoc Evans
Wales. Vol. V, no. 7, 1945. pp. 61—64.

B 117 : Rees, J. Seymour
Caradoc Evans. [Article in Welsh].
Yr Ymofynnydd. LII, no. 12, 1952. pp. 204—8.

B 118 : "Sandys, Oliver" (*i.e. Marguerite Florence Evans*)
Caradoc Evans.
London, New York, etc. ; Hurst and Blackett,
[1946].
[4], 5—167p. front. (port.) plates, 21½cm.
cloth.

B 119 : Wright, Edward
Caradoc Evans.
Bookman, Oct. 1917. pp. 6—7 (with portrait).

EVANS, George Ewart

B 120 : Evans, George Ewart
Replies to ' Wales ' Questionnaire.
Wales. No. 8/9, 1939. pp. 225—226.
(Considers the writer's own position in Anglo-
Welsh literature).

EVANS, Margiad

B 121 : [Bibliography].
Wales, No. 5, Summer 1938. pp. 181—2.

B 122 : Savage, Derek Stanley
The withered branch : six studies in the modern
novel.
London ; Eyre & Spottiswoode, 1950.
pp. 106—128 : Margiad Evans.

EVANS, William   ' *Wil Ifan* '

B 123 : Glamorgan County Council. *County Library.*
Wil Ifan : [a] bibliography of Welsh and
English works ; [edited by] H. J. Williams,
B.A., F.L.A.
Bridgend, Glam. ; Glamorgan County Library,
1959.
[3], ii, [1], 46p. 21½cm. wrappers.
Second t.p. in Welsh. pp. 36—46 : Title and
first line index to Wil Ifan's English poetry
and prose.

FRANCIS, John Oswald

B 124 : [Anon]
J. O. Francis : (a profile).
Y Ddinas. Vol. 9, no. 2, 1954, pp. 4, 9 (with
portrait).

B 125 : "E.T.R."
[Review of four plays of J. O. Francis].
Y Ddolen. Vol. 2, no. 14, 1927. p. 19.
[Reviews of : The beaten track ; The perfect
husband ; Birds of a feather ; John Jones].

B 126 : Jones, Idwal
[Review of four plays of J. O. Francis : Birds
of a feather ; John Jones ; The beaten
track ; The perfect husband].
The Dragon, Michaelmas Term 1927. pp. 33—4.

B 127 : Obituary.
Y Ddinas. Vol. II, no. 2, Nov. 1956. p. 10.

GALLIE, Menna

B 128 : Stephens, Raymond
The novelist and community : Menna Gallie.
Anglo-Welsh Review. Vol. 14, no. 34. pp. 52-63.

GLYNNE-JONES, William

B   129 : [Anon]
You meet them here : [a portrait of W.G.-J.].
Y Ddinas. Vol. 1, no. 2. Nov. 1946. p. 8.

GRIFFITH, Llewelyn Wyn

B   130 : Griffith, Llewelyn Wyn
Reply to ' Wales ' Questionnaire.
Wales. Vol. VI, no. 3, 1946. p. 26.

HAYCOCK, B. Myfanwy

B   131 : Collins, William John Townsend
Myfanwy Haycock.
Monmouthshire Writers.   Newport, Mon.,
R. H. Johns, 1945. pp. 151—3.
(Includes the poems *Christmas Story, Snow, June
Thoughts*).

HERBERT, Evelyn

B   132 : Collins, William John Townsend
Evelyn Herbert.
Monmouthshire Writers.   Newport, Mon.,
R. H. Johns, 1945. pp. 127—131.
(Includes extracts entitled : A derelict town ;
The canal at Govilon ; The eisteddfod).

HOCKEY, Lawrence William

133 : Collins, William John Townsend
Lawrence William Hockey.
Monmouthshire Writers.   Newport, Mon.,
R. H. Johns, 1945. pp. 132—5.
(Includes the poems ' *Riches* ', ' *Clouds and Sun* ',
' *Full Moon* ', ' *Felling trees* ', ' *Farewell* ' and
' *The Master* ').

HUGHES, Richard Arthur Warren

B   134 : [Bibliography]
Wales. No. 4, March 1938. p. 156.
(No. 3 in series of "Bibliographies of Modern
Welsh Authors").

B   135 : Bosano, J.
Richard Hughes.
Études Anglaises, XVI, 1963. pp. 262—9.

B   136 : Kermode, Frank
[A fox in the attic] reviewed in Partisan
Review, Vol. 29, 1962, pp. 466—75 (in part).

HUGHES, Thomas Rowland

B   137 : Ruck, Richard C.
T. Rowland Hughes and his five novels.
Anglo-Welsh Review. Vol. 9, no. 24, 1958.
pp. 22—29.

HUMPHREYS, Emyr

B   138 : Humphreys, Emyr
Reply to ' Wales ' Questionnaire.
Wales. Vol. VI, no. 3, 1946. p. 27.

B   139 : Jones, John Gwilym
Dawn Emyr Humphreys. [Article in Welsh].
Yr Arloeswr Newydd. Rhif 1, 1959. pp. 17—18.
[Forms a critical assessment of *The Toy Epic* :
Welsh version *Y Tri Llais*].

JONES, David

B   140 : Bergonzi, Bernard
Heroes' twilight : a study of the literature of the
Great War.
London, Constable, 1965.
Chap. 10 : Remythologizing : David Jones'
In Parenthesis. pp. 198—212.

B   141 : Braybrooke, Neville
David Jones, painter and poet.
Queen's Quarterly, 70, Winter 1964.   pp.
508—14.

B   142 : Davie, Donald
In the pity.
New Statesman, Aug. 28, 1964. pp. 282—3.

B   143 : Davies, Aneirin Talfan
Awenydd y ' Pethe '.
"Western Mail", November 22, 1965. p. 8.
[Welsh descriptive article on the occasion of
the 70th birthday of David Jones].

B   144 : Eliot, Thomas Stearns
A note on ' In Parenthesis ' and ' The Anath-
emata '.
Dock Leaves. Vol. 6, no. 16, 1955. pp. 21—23.

B   145 : Hague, René
David Jones : a reconnaissance.
Twentieth Century. July 1960. pp. 27—45.

B   146 : Hollander, John
A raid on the inarticulate.   [Reviews ' In
Parenthesis '].
Partisan Review.   Vol. 29, no. 3, 1962. pp.
451—3.

B   147 : Holloway, John
A perpetual showing.
Hudson Review, Vol. 16, 1963. pp. 122—130.
[Reviews ' In Parenthesis ' and ' The Ana-
themata '].

B   148 : Johnston, John H.
English poetry of the First World War.
Princeton, New Jersey, Princeton U.P. ;
London, Oxford U.P., 1964.
pp. 284—340 : *The heroic vision : David Jones*.

B 149 : Jones, David
History and pre-history.
Dock Leaves. Vol. 6, no. 16, 1955. pp. 18—21.
[David Jones outlines his own Welsh background].

B 150 : Jones, David
Replies to ' Wales ' Questionnaire.
Wales. Vol. VI, no. 2, 1946. pp. 84—88.
[Considers the writer's own attitude to Anglo-Welsh writing].

B 151 : Petts, John
David Jones : an introduction.
Dock Leaves. Vol. 6, no. 16, 1955. pp. 10—17.

B 152 : Rees, David
Profile I : David Jones.
Wales. No. 41, 1959. pp. 74—8.

B 153 : Speaight, Robert
The anathemata [Personal Preference].
TLS., Aug. 6, 1954. pp. xxxii—xxxiii.

JONES, Glyn

B 154 : Jones, Glyn
Reply to ' Wales ' Questionnaire.
Wales. Vol. VI, no. 3, 1946. pp. 26—27.

JONES, Gwyn

B 155 : Collins, William John Townsend
Gwyn Jones.
Monmouthshire Writers.   Newport, Mon.,
R. H. Johns, 1945. pp. 140—147.
[Includes extracts from *Times Like These* :
Caradoc Evans (*Welsh Review* article) : *Son of
the late Earl Rivers* (*Welsh Review* article)].

JONES, Jack

B 156 : [Anon]
Welsh profile, 7 : Jack Jones.
Welsh Review, Vol. VI, no. 3, 1947. pp.
168—71.

B 157 : Davies, Anthony
A mirror of Welsh life : Jack Jones at home and
abroad.
Y Ddinas. Vol. 1, no. 4, 1947. pp. 6, 12.
[Includes excerpts from "*Me and Mine*"].

B 158 : Davies, Anthony
When Dr. Joseph Parry came to London to
win fame.
Y Ddinas. Vol. 2, no. 2, 1947. pp. 2, 12.
[Descriptive article on "*Off to Philadelphia in the
Morning*"].

B 159 : Jones, Jack
My literary life.
Western Mail, Nov. 25, 1957, p. 4 ; Nov. 26,
p. 4 ; Nov. 27, p. 6 ; Nov. 28, p. 6.

B 160 : "W.G." [William Griffiths]
A distinguished Welshman.
Y Ddinas. Vol. 5, no. 2, 1950. pp. 10, 11.

B 161 : Williams, [George] Emlyn
Jack Jones.
Welsh Review. Vol. 1, no. 4, 1939. pp.
205—208.

JONES, Lewis

B 162 : Garman, Douglas
A revolutionary writer.
Welsh Review. Vol. 1, no. 5. pp. 263—267.
[An assessment of the novelist Lewis Jones and
his work, *Cwmardy* and *We Live*].

JONES, Thomas Gwynn

B 163 : Denbighshire County Council. *County Library*.
A bibliography of Thomas Gwynn Jones,
reprinted from "The Bibliography of Denbighshire, Part 3", together with a biographical note and an index compiled by Owen
Williams . . .
Wrexham, Principality Press, 1938.
[2], 3—53p. 21½cm. cloth.
Also : Atodiad (Supplement), 1956.
Notes T.G.J.'s English contributions to periodicals and newspapers.

JONES, Thomas Henry

B 164 : Jones, Gwyn
T. H. Jones : [obituary].
Poetry Wales, I, Spring 1965. p. 16.

B 165 : Partridge, Colin John
The verse of T. H. Jones.
Poetry Wales, I, no. 2, 1965. pp. 3—7.

LEWIS, Alun

B 166 : Duncan, Ronald H.
Towards a re-examination of Alun Lewis.
Chance [No. 4], Autumn 1953. pp. 87—92.

B 167 : Evans, George Ewart
The foils are poisoned that the good might die.
[An obituary of Alun Lewis].
Wales. New Series, 4. Summer 1944. pp. 4—5.

B 168 : Hamilton, Ian
Poetry : the Forties—I.
London Magazine.   Vol. 4, no. 1, 1964.
pp. 81—89.
[Includes assessment of the writings of Alun
Lewis].

B 169 : Harding, Joan
Welsh poet with the magic of Keats.
Western Mail Literary Review, Aug. 7, 1965.
p. 9.

B 170 : Hutton, W. R.
The poetry of Alun Lewis.
Bristol Writers and Artists Association.
Bristol Packet, (no. 2, 1945). 73 et seq.

B 171 : Jones, Gwyn
Alun Lewis (1915—1944).
Welsh Review. Vol. III, no. 2, 1944. pp.
118—121.

B 172 : Morgan, Gerald
Alun Lewis, 1915—44. [Welsh article].
Barn. Rhagfyr (Dec.) 1965. pp. 43—4.

B 173 : Ross, Julien Maclaren
Second Lieutenant Lewis : a memoir.
The Funny bone.   London, Elek, 1956.
pp. 175—184.

B 174 : Stephens, Myfanwy
Two Welsh poets.   [Edward Thomas and
Alun Lewis].
Y Ddinas. Vol. 4, no. 8, 1950. p. 8.
[Reviews Collected Poems and The Trumpet and
other poems (Edward Thomas) and Raiders'
Dawn and Ha ! Ha ! Among the Trumpets
(Alun Lewis)].

B 175 : Symes, Gordon
Muse in India : an aspect of Alun Lewis.
English. Vol. 6, no. 34, 1947. pp. 191—5.

B 176 : Williams, John Stuart
The short stories of Alun Lewis.
Anglo-Welsh Review, Vol. 14, no. 34, 1964-5.
pp. 16—25.

The poetry of Alun Lewis.
Anglo-Welsh Review, Vol. 14, no. 33, 1964.
pp. 59—71.

LEWIS, Howell Elvet

B 177 : A bibliography.
Journal of the Welsh Bibliographical Soc., 1954,
Vol. 8, no. 1. pp. 7—23 ; Vol. 8, no. 3, 1955.
p. 106.

LEWIS, John Saunders

B 178 : [Anon]
Welsh profile : Saunders Lewis.
Welsh Review. Vol. V, no. 4, 1946. pp. 258—
263.

B 179 : Jones, Percy Mansell
Sketches for a portrait.
Davies, W. T. Pennar, ed. Saunders Lewis : ei
feddwl a'i waith [Welsh volume].
Denbigh, Gee, 1950. pp. 18—27.

B 180 : Wynne, R. O. F.
Saunders Lewis [Essay in English].
ibid. pp. 28—31.

MACHEN, Arthur

For a detailed bibliography of Arthur Machen critic-
ism, see Goldstone, Adrian and Sweetser, Wesley D. (B 184).
The entries below represent a brief selection only of
Machen bibliography and criticism.

B 181 : Collins, William John Townsend
Arthur Machen.
Monmouthshire Writers, Newport, Mon. ;
R. H. Johns, 1945.
pp. 90—94 (with photograph).
[Includes an extract from "The Hill of Dreams"
and from "Far-off Things"].

B 182 : Danielson, Henry, comp.
Arthur Machen : a bibliography with notes,
biographical and critical, by A. Machen and
an introduction by Henry Savage.
London ; H. Danielson, 1923.
x, [1], 59p. front. (port.) facsim. 21½cm. cloth.
Publ. in a limited ed. of 500 copies.

B 183 : Fletcher, Ifan Kyrle
Arthur Machen.
Welsh Outlook. Vol. 13, 1926. pp. 134—5.

B 184 : Goldstone, Adrian and Sweetser, Wesley D.
A bibliography of Arthur Machen.
Austin, Texas ; The University of Texas, 1965.
180, [2]p. illus. ports. facsims. 25cm. cloth.
Title-page reproduces the frontispiece to
Machen's The Shining Pyramid. 500 copies of
this bibliography were printed. pp. 146—
164 : select bibliog. of criticism and commentary on the works of Machen.

B 185 : Holroyd, J. E.
Apostle of wonder.
The Guardian, March 2, 1963. p. 5.

B 186 : John, Alun
Arthur Machen and ' The Angels of Mons '.
Anglo-Welsh Review, Vol. 14, no. 34, 1964—5.
pp. 10—14.

B 187 : Mais, Stuart Petre Brodie
Some modern authors.
London, Grant Richards, 1923. pp. 211—17 :
Arthur Machen.

B 188 : Mathias, Roland
Editorial [on the work of Arthur Machen].
Anglo-Welsh Review. Vol. 14, no. 33, 1964,
pp. 3—5.

B 189 : Michael, D[avid] Parry M[artin]
Machen centenary.
Western Mail, March 2, 1963. p. 5.
Also : Poem by Lawrence W. Hockey. The
Master : In Memoriam, Arthur Machen,
born March 3, 1863. The above article
includes publication history of Machens'
major works.

B 190 : Sweetser, Wesley D.
Arthur Machen.
New York, Twayne Publishers Inc., 1964.
[16], 17—175p. 20½cm. cloth.
(Twayne's English Authors Series, no. 8).
Includes : Chronology of Machen's life and
publications.
pp. 157—165 : Selected bibliography, primary and secondary sources.

B 191 : Sweetser, Wesley D.
Arthur Machen [London]. 1960. 24p. 22cm.
(Lib. of Congress National Union Catalogue,
1958—62).

B 182 : Sweetser, Wesley D.
Arthur Machen : a miscellany.
[Llandeilo, St. Albert's Press, 1960].
43p. 22cm.
Reprinted, with additions, from the *Aylesford
Review*.
350 copies printed. (Lib. of Congress National
Union Catalogue, 1958—62).

B 193 : Sweetser, Wesley D.
The works of Arthur Machen : an analysis and
bibliography : a thesis . . . of the University
of Colorado . . . 1958.
Ann Arbor, Michigan ; University Microfilms
Inc., 1958.
[7], 479p. 22½cm. wrappers.
pp. 374—479 : Bibliographical apparatus, incl.
primary and secondary sources.

B 194 : Wells, Geoffrey H.
A Welsh border writer.
Welsh Outlook. Vol. 11, 1924, pp. 15—16.

MORGAN, Elaine

B 195 : Lipman, Beata
A playwright's life of chasing deadlines.
[Descriptive article, with portrait].
Western Mail, April 21, 1964. p. 7.

MORGAN, Evan   *Viscount Tredegar*

B 196 : Collins, William John Townsend
Evan Morgan, Viscount Tredegar.
Monmouthshire Writers, Newport, Mon. ;
R. H. Johns, 1945. pp. 120—124 (with
photograph). [Includes poems ' The Eel ',
' Dragonfly ', ' A Saturday ', ' My Bed ' and
' Little Fish '].

OWEN, Alun

B 197 : Taylor, John Russell
Anger and after : a guide to the new British
drama.
London, Methuen, 1962. (repr. 1963).
pp. 183—202 : *Alun Owen.*

POWYS, John Cowper

B 198 : Aury, Dominique
Reading Powys ; translated by Margaret
Davies.
A Review of English Literature. Vol. 4, no. 1,
1963. pp. 33—37.

B 199 : Braybrooke, Neville
Tribute to Powys.
Western Mail Literary Review, June 11, 1964.
p. 1.

B 200 : Ghose, Zulfikar
Powys—a poetical failure.
Western Mail Literary Review, Dec. 5, 1964,
p. 1.

B 201 : Hanbury, Michael
John Cowper Powys and some Catholic
contacts.
The Month, No. 30, Nov. 1963. pp. 299—303.

B 202 : Hanley, James
The man in the corner.
Dock Leaves. Vol. 7, no. 19, 1956. pp. 2—7.

B 203 : Hicks, Eric
John Cowper Powys at eighty-six.
Wales, 1958. No. 3. pp. 60—4.

B 204 : Hopkins, Kenneth
A note on the poetry of John Cowper Powys.
Dock Leaves. Vol. 7, no. 19, 1956. pp. 10—17.

B 205 : Knight, G. Wilson
Owen Glendower.
A Review of English Literature. Vol. 4, no. 1,
1963. pp. 41—52.

B 206 : Mathias, Roland
[Editorial assessment of the work of J. C.
Powys].
Anglo—Welsh Review. Vol. 13, no. 32, 1963.
pp. 3—6.

B 207 : Mathias, Roland
Gwlad-yr-Haf.
Dock Leaves. Vol. 7, no. 19, 1956. pp. 20—29.
[Critical article on J. C. Powys' ' A Glastonbury
Romance '].

B 208 : Miller, Henry
The immortal bard.
A Review of English Literature. Vol. 4, no. 1,
1963. pp. 21—24.

B 209 : O'Connor, Philip
[Obituary of J. C. Powys].
The London Welshman. Vol. 18, no. 8,
Aug. 1963. p. 20.

B 210 : Painter, George D.
The oar and the winnowing fan.
Dock Leaves. Vol. 7, no. 19, 1956. pp. 32—45.

B 211 : Peate, Iorwerth Cyfeiliog
John Cowper Powys : letter writer.
A Review of English Literature. Vol. 4, no. 1,
1963. pp. 38—40.
Appended are two plates, I and II : showing
Gertrude Powys' portrait of J.C.P. and
holograph first and last leaves of a letter
from Powys to Peate in November 1947.

B 212 : Powys, John Cowper
Answer to ' Wales ' questionnaire.
Wales. No. 10, 1939. pp. 280—281.

B 213 : Priestley, John Boynton
The happy introvert.
A Review of English Literature. Vol. 4, no. 1,
1963. pp. 25—32.

B 214 : Russell, Robert
John Cowper Powys : [a tribute].
Dock Leaves. Vol. 3, no. 7, 1952. pp. 7—10.

B 215 : Wilson, Angus
' Mythology ' in John Cowper Powys ' novels.
A Review of English Literature. Vol. 4, no. 1,
1963. pp. 9—20.

POWYS FAMILY

B 216 : Marlow, Louis
Welsh ambassadors.
London, Chapman & Hall, 1936.
xi, [1], 284p. front. plates. 21½cm. cloth.
A study of John, Theodore Francis and
Llewelyn Powys.
pp. 269—275 : Bibliography of J. C. Powys.

B 217 : Powys, Littleton C.
The Powys family.
Little Reviews Anthology, 1949. pp. 154—176.
Welsh Review, Vol. VII, no. 1, 1948. pp. 3—19.

B 218 : Ward, Richard Heron
The Powys brothers : a study.
London, Bodley Head, 1935.
xvii, [3], 201, [3]p. illus. (ports.) 21½cm. cloth.
pp. 1—80 : John Cowper Powys.

B 219 : Wilkinson, Louis Unfreville
The brothers Powys.
Essays by divers hands. New Series, Vol. 24,
1948. pp. 40—62.

PRYS-JONES, Arthur Glyn

B 220 : Reid, E. A.
Modern poetry and a Welsh poet.
Welsh Outlook. Vol. 13, 1926. pp. 45—47.
[Review article on A. G. Prys-Jones' *Poems of
Wales*].

"RAINE, Allen" (*i.e. Anne Adalisa Puddicombe*)

B 221 : Griffiths, William
Ada Evans . . . a dream . . . and success.
Y Ddinas. Vol. 2, no. 10, 1948. p. 8.

B 222 : Rhys, Ernest
A bibliography.
Manchester Guardian, June 24 and 27, 1908.

RHYS, Ernest

B 223 : [Anon.]
[Ernest Rhys and the Everyman Series :
[a tribute].
Y Ddinas. Vol. 11, no. 7, May 1956. p. 3.

B 224 : Griffith, Llewelyn Wyn
Ernest Rhys.
The British Annual of Literature, 1939. Vol. 2.
pp. 16—19 (with a portrait of E.R.)

ROBERTS, Kate

B 225 : Jones, R. Gerallt
An introduction to the work of Kate Roberts.
Anglo-Welsh Review. Vol. 9, no. 24 (undated).
pp. 10—21.

THOMAS, Dylan [Marlais]

A comprehensive bibliography of Dylan Thomas's
original works will be found in Rolph, John Alexander :
Dylan Thomas : a bibliography (B 303) but this bibliography
does not record criticism of Thomas's work. In view of the
now extensive nature of this commentary and criticism,
which would properly form the subject of a complete
bibliography in its own right, the entries appended
below represent only a selection of the critical volumes and
articles most readily accessible in British libraries.

B 226 : [Anon.]
Dylan Thomas, 1914—1953.
Gower (magazine of the Gower Society), 1953.
6 : pp. 2—6 (incl. portrait).

B 227 : Ackerman, John (*i.e. John Ackerman Jones*)
Dylan Thomas : his life and work.
London, New York (etc.) ; Oxford U.P., 1964.
[14], 201p. front. (port.) 4 facsims. 21½cm.
cloth. pp. 191—194 : Select bibliography.

B 228 : "Adam" (*magazine*)
Adam International Review : Dylan Thomas
memorial number. No. 238. London, 1953.

B 229 : Arlott, John
Dylan Thomas and radio.
Adelphi, Vol. 30, no. 2, 1954. pp. 121—4.

B 230 : Blackburn, Thomas
The price of an eye.
London, Longmans, 1961.   *pp.* 111—123 :
Dylan Thomas.

B 231 : Breit, Harvey
The writer observed.
London ; A. Redman, 1957.   *pp.* 123—5 ;
231—3 : *Dylan Thomas.*

B 232 : Brinnin, John Malcolm, *editor.*
A casebook on Dylan Thomas.
New York ; Thomas Y. Crowell Company,
1960.
xiii, 322p. 21cm. Paper cover.
Another impression : 1961.
     „   „   1964.
[Analyses of ten poems, with a collection of
critical articles and observations : pp. 295—
310 : Bibliog. of primary and secondary
sources].

B 233 : Brinnin, John Malcolm
Dylan Thomas in America : an intimate
journal.
Boston ; Little, Brown, 1955.
Reprinted November and December, 1955.
[14], 303p. front (port.), plates, facsim. 20cm.
cloth.
—Another edition, London, Dent, 1956.
ix, [1], 245p. front (port.), plates. 21cm. cloth.

B 234 : Campbell, Roy, *and others*
O weep for Adonais : tribute to Dylan Thomas
by Roy Campbell, Elizabeth Lutyens, John
Lehmann, Emanuel Litvinoff [and] Stephen
Spender.
Adam International Review.   Nos. 235—7,
1953. pp. 3—5.

B 235 : Church, Richard
Dylan Thomas : the early poems.
Adelphi, Vol. 30, no. 2, 1954. pp. 118—20.

B 236 : Corman, Cid
Dylan Thomas : rhetorician in mid-career.
Accent. Vol. 13, no. 1, 1953. pp. 56—59.
[Forms a review of *Collected Poems, 1934—1953*].

B 237 : Cox, Charles Brian
Dylan Thomas's *Fern Hill.*
Critical Quarterly.   Vol. 1, no. 2, 1959.
pp. 134—138.

B 238 : Cox, Charles Brian *and* Dyson, Anthony
Edward
The practical criticism of poetry.
London, Edward Arnold, 1965.
pp. 162—5 : Dylan Thomas's "Fern Hill", with
critical and analytical questions.

B 239 : Daiches, David
The poetry of Dylan Thomas.
Literary Essays. Oliver & Boyd, 1956.
pp. 50—61.
[First publ. in *The English Journal* (Chicago)
October, 1954].

B 240 : Davies, Aneirin Talfan
Dylan : Druid of the broken body.
London ; Dent, 1964.
ix, [1], 75p. 18cm. cloth.
Wrapper : ". . . an assessment of Dylan Thomas
as a religious poet . . . originally given in two
lectures at the invitation of the Honourable
Society of Cymmrodorion and at the State of
New York University at Buffalo . . ."

B 241 : Davies, Aneirin Talfan
The golden echo.
Dock Leaves. Vol. 5, no. 13, 1954. pp. 10—17.
Discusses four anthologies of modern poems
read by the poet for the B.B.C., March 1953.

B 242 : Davies, William Thomas Pennar
Sober reflections on Dylan Thomas.
Dock Leaves. Vol. 5, no. 15, 1954. pp. 13—17.

B 243 : Emery, Clark
The world of Dylan Thomas.
Florida ; University of Miami Press, 1962.
[14], 319p. 22½cm. cloth.
(University of Miami Publications in English
and American Literature, No. 6, 1962).

B 244 : Firmage, George J., *compiler*
A garland for Dylan Thomas.
Advisory editor, Oscar Williams.
New York ; Clarke & Way, 1963.
xvi, 171p. 19½cm. boards.
[Selected tributes to the memory of Dylan
Thomas].
Includes poems by Dannie Abse, Anthony
Conran, Ken Etheridge, T. H. Jones, T.
James Jones, Leslie Norris and Vernon
Watkins.

B 245 : Fitzgibbon, Constantine
The life of Dylan Thomas.
London, Dent, 1965.
ix, 422p. front. plates, facsims., 21cm. cloth.

B 246 : Fraser, George Sutherland
Dylan Thomas.
London, New York, [etc.] ; Longmans, Green,
for the British Council and the National Book
League, 1957.
[4], 5—36p. front (port.) 21½cm. wrappers.
(Writers and Their Work Series, no. 90).
pp. 35—6 : Bibliography.

B 247 : Fraser, George Sutherland
Vision and rhetoric.
London, Faber, 1959.   *pp.* 211—241 : *Dylan
Thomas.*

B 248 : Garlick, Raymond
Editorial notice : obituary.
Dock Leaves. Vol. 5, no. 13, 1954. pp. 1—5.

B 249 : Garlick, Raymond
The endless breviary : aspects of the work of
Dylan Thomas.
The Month, New Series, Vol. 11, no. 3,
March 1954, pp. 143—53.

B   250 : Garlick, Raymond
The interpreted evening : a note on Dylan
Thomas' pattern-poem.
Adam International Review, No. 257, 1956,
pp. 10—15.
[A critical appreciation of the poem ' Vision
and Prayer '].

B   251 : Goodwin, J. C. H.
Interpretations. 1. Dylan Thomas.
Prospect, Vol. 2, no. 12, 1949, pp. 4—6.

B   252 : Graddon, John and Johnson, Geoffrey
Dylan Thomas yes and no : [reviews of
Collected Poems, 1934—1952].
The Poetry Review, Vol. 44, 1953. pp. 338—
342, followed by readers' comments.

B   253 : Griffiths, Bryn
Ten years after.
The London Welshman. Vol. 18, no. 12, 1963.
p. 4.

B   254 : Grigson, Geoffrey
Dylan and the dragon.
New Statesman, Dec. 18, 1964. pp. 968—9.

B   255 : Grigson, Geoffrey
Recollections of Dylan Thomas.
London Magazine.   Vol. 4, no. 9, 1957.
pp. 39—45.

B   256 : Hardwick, Elizabeth
America and Dylan Thomas.
Partisan Review. Vol. 23, no. 2, 1956.
pp. 258—264.

B   257 : Hawkes, Terence
Dylan Thomas' Welsh.
College English. Vol. 21, March 1960.
pp. 345—7.

B   258 : Heppenstall, Rayner
Four absentees.
London ; Barrie & Rockliff, 1960.
pp. 9—96 : Dylan Thomas.

B   259 : Heppenstall, Rayner
My bit of Dylan Thomas.
[No imprint].
[24]p. facsim. 21½cm. limp cloth.
Limited ed. of 80 copies for private circulation.

B   260 : Holbrook, David
Llareggub revisited : Dylan Thomas and the
state of modern poetry.
London, Bowes and Bowes, 1962.
[14], 15—255p. 21½cm. cloth.

B   261 : Horan, Robert
In defense of Dylan Thomas.
Kenyon Review, Vol. VII, Spring 1945.
pp. 304—10.

B   262 : Hornick, L. R.
The intricate image : a study of Dylan Thomas.
Ann Arbor, U.S.A. ; University Microfilms,
1958.
[Copy of this microfilm deposited in NLW].

B   263 : Huddlestone, Linden
An approach to Dylan Thomas.
Penguin New Writing, no. 35, 1948. pp. 123-60.

B   264 : Huddlestone, Linden
To take to give is all.
Adam Int. Rev., No. 238, 1953. pp. 44—7.

B   265 : James, Dwynwen
' I have longed to move away ' : an appreciation of Dylan Thomas.
Y Ddinas. Vol. 8, no. 3, 1953. p. 5 (with
portrait).

B   266 : Jenkins, David Clay
Dylan Thomas and Wales magaz'ne, with the
first complete list of Thomas' contribution to
Wales.
Trace, no. 30, 1959. pp. 1—8.

B   267 : Jenkins, David Clay
Dylan Thomas' Under Milk Wood : the Ameri-
can element.
Trace, no. 51, 1964. pp. 325—35.

B   268 : John, Augustus
The monogamous Bohemian.
Adam Int. Rev., No. 238, 1953. pp. 9—10.

B   269 : Jones, Daniel, and others
Memories and appreciations.
Encounter, Vol. II, no. 1, 1954.
pp. 9—17 : by Daniel Jones, Theodore
Roethke, Louis MacNeice, Marjorie Adix
and George Barker.

B   270 : Jones, Daniel and Davies, Aneirin Talfan
Obituary notices. 1 : by Daniel Jones, 2 : by
Aneirin Talfan Davies.
Dock Leaves. Vol. 4, no. 12, 1953. pp. 4—7.

B   271 : Jones, Glyn
Dylan Thomas and Welsh.
Dock Leaves. Vol. 5, no. 13, 1954. pp. 24—25.

B   272 : Jones, Gwyn
Welsh Dylan.
Adelphi. Vol. 30, no. 2, 1954. pp. 108—117.

B   273 : Jones, Thomas Henry
Dylan Thomas.
London, Oliver & Boyd, 1963.
[6], 118p. 18cm. wrappers. (Writers and
Critics Series, No. 23).
Bibliography (2pp.) of Dylan Thomas's princi-
pal works, and a selection of criticism.

B 274 : Kleinman, H. H.
The religious sonnets of Dylan Thomas : a
study in imagery and meaning.
Berkeley and Los Angeles ; University of
California P., 1963.
xii, [2], 153p. 21½cm. cloth. (Perspectives in
Criticism Series, 13). p. 147 : Brief bibli-
ography.

B 275 : Korg, Jacob
Imagery and universe in Dylan Thomas's
18 *Poems*.
Accent, Vol. 17, no. 1, 1957, pp. 3—15.

B 276 : Lewis, Evan Glyn
Dylan Thomas.
Welsh Review. Vol. 7, no. 4, 1948. pp. 270-281.

B 277 : Lewis, Lewis Haydn
Dylan Thomas a'i feirniaid. [Dylan Thomas
and his critics].
(Welsh article).
Y Traethodydd (The Essayist). Vol. 118, 1963,
pp. 79—89.

B 278 : Lewis, Saunders
Obituary notice.
Dock Leaves. Vol. 5, no. 13, 1954. Welsh &
English version.
[Text of a talk broadcast by the B.B.C.].

B 279 : Macleod, Runia Sheila
The Dylan I knew.
Adam Int. Rev., No. 258, 1953. pp. 17—23.
[Reproduces the poem 'That Sanity Be Kept',
Dylan Thomas's first published poem in the
Sunday Referee, 3rd Sept., 1933, together with
other poems].

B 280 : Mathias, Roland
A merry manshape (or, Dylan Thomas at a
distance).
Dock Leaves. Vol. 5, no. 13, 1954. pp. 30—39.

B 281 : Maud, Ralph N.
Dylan Thomas' first published poem.
Modern Language Notes, vol. 74, 1959.
pp. 117—8.

B 282 : Maud, Ralph N.
Dylan Thomas' *Collected Poems* : chronology of
composition.
PMLA, Vol. LXXVI, 3 : June 1961. pp. 292-7.

B 283 : Maud, Ralph N.
Dylan Thomas's poetry.
Essays in Criticism, Vol. IV, Oct. 1954.
pp. 411—420.

B 284 : Maud, Ralph N.
Entrances to Dylan Thomas' poetry.
Pittsburgh, Univ. of Pittsburgh Press.
Lowestoft, Suffolk ; Scorpion Press, 1963.
ix, [1], 175p. 19½cm. cloth.
Includes : pp. 121—148 : Chronology of
composition of Dylan Thomas' works.

B 285 : Melchiori, Giorgio
The tightrope walkers.
London, Routledge & K. Paul, 1956.
pp. 213—42 : *Dylan Thomas : the poetry of vision.*

B 286 : [Memoirs and obituaries]
Adam Int. Rev. No. 238, 1953. pp. 11—13.
By Philip Lindsay, David Daiches and Glyn
Jones. pp. 24—39, by Pamela Hansford
Johnson, [and others].

B 287 : Merwin, William Stanley
The religious poet.
Adam Int. Rev., No. 238, 1953. pp. 73—78.

B 288 : Mills, Ralph J., *jnr*.
Dylan Thomas : the endless monologue.
Accent, Vol. 20, no. 2, 1960. pp. 114—136.

B 289 : Moore, Geoffrey
Dylan Thomas.
Kenyon Review.   Vol. XVII, no. 2, 1955.
pp. 258—77.

B 290 : Moore, Nicholas
The poetry of Dylan Thomas.
Poetry Quarterly.   Vol. 10, no. 4,   1948.
pp. 229—236.

B 291 : Morton, Richard
Notes on the imagery of Dylan Thomas.
English Studies, 1962 : Vol. 43. pp. 155—164.

B 292 : Moynihan, William T.
Dylan Thomas and the ' Biblical Rhythm '.
PMLA. Vol. 79, 1964. pp. 631—47.
[The themes of Creation, Fall and Redemption
in Dylan Thomas's work].

B 293 : Olson, Elder
The poetry of Dylan Thomas.
Chicago, University of Chicago Press ;
London, Cambridge U.P., 1954.
vii, [1], 164p. 21½cm. cloth.
pp. 102—146 : Bibliography by William H.
Huff.

B 294 : Orwell, Charles
' Labour by singing light '.
Outposts, No. 13, 1949. pp. 26—28.

B 295 : Peschmann, Hermann
Dylan Thomas, 1912 (sic)—1953 : a critical
appreciation.
English. Vol. 10, 1954. pp. 84—87.

B 296 : Pike, Stephen *and* Holroyd, Stuart
Under Milk Wood yes and no : [reviews by S.
Pike and S. Holroyd]. The Poetry Review,
Vol. 45, 1954. pp. 164—7.

B 297 : Prys-Jones, Arthur Glyn
Death shall have no dominion : a tribute paid
to [Dylan Thomas] at the Memorial Recital
organised by the Cardiff Branch of the
Poetry Association, December 7th, 1953.
Dock Leaves. Vol. 5. no. 13, 1954. pp. 26—29.

B 298 : Prys-Jones, Arthur Glyn
No drums for Dylan.
The London Welshman. Vol. 17, no. 6, 1962.
p. 14.
[Forms review of Holbrook, David. *Llareggub Revisited*].

B 299 : Raymond, David
Lament for a poet.
Y Ddinas. Vol. 8, no. 3, 1953. pp. 1—2.

B 300 : Read, Bill
The days of Dylan Thomas, by Bill Read, with
photographs by Rollie Mckenna and others.
London, Weidenfeld & Nicolson, 1965.
[21], 22—184, [5]p. map. photos. 20½cm.
cloth. pp. 182—4 : Bibliography.

B 301 : Rhys, Keidrych
Old hat on Dylan.
The London Welshman. Vol. 16, no. 5, 1961.
pp. 9—10.
Review article on Tedlock, E. W., *Dylan Thomas, the legend and the poet*.

B 302 : Rodgers, W. R.
Dylan Thomas.
Listener, May 27, 1954. pp. 913—14.

B 303 : Rolph, John Alexander
Dylan Thomas : a bibliography.
Foreword by Dame Edith Sitwell.
London, Dent ; New York, New Directions,
1956.
xix, [1], 108p. front (port.), plates. 21cm.
cloth.

B 304 : Ross, Ethel
Dylan Thomas and the amateur theatre.
The Swan : magazine of the Swansea Training
College.
No. 2 (3rd Series), March 1958. pp. 15—21.

B 305 : Ross, J. E.
"We had evidence and no doubt".
Gower, Vol. XVI, 1964. pp. 147—50.
[Records impressions and memories (by others)
of Dylan Thomas as a child].

B 306 : Rothberg, Winterset (*i.e. Theodore Roethke*)
One ring-tailed roarer to another.
Poetry (Chicago). Vol. 81, no. 3, 1952.
pp. 184—6.
[Forms review of *In Country Sleep, and other Poems*. N.Y., New Directions, 1952].

B 307 : Rousillat, Suzanne
(D.T.) His work and background.
Adam Int. Rev. No. 238, 1953. pp. 66—72
(with bibliography).

B 308 : Rowlands, Sheila
The literary topography of Laugharne.
Dock Leaves. Vol. 5, no. 15, 1954. pp. 38—40.

B 309 : Sanesi, Roberto
Dylan Thomas.
Milan ; Larici, 1960.
200, [2]p. 21½cm. Paper.

B 310 : Saroyan, William
The wild boy.
Books and Bookmen. July 1964. pp. 5—7.

B 311 : Savage, D[erek] S[tanley]
Dylan Thomas.
Little Reviews Anthology, 1947-48. pp. 201—6.

B 312 : Scarfe, Francis
Auden and after : the liberation of poetry,
1930—1941.
London, Routledge, 1942.
pp. 101—117 : *Dylan Thomas (with portrait)*.

B 313 : Scarfe, Francis
The poetry of Dylan Thomas.
Horizon, Nov. 1940. pp. 226—39.

B 314 : Scott, Hardiman
From death to entrance.
Outposts, No. 7, 1947. pp. 12—14.

B 315 : Sergeant, Howard
The religious development of Dylan Thomas.
A Review of English Literature. Vol. 3, no. 2,
1962. pp. 59—67.

B 316 : Smith, A. J.
Ambiguity as poetic shift.
Critical Quarterly. Vol. 4, no. 1, 1962.
pp. 68—74.
[Forms an assessment of D.T.'s poem ' Our
Eunuch Dreams ', from 18 *poems*. The poem
orig. publ. in New Verse, no. 8, April 1934].

B 317 : Stanford, Derek
Dylan Thomas : a literary study.
London ; Spearman, 1964.
[8], 212p. 20½cm. cloth.
pp. 207—210 : Selected bibliography.
1st American ed. published New York, Citadel
Press, 1954.

B 318 : Stephens, John Oliver
Dylan Thomas (1914—1953). [In Welsh].
Y Genhinen, Gwanwyn (Spring) 1954.
pp. 65—73.

B 319 : Symons, Julian
Obscurity and Dylan Thomas.
Kenyon Review, Vol. II, 1940. pp. 66—71.

B 320 : Symons, Julian
Words as narrative.
Twentieth Century Verse. No. 1, 1937. (Pages
unnumbered).
[Forms a review of *Twentyfive Poems*].

B 321 : Tedlock, E. W., *editor*
Dylan Thomas : the legend and the poet : a
collection of biographical and critical essays.
London, Melbourne, [etc.] ; Heinemann, 1960.
x, [2], 3—283p. 21½cm. cloth.
Pt. I consists of biographical essays (pp. 3—87) :
Pt. II : 17 critical assessments of the literary
work of Dylan Thomas.

B 322 : Tellier, A. R.
La poésie de Dylan Thomas (Thémes et formes).
Paris ; Presses Universitaires de France, 1963.
248, [4]p. 25cm. wrappers.
(Publications de la Faculté des Lettres de
L'Universitie de Clermont.   2ième série,
fasc. 18). pp. 237—48 : Bibliog. of poetical
works of Dylan Thomas and of critical
articles).

B 323 : Thomas, R. George
Bard on a raised hearth : Dylan Thomas and
his craft.
A-W.R., Vol. 12, no. 30, [1964], pp. 11—20.

B 324 : Thomas, R. George.
Dylan Thomas : a poet of Wales ?
English. Vol. 14, Spring 1963. pp. 140—5.

B 325 : Thompson, Kent
An approach to the early poems of Dylan
Thomas.
A-W.R. Vol. 14, no. 34, 1964—65. pp. 81—88.

B 326 : Tindall, William York
A reader's guide to Dylan Thomas.
London ; Thames & Hudson, 1962.
[6], 7—317p. 20cm. cloth.
pp. 311—12 : Bibliography.

B 327 : Treece, Henry
Chalk sketch for a genius.
Dock Leaves. Vol. 5, no. 13, 1954. pp. 18—23.

B 328 : Treece, Henry
Dylan Thomas : ' dog among the fairies '.
London ; Lindsay Drummond, 1949.
xiii, [1], 15—159p. 18cm. cloth.
Appendix I : ' A new poet ', by Edith Sitwell.
[From Sunday Times, 1936 : a review of
Twenty-five Poems].
Appendix II : Reply by Dylan Thomas.
Appendix III : A critic interprets a poem, by
Marshall Stearns (from ' Transformation 3 ').

—Another edition.   2nd ed. rev.   London,
Ernest Benn, 1956.
[8], 9—158p. 18½cm. cloth.
Appendix I : Analysis of a poem (Jan. 1939).
Appendix II : An analysis of ' Light Breaks ', by
M. Stearns (from ' Transformation 3 ').

B 329 : Wain, John
Dylan Thomas : a review of his *Collected Poems*.
Preliminary Essays.
London, Macmillan, 1957. *pp.* 180—185.

B 330 : Williams, A. R.
A dictionary for Dylan Thomas.
Dock Leaves. Vol. 3, no. 9, 1952. pp. 30—36.

B 331 : Williams, Raymond
Dylan Thomas's play for voices.
Critical Quarterly.   Vol. 1, no. 1, 1959.
pp. 18—26.

THOMAS, Ronald Stuart

B 332 : Cox, Charles Brian *and* Dyson, Anthony
Edward
The practical criticism of poetry.
London, Edward Arnold, 1965.
pp. 35—45 comprise part of a seminar dis-
cussion at the University of East Anglia on
R. S. Thomas' poem *Here* (p. 36).

B 333 : Garlick, Raymond
Editorial.
Dock Leaves. Vol. 6, no. 18, 1955. pp. [1]—9.
[Critical assessment of the poetry of R. S.
Thomas].

B 334 : Garlick, Raymond
Editorial article.
Anglo-Welsh Review.   Vol. 9, no. 24, n.d.
pp. 3—8.
[Critical assessment of the poetry of R. S.
Thomas and a review of *Poetry for Supper*].

B 335 : Hainsworth, J. D.
Extremes in poetry—R. S. Thomas and Ted
Hughes.
English, XIV, no. 84, 1963. pp. 226—30.

B 336 : Mathias, Roland
[Editorial article].
Anglo-Welsh Review. Vol. 13, no. 31, undated.
[pp. 4—12 of this article comprise a critical
assessment of the work of R. S. Thomas].

B 337 : Merchant, William Moelwyn
The art of R. S. Thomas.
Province, Vol. 9, 1958. pp. 116—125.

B 358 : Merchant, William Moelwyn
R. S. Thomas.
Critical Quarterly.   Vol. 2, no. 4, 1960.
pp. 341—51.

B 339 : Price, Cecil
The poetry of R. S. Thomas.
The Welsh Anvil, No. IV, [1952]. pp. 82—86.

B 340 : Nightingale, Benedict
Hewer of verses : the poet of Eglwysfach.
Guardian, 4 March, 1964. p. 9 (with photo-
graph).

B 341 : Nye, Robert
A proper language for the telling of truth.
Western Mail Literary Review, July 17, 1964.
p. 7.

B   342 : Thomas, R. George
The poetry of R. S. Thomas.
A Review of English Literature. Vol. 3, no. 4,
1962. pp. 85—95.

B   343 : Thomas, R. George
R. S. Thomas. *In* Clark, Leonard *and* Thomas,
R. G.
Andrew Young and R. S. Thomas.
London, Longmans for the British Council and
NBL, 1964.
pp. 27—41 (also bibliography).
(Writers and their Works Series, No. 166).

B   344 : Thomas, Ronald Stuart
Reply to ' Wales ' Questionnaire.
Wales. Vol. VI, no. 3, 1946. pp. 22—23.

VAUGHAN, Herbert Millingchamp

B   345 : Williams, William
H. M. Vaughan.
National Library of Wales Journal, Winter 1949.
pp. 166—169 (with portrait).

WATKINS, Vernon

B   346 : Flint, R. W.
Poets of the '50's.
Partisan Review. Vol. 21, no. 6, 1954.
pp. 676—82.
[Includes review of Watkins, Vernon. *The
death bell*. New Directions ed.].

B   347 : Heath-Stubbs, John
Pity and the nxed stars : an approach to Vernon
Watkins.
Poetry Quarterly. Vol. 12, no. 1, 1950.
pp. 18—23.

B   348 : Mathias, Roland
A note on some recent poems by Vernon
Watkins.
Dock Leaves. Vol. 1, no. 3, 1950. pp. 38—49.
[Considers text of poems publ. in *The Listener*
after the date of the first publication of
The Lady with the Unicorn].

B   349 : Raine, Kathleen
Vernon Watkins : poet of tradition.
Texas Quarterly, Vol. VII, no. 2, 1964.
pp. 173—189.
Anglo-Welsh Review. Vol. 14, no. 33, 1964.
pp. 20—38.

B   350 : Watkins, Vernon
Context ; [replies by V.W. to questions
concerning poetry].
The London Magazine. (N.S.) Vol. 1, no. 11,
1962. pp. 43—4.

B   351 : Watkins, Vernon
Reply to ' Wales ' Questionnaire.
Wales. Vol. VI, no. 3, 1946. pp. 23—4.

WILLIAMS, Emlyn

B   352 : Findlater, Richard
Emlyn Williams.
London ; Rockliff, 1956.
[4], 5—112p. front. (port.) photos. 21½cm.
cloth. pp. 101—112 : Appendix : chronology
of stage and film career of Emlyn Williams.

B   353 : Fletcher, Ivan Kyrle
An Oxford expedition.
Welsh Outlook. Vol. 14, 1927. pp. 185—6.
[Forms a review article of a performance at the
Oxford Playhouse in 1927 of Emlyn Williams'
Full Moon].

B   354 : Goodwin, Geraint
A new Welsh dramatist.
Welsh Outlook. Vol. 15, 1928. pp. 344—5.

B   355 : Trewin, John Courtenay
Dramatists of today.
London, Staples Press, 1953.
pp. 162—169 : Theatre theatrical : Emlyn Williams

WILLIAMS, Hugh Menai   *"Huw Menai"*

B   356 : Williams, Hugh Menai
The bilingual mind : my early background of
cynghanedd.
Wales, 1958, no. 1. pp. 31—34 ; no. 2.
pp. 8—14.
Wales, 1959, no. 6. pp. 23—27 ; no. 8.
pp. 36—39.

WILLIAMS, Raymond

B   357 : Kermode, Frank
[Border country] review.
Partisan Review, Vol. 29, no. 3, 1962.
pp. 466—475 (in part).

B   358 : Mathias, Roland
Editorial article.
Anglo-Welsh Review. Vol. II, no. 27, undated.
pp. 5—13.
[Reviews the work of Raymond Williams, in
particular the novel *Border Country*].

DISSERTATIONS AND UNPUBLISHED SOURCES

I.   UNIVERSITY THESES

B   359 : Edwards, James Haydn Keri
The life and works of three Anglo-Welsh
writers of East Glamorgan : Joseph Keating,
Jack Jones, Lewis Jones. M.A. thesis in the
University of Wales (Aberystwyth), 1962.
pp. 367—375 : Bibliographies of the above
authors.

pp. 376—382 : Bibliography of other Anglo-Welsh works and critical articles.
Thesis refers to "holograph mss. and (mostly) typescripts" of Jack Jones' unpublished works. A detailed schedule of this material, including radio scripts, will be found in *A Schedule of Manuscripts Presented (to the National Library of Wales) by Jack Jones, Esq., Rhiwbina, 1961* ; compiled by B. G. Charles. Aberystwyth, National Library of Wales, 1961.

B   360 : Jenkins, David Clay
Writing in 20th century Wales : a defence of the Anglo-Welsh. Ph.D. dissertation of the Iowa State University. (Summarised in Dissertation Abstracts, Vol. 16, no. 10, 1955—6. p. 1906). Microfilm copy in N.L.W. Treats in particular of Caradoc Evans, Richard Hughes, Dylan Thomas and the magazines *Wales* and *The Welsh Review*. Includes also :
Appendix A : p. 250 : Dylan Thomas' contributions to *Wales*.
Appendix B : pp. 251—4 : Annals of modern Anglo-Welsh writing.
Appendix C : pp. 255—271 : Bibliography.
pp. 272—295 : Bio-bibliography of modern Welsh authors.
Supplement : (pp. 1—50) : *An index to The Welsh Review* (cf. B 2).

B   361 : Williams, David Marcel
The presentation of character in the Anglo-Welsh novel : a study of techniques and influences.
M.A. thesis in the University of Wales (Swansea), 1959.
An assessment of the novels of Caradoc Evans, Rhys Davies, Gwyn Thomas, Emyr Humphreys, Cledwyn Hughes, Geraint Goodwin, Gwyn Jones, Glyn Jones, Richard Vaughan, Jack Jones, Richard Llewellyn, Eiluned Lewis, Hilda Vaughan.
pp. 141—43 : Bibliography of the above authors arranged chronologically. Copy deposited in National Library of Wales.

AMIS, Kingsley

B   362 : Smith, Robert Bruce
An analysis of the works of Kingsley Amis. Ph.D. dissertation of the University of Washington, 1965.
Summarised in Dissertation Abstracts, Vol. 26, no. 5, 1965, 2762.

DAVIES, Idris

B   363 : Jenkins, Islwyn
The life and works of Idris Davies, Rhymney. M.A. thesis in the University of Wales, 1957.
pp. 282—4 comprise a bibliography of published and unpublished works of Idris Davies :

A : Ms. sources of unpublished poetry and prose, incl. poems sequences and a verse play in ms. at N.L.W.
B : Published works, incl. periodicals to which Idris Davies contributed.
Copy deposited in National Library of Wales.

DAVIES, William Henry

B   364 : Hockey, Lawrence William
The life and work of W. H. Davies. M.A. thesis in the University of Wales (Cardiff), 1956.
pp. 276—285 comprise a bibliography of W. H. Davies, including unpublished material in ms., correspondences, original works by date of first publication, and references to critical articles on the work of W.H.D. Copy deposited in National Library of Wales.

MACHEN, Arthur

B   365 : Michael, David Parry Martin
The life and works of Arthur Machen, with special reference to his novels and tales. M.A. thesis in the University of Wales (Cardiff), 1940.
Appendix A : Bibliography of Arthur Machen.
Appendix B : List of books and articles referring directly to Arthur Machen.
Appendix C : Chronological list of principal works of Arthur Machen.
Copy deposited in National Library of Wales.

POWYS, John Cowper

B   366 : Going, Margaret Elizabeth Moore
John Cowper Powys, novelist. Ph.D. dissertation of the University of Michigan, 1955. Summarised in Dissertation Abstracts, Vol. 15, no. 4, 1955, 582.

THOMAS, Dylan

B   367 : Dhall, A. D.
Dylan Thomas : a critical analysis and re-appraisal of his earlier poetry. M.A. thesis in the University of Manchester, 1962—63.

B   368 : Jones, J. Ackerman
The works of Dylan Thomas in relation to his Welsh environment. M.A. thesis in King's College, London, 1958—59. [See also B 227].

Section C : Children's Stories

The titles listed below consist of children's stories by Anglo-Welsh authors, and by other non-Welsh authors who have located their narratives against a Welsh background.

ALLAN, Mabel Esther

C 1 : Catrin in Wales.
London, Bodley Head, 1959.
Location : "Nant Gwyncefn", N. Wales.
—Another edition. Brockhampton Press, 1965.
(Hampton Library Series).

C 2 : School under Snowdon.
London, Hutchinson, [1950].
Location : Caernarvonshire ("Llanrhysydd Castle").

C 3 : The Wyndhams went to Wales.
London, Sylvan Press, 1948.
Location : "Llanechlin", North Wales.

BELL, Kathleen M.

C 4 : The talisman of Sundu.
London, Carey Press, 1921.
Location : Partly N. Wales.

BIRBECK, Antonia

C 5 : A fairy tale of St. David's.
London, Philip Allan, 1933.

BRENT-DYER, Elinor Mary

C 6 : The Highland twins at the Chalet School.
London, Chambers, 1942.

C 7 : The lost staircase.
London, Chambers, 1946.

CRAWSHAY-WILLIAMS, Eliot

C 8 : Hywel and Gwyneth : a modern fairy tale.
Cardiff, William Lewis, [1945].

DALE, Gareth

C 9 : Bracken horse.
London, Lutterworth Press, 1960.

DUNN, Mary

C 10 : Mountain mystery.
London, Lutterworth Press, 1951.
Location : Near Dolgelley, N. Wales.

FARJEON, Joseph Jefferson

C 11 : The Llewellyn Jewel mystery.
London, Glasgow, Collins, 1948.
Location : "Pendragon, Aberwys".

GLYNNE-JONES, William

C 12 : Brecon adventure : a story for boys.
London, Lutterworth Press, 1945.
—Another edition. New ed., 1951. (Dominion Library Series).

C 13 : Dennis and Co.
London, New York, Warne, 1947.
Location : "Abermouth".

C 14 : Legends of the Welsh hills.
London, Mowbray, 1957.

C 15 : The magic forefinger, and other Welsh fairy stories.
London, Boardman, 1949.

GREEN, Roger Lancelyn

C 16 : The secret of Rusticoker.
London, Methuen, 1953.
Location : Beaumaris Castle, Anglesey.

GRIFFITHS, John

C 17 : Griff and Tommy.
London, Dent, 1956.
Location : "Pantyglo", S. Wales mining village.

HALL, Aylmer

C 18 : The Sword of Glendower.
London, Methuen, 1960.
Location : "Llanvair Castle", near "Llanwern".

HENSON, Jean

C 19 : Detectives in Wales.
London, Faber, 1953.

JONES, Beryl Marian

C   20 : Adventurers from Wales. (Vols. I—V).
Cardiff, Hughes & Son, undated [1953—4 ?].

C   21 : The enchanted harp.
Leeds, E. J. Arnold, [1949].

C   22 : Tales of magic and romance.
Cardiff, University of Wales Press, 1964.

JONES, Gwyn

C   23 : Welsh legends and folk tales.
Oxford University Press, 1955.

KENYON, Edith Caroline

C   24 : Two girls in a siege : a tale of the great Civil War.
London, "Leisure Hour Library Office", n.d.
—London, Religious Tract Society, [1915].

LEE, Lisa

C   25 : Owen's second story book.
Shrewsbury, Wilding, 1962.

C   26 : Owen's story book.
Shrewsbury, Wilding, 1955.

OLDMEADOW, Katherine

C   27 : The three Mary Anns.
London, Cassell, 1948.
Part I : Mary Ann, South Wales, 1796—7 :
Part II : Mary Ann, England, 1833 : Part III :
Mary Ann, South Wales, 1941.

OWEN, Gwen

C   28 : Helen of the hills.
Denbigh, Gee, 1958.
Location : ' Havodfelyn ', Aber valley, N. Wales.

"OXENHAM, Elsie" [*i.e. Elsie Jeanette Dunkerley*)

C   29 : The Girls of Gwynfa.
London, Warne, 1924.
Location : House of Gwynfa, Caernarvonshire.

PRICE, Christine

C   30 : David and the mountain.
London, New York, Longmans, 1959.
Location :   "Cwmffynnon"   Farm.   (Black
Mountains area).

RIDGE, Antonia

C   31 : The thirteenth child.
London, Faber, 1962.
(Owen Tudor and Katherine de Valois).

RUSSELL, Ivy

C   32 : Megan of the Welsh hills.
London, Latimer House, [1952].
Location : North Wales Coast.

SAUNDERS, Roy

C   33 : Craig of the Welsh hills.
London, Oldbourne, 1958.
Location : Breconshire and Radnorshire hills.

SHEPPARD-JONES, Elizabeth

C   34 : The search for Mary.
London, Nelson, 1960.
Location : Partly South Wales.

SLEIGH, Lynwood

C   35 : The tailor's friends.
London, Faber, 1956.

SPURRELL, Rosalind

C   36 : Welsh adventure.
London, Epworth Press, 1961.

STYLES, Frank Showell

C   37 : The Shop in the mountain.
London, Gollancz, 1961.

THEOBALD, Tessa

C   38 : A shadow on the sea.
London, Oxford University Press, 1957.
Location : Pembrokeshire.

THOMAS, William Jenkyn

C   39 : More Welsh fairy and folk tales.
Cardiff, University of Wales Press, 1957.

C   40 : The Welsh fairy book.
London, Fisher Unwin, 1907.
—Another impression, 1908 ; 1912.

THOMPSON, Honora Elizabeth

C 41 : Dick, Gerry and Miranda.
London, Elliot Stock, 1910.
Location : A Welsh village.

TURNBULL, Eleanor Lucia

C 42 : Bingo and the fox : a Welsh folk tale.
The shepherd of Myddvəi : a Welsh legend.
Oxford University Press, 1954.   (Traditional
Tales, nos. 13 and 16).

VEREKER, Barbara

C 43 : Caroline in Wales.
London, Melbourne [etc.], Ward, Lock, 1959.
Location : Mining village of "Llandrydch".

VILLIERS, Alan

C 44 : And not to yield : a story of the ' Outward
Bound '.
London, Hodder & Stoughton, 1953.
Location : Off the Welsh Western sea coast.

WATKINS, Tudur

C 45 : The Spanish galleon : an adventure story.
London, Peter Lunn, 1945.
Location : S. Wales, Channel coast. Originally
broadcast by B.B.C.

WELCH, Ronald

C 46 : The gauntlet.
London, Glasgow [etc.], Oxford U.P., 1951.
Location : Carreg Cennen Castle, Carms.

WILLIAMS, A. J. Bailey

C 47 : The enchanted wood, and other stories.
Newtown, Montgomeryshire Printing Company
[1948].

Indexes

(1) REGIONAL INDEX

This index lists the names of authors whose prose fiction and drama can be assigned to definite county areas. Indeterminate locations such as "North Wales" or "South Wales" are excluded.

Anglesey
Arnold, *Mrs.* A. V.
Elias, Frank
Glyn, Megan
Hughes, Eilian
Pryce, Gwendolen
Roberts, Barbara Dew

Border Counties
Andrew, P.
Ashton, Helen
Berridge, E.
Evans, Margiad
Fletcher, H. L. V.
Goodwin, Geraint
Lewis, Helen P.
Newby, P. H.
Onions, Oliver
Pargeter, Edith
Webb, Mary
Williams, Raymond

Breconshire
Carter, Barbara
Davies, Gwyn
Hughes, David
Jacob, Violet
Thomas, H. Elwyn
Vaughan, Hilda
Williams, Alis Mallt

Caernarvonshire
Ashby, R. C.
Brooks, Jeremy
Canaway, W. H.
Carr, Glyn
Firbank, Thomas
Fletcher, J. K. *and* J. S.
Griffith, Ll. Wyn
Hales, Alfred G.
Hughes, Richard
Hughes, T. Rowland
Humphreys, Emyr
Kendrick, T. D.
Lloyd, J. H.
Moray, Ann
Nepean, Edith
Powys, John Cowper
Pryce, Gwendolen
Quin, Shirland

Radcliffe, G.
Rees, Goronwy
Roberts, Barbara Dew
Styles, F. Showell
Tucker, Norman
Val Baker, Denys
Ward, Edith M.
West, Frederick W.
Williams, J. Ellis
Williams, Trevor
Woolland, Henry

Cardiganshire
Askew, A. J. de. C.
Boore, W. H.
Davies, Naunton
Evans, Caradoc
Evans, Marguerite Florence
Finnemore, J.
Harris-Burland, J. B.
Inglis-Jones, Elizabeth
James, Margot
Kenyon, Edith C.
Macdonald, Tom
Raine, Allen
Ward, Edith M.
Williams, Elma M.
Yorke, C.

Carmarthenshire
Beale, Anne
Cordell, Alexander
Glynne-Jones, W.
Montgomery, K. L.
Morgan, D. Derwenydd
Saunders, Roy
Thomas, H. Elwyn
Thomas, R. M.
Vaughan, Richard

Denbighshire
Charles, T. O.
Ellis, Joseph E.
Jones, Ivan M.
Roberts, Grace

Flintshire
Bellys, Gwilym
Humphreys, Emyr

Glamorgan
Abse, Dannie
Amis, Kingsley
Burton, P. H.
Davies, Gwyn
Davies, Naunton
Davies, Rhys
Dyer, John
Eustace, Alice
Gallie, Menna
Hughes, Isaac Craigfryn
Jones, Glyn
Jones, Gwyn
Jones, Jack
Jones, Lewis
Keating, Joseph
Lewis, Miles
Llewellyn, Richard
Llewelyn, M. Gareth
Martin, David
Onions, Oliver
Parker, John
Robertson, G.
Smart, Arthur D.
Spring, Howard
Taylor, Margaret S.
Thomas, Gwyn
Walsh, J. M.

Merionethshire
Evans, Evan R.
Griffith, Ll. Wyn
Thomas, Murray
Williams, Elma M.

Monmouthshire
Bairacli-Levy, J. de
Butler, Suzanne
Castle, Agnes *and* Egerton
Cordell, Alexander
Fisher, Alan M.
Herbert, Evelyn
Newby, P. H.
Traherne, *Mrs.* Arthur

Montgomeryshire
Everett-Green, E.
Goodwin, Geraint
Lewis, Eiluned

Pembrokeshire
Bannerman, Alexander
Bowen-Rowlands, L.
Broster, D. K.
Davies, D. (*of Molleston*)
Dorling, H. T.
Howell, Florence

Knight, L. A.
Jones, Gwyn
Lewis, Eiluned
Llewellyn, Richard
Morgan-Richardson, C.
Richards, David Seaborne
Williams, Islwyn

Radnorshire
Fletcher, H. L. V.
Hereford, John
Littlestone, G.
Llewellyn, Alun
Vaughan, Hilda
Young, Francis Brett

(2) GENERAL INDEX

The numbers refer to bibliographical items in Sections A—C and not to the pagination of the volume.
' A ' numbers denote (1) collections and anthologies and (2) original works by individual authors.
' B ' numbers denote critical, bibliographical and certain biographical works.
' C ' numbers denote the authors of children's stories.

Index entries are *not* made for the authors of critical articles on individual writers. References to criticism of the works of a particular author will be found at the appropriate B numbers listed after the name of the author, which is used as a subject-heading. Authors of general criticism of the Anglo-Welsh school and of university theses have been included in the general index.

Pryce, Gwendolen — A 1127-1129
Pryce, Myfanwy — A 1130
Pryce, Richard — A 1
Prys-Jones, A. G. — A 14, 1131-1136 ; B 33, 220
Prys-Williams, Marion — A 1137-1140
Puddicombe, Anne A.
  see Raine, Allen
Pugh, Jonathan A. — A 1141
Pughe, Ifan — A 1
Quin, Shirland — A 1142-1144
Radcliffe, Garnett — A 1145
Raine, Allen — A 1, 1146-1158 ; B 11, 221-222
Ray, Jane — A 1159
Rees, Alun — A 1160-1161
Rees, Enoch — A 1162-1166
Rees, Goronwy — A 1167-1171
Rees, Ioan Bowen — B 35
Rees, Morwyth — A 1172-1175
Rees, Thomas Hardy — A 1176
Remenham, John — A 1177
Rhoscomyl, Owen
  see Vaughan, Arthur O.
Rhys, Cadvan — A 1178
Rhys, Edward Prosser — A 1179-1180
Rhys, Ernest — A 1181-1186 ; B 223-224
Rhys, Keidrych — A 15, 1187-1191 ; B 36
Richards, A. Edward — A 3, 4, 1192-1196
Richards, Alun — A 1197-1200 ; B 37
Richards, Ann — A 1201
Richards, D. L. S. — A 1202
Richards, Frank — A 1
Richards, Hedley — A 1203
Richardson, C. Morgan-
  see Morgan-Richardson, C.
Ridge, Antonia — C 31
Roberts, Arthur O. — A 1204
Roberts, Barbara D. — A 1205-1208
Roberts, Glyn — B 38
Roberts, Grace — A 1209-1213
Roberts, Hugh P. — A 1214
Roberts, Kate — A 1-4, 1215-1220 ; B 225
Roberts, Lewis M. — A 1221
Roberts, Lynette — A 1222-1225
Roberts, Mary Elizabeth — A 1226-1227
Roberts, Rhian — A 1228-1230
Roberts, Sally — A 1231
Robertson, Graham — A 1232
Rowe, Dilys — A 2 ; B 39
Rowlands, L. Bowen-
  see Bowen-Rowlands, L.
Ruck, Berta — A 1233-1238
Russell, Ivy — C 32
Sandeman, Robert G. — A 1239
Sandys, Oliver
  see Evans, Marguerite Florence
Saunders, Roy — A 1240 ; C 33
Saunderson, Irene — A 1241
Scott-Ellis, T. Evelyn, 8th
  Baron Howard de Walden
  see Ellis, T. Evelyn
"Scrutator" — A 1242
Sheppard-Jones, Elizabeth — C 34
Shirley, Rae — A 1243
Slater, Montagu — A 1244

Sleigh, Lynwood — C 35
Smart, Arthur D. — A 1245
Smith, M. Josephine — A 1246
Smith, Robert B. — B 362
Sneyd-Kynnersley, E. M. — A 1247
Somerset, Raglan — A 1248
Sparroy, Wilfrid — A 1248
Spring, Howard — A 1250-1252
Spurrell, Rosalind — C 36
Steel, Flora A. — A 1253
Stephens, Meic — A 8, 1254
Street, Lucie — A 1255
Styles, F. Showell — A 1256-1257 ; C 37
Tabori, Paul — A 1258
Taffrail
  see Dorling, H. T.
Taylor, Frederick — A 1259
Taylor, Margaret S. — A 1260-1261
Tegart, Kathleen F. — A 1262
Theobald, Tessa — C 38
Thomas, Alfred — A 1263
Thomas, Bertha — A 1264
Thomas, D. Brychan — A 1265
Thomas, Dylan — A 1-4, 1266-1290 ; B 7, 18, 21, 22, 40, 226-331, 360, 367-368
Thomas, Ernest Lewis
  see Vaughan, Richard
Thomas, Evan Edward — A 1291
Thomas, Gwyn — A 2, 4, 1292-1328 ; B 21, 22, 361
Thomas, H. Elwyn — A 1329-1330
Thomas, Howard — A 1331
Thomas, J. R. — A 1332
Thomas, John — A 1333
Thomas, L. Byrne-
  see Byrne-Thomas, L.
Thomas, Mrs. O. — A 1333
Thomas, John Mansel — A 1334-1337
Thomas, John Ormond — A 1338
Thomas, Luther — A 1339
Thomas, Maude M. — A 1340
Thomas, Muriel M. — A 1341
Thomas, Murray — A 1342
Thomas, Nathaniel — A 1343
Thomas, Norman — A 1344
Thomas, R. M. — A 1345
Thomas, R. S. — A 1346-1357 ; B 21, 41, 332-344
Thomas, T. C. — A 1358-1360
Thomas, W. Jenkyn — C 39-40
Thompson, Honora E. — C 41
Thorne, Guy — A 1361
Times Literary Supplement — B 42
Toriel
  see Williams, John Toriel
Traherne, Mrs. Arthur — A 1362
Tredegar, Evan Morgan,
  Viscount
  see Morgan, Evan
Treece, Henry — A 5
Trefor, Eirlys — A 1363-1365
Tucker, Norman — A 1366-1370
Turnbull, E. L. — C 42
Turner, M. L. — A 5